MAC

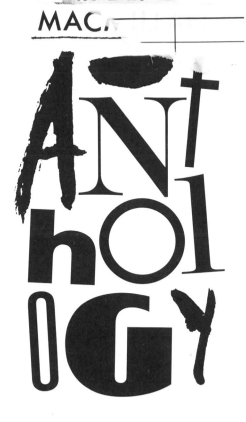

ANTHOLOGY

Edited by

John Metcalf and Leon Rooke

Macmillan of Canada
A Division of Canada Publishing Corporation
Toronto, Ontario, Canada

Canadian Cataloguing in Publication Data

The National Library of Canada has cata-
logued this annual as follows:

Main entry under title:

The Macmillan anthology

Annual.
1-
ISSN 0841-7431
ISBN 0-7715-9202-7 (no. 2).

1. Canadian literature (English) — 20th
century — Periodicals.

PS8233.M32   C810'.8'0054   C89-030005-4
PR9180.M32

Design: *Craig Allen/The Richmond Studio*

Macmillan of Canada
A Division of Canada Publishing Corporation
Toronto, Ontario, Canada

Printed in Canada

ACKNOWLEDGEMENTS

"Good Manners" by Carol Shields first appeared in *West Coast Review.*

The following **"America"** poems by Jena Hamilton first appeared in *The Malahat Review:* **"Amaranth"**, **"Moonwalk"**, **"Spark Plugs"**, **"Honey God"**, **"four a.m. feeding"**.

The quotations in *The America Poems* were selected from Harper's Index 1988 and are reproduced with the permission of *Harper's Magazine.*

"Oranges and Apples" and **"Oh, What Avails"** by Alice Munro first appeared in *The New Yorker.*

CONTENTS

GOOD MANNERS

By *CAROL SHIELDS*

T he stern, peremptory social arbiter Georgia Willow has been overseeing Canadian manners for thirty-five years. She did it in Montreal during the tricky fifties and she did it in Toronto in the unsettled sixties. In the seventies she operated underground, so to speak, from a converted Rosedale garage, tutoring the shy wives of Japanese executives and diplomats. In the eighties she came into her own; manners were rediscovered, particularly in the West, where Mrs. Willow has relocated.

Promptly at three-thirty each Tuesday and Thursday, neatly dressed in a well-pressed navy Evan-Picone slub-silk suit, cream blouse, and muted scarf, Georgia Willow meets her small class in the reception area of the Macdonald Hotel and ushers them into the long, airy tearoom — called, for some reason, Gophers — where a ceremonial spread has been ordered.

Food and drink almost always accompany Mrs. Willow's lectures. It is purely a matter of simulation, since, wherever half a dozen people gather, there is sure to be a tray of sandwiches to trip them up. According to Mrs. Willow, food and food implements are responsible for fifty per cent of social unease. The classic olive-pit question. The persisting problem of forks, cocktail picks, and coffee spoons. The more recent cherry-tomato dilemma. Potato skins, eat them or leave

Carol Shields was born in Oak Park, Illinois, and has lived in Canada since 1957. She teaches at the University of Winnipeg. Her last book was *Swann: A Mystery*. Her story "Good Manners" will be appearing this spring in a new story collection called *The Orange Fish*.

them? Saucers, the lack of. The challenge of the lobster. The table-napkin quandary. Removing parsley from between the teeth. On and on.

There are also sessions devoted to hand-shaking, door-opening, and rules regarding the wearing and non-wearing of gloves. And a concluding series of seminars on the all-important *langue de la politesse,* starting with the discourse of gesture, and moving on quickly to the correct phrase for the right moment, delivered with spiritual amplitude or imprecation or possibly something in between. Appropriateness is all, says Georgia Willow.

Our *doyenne* of good manners takes these problems one by one. She demonstrates and describes and explains the acceptable alternatives. She's excellent on fine points, she respects fine points. But always it's the philosophy *behind* good manners that she emphasizes.

Never forget, she tells her audience, what manners are *for.* Manners are the lubricant that eases our passage through life. Manners are the first-aid kit we carry out on to the battlefield. Manners are the ceremonial silver tongs with which we help ourselves to life's most alluring moments.

She says these things to a circle of puzzled faces. Some of those present take notes, others yawn; all find it difficult to deal with Mrs. Willow's more exuberant abstractions. As a sensitive person, she understands this perfectly well; she sympathizes and, if she were less well-mannered, would illustrate her philosophy with personal anecdotes culled from her own experience. Like everyone else, her life has been filled with success and failure, with ardor and the lack of ardor, but she is not one of those who spends her time unpicking the past, blaming and project-ing and drawing ill-bred conclusions or dragging out pieces of bloodied vision or shame. She keeps her lips sealed about personal matters and advises her clients to do the same. Nevertheless, certain of her experiences refuse to dissolve. They're still on center stage, so to speak, frozen tableaux waiting behind a thickish curtain. Only very occasionally do they press their way forward.

It is an hour before dusk on a summer evening. She is ten years old. The motionless violet air has the same density and permanence as a word she keeps tripping over in storybooks, usually on the last page, the word *forever*. She intuitively, happily, believes at this moment that she will be locked forever into the simplicity of the blurred summer night, forever throwing a rubber ball against the side of her house and disturbing her mother with the sound of childish chanting. It is impossible for her to know that the adult world will some day, and soon, carry her away, reject her thesis on the *Chanson de Roland* and the particular kind of dated beauty her features possess; that she will be the protagonist of an extremely unpleasant divorce case and, in the end, be forced to abandon a studio apartment on the twenty-fourth floor of an apartment building in a city two thousand miles from the site of this small wooden house; that she will feel in her sixtieth year as tired and worn down as the sagging board fence surrounding the house where she lives as a child, a fence that simultaneously protects and taunts her ten-year-old self.

On the other side of the fence is old Mr. Manfred, sharpening his lawn mower. She puts down her ball and watches him cautiously, his round back, his chin full of gray teeth, the cloud of white hair resting so lazily on top of his head, and the wayward, unquenchable dullness of his eyes. Twice in the past he has offered her peppermints, and twice, mindful of her mother's warnings, she has refused. "No, thank you," she said each time. But it had been painful for her, saying no. She had felt no answering sense of virtue, only the hope that he might offer again.

Tonight Mr. Manfred walks over to the fence and tells her he has a secret. He whispers it into her ear. This secret has a devious shape: grotesque flapping ears and a loose drooling mouth. Mr. Manfred's words seem ghosted by the scent of the oil can he holds in his right hand. In his left hand, in the folds of his cotton work-pants, he grasps a tube of pink snouty dampish flesh. What he whispers is formlessly narrative and involves the familiar daylight objects of underwear and fingers and the reward of peppermint candy.

But then he draws back suddenly as though stung by a wasp. The oil can rolls and rolls and rolls on the ground. He knows, and Georgia, aged ten, knows, that something inadmissible has been said, something that cannot be withdrawn. Or can it? A dangerous proposition has been placed in her hand. It burns and shines. She wants to hand it back quickly, get rid of it somehow, but etiquette demands that she first translate it into something bearable.

The only other language she knows is incomprehension, and luckily she's been taught the apt phrase. "I beg your pardon?" she says to Mr. Manfred. Her face does a courteous twist, enterprising, meek, placatory, and masked with power, allowing Mr. Manfred time to sink back into the lavender twilight of the uncut grass. "I'm afraid I didn't quite hear . . ."

Later, twenty-three years old, she is on a train, the Super Continental, traveling eastward. She has a window seat, and sunlight gathers around the crown of her hair. She knows how she must look, with her thin, clever mouth and F. Scott Fitzgerald eyes.

"I can't resist introducing myself," a man says.

"Pardon?" She is clearly flustered. He has a beautiful face, carved cheeks, crisp gray hair curling at the forehead.

"The book." He points. "The book you're reading. It looks very interesting."

"Ah," she says.

Two days later they are in bed together, a hotel room, and she reflects on the fact that she had not finished the book, that she doesn't care if she ever does, for how can a book about love compare with what she now knows.

"I'm sorry," he says then. "I hadn't realized I was the first."

"Oh, but you're not," she cries.

This curious lie can only be accounted for by a wish to keep his love. But it turns out she has never had it, not for one minute, not love as she imagines it.

"I should have made things clear to you at once," he says. How was he to know she would mistake a random disruption for lasting attachment? He is decent enough to feel ashamed. He only wanted. He never intended. He has no business in a hotel with. If only she.

She seems to hear cloth ripping behind her eyes. The syntax of culpability — he's drowning in it, and trying to drown her too. She watches him closely, and the sight of his touching, disloyal mouth restores her composure.

Courtesy demands that she rescue him and save herself at the same time. This isn't shrewdness talking, this is good manners, and there is nothing more economical, she believes, than the language of good manners. It costs nothing, it's portable, easy to handle, malleable, yet pre-formed. Two words are all that are required, and she pronounces them slippingly, like musical notes. "Forgive me," she says. There. It's said. Was that so hard?

There is a certain thing we must all have, as Georgia Willow has learned in the course of her long life. We may be bankrupt, enfeebled, ill, or depraved, but we must have our good stories, our moments of vividness. We keep our door closed, yes, and move among our scratched furniture, old photographs, calendars and keys, ticket stubs, pencil ends and lacquered trays, but in the end we'll wither away unless we have a little human attention.

But no one seems to want to give it away these days, not to Georgia Willow. It seems she is obliged to ask even for the unpunctual treats of human warmth. A certain amount of joyless groping is required and even then it's hard to get enough. It is especially painful for someone who, after all, is a personage in her country. She has her pride, her reputation — and a scattering of small bruise-colored spots on the backs of her long, thin hands. It makes you shudder to think what she must have to do, what she has to say, how she is obliged to open her mouth and say *please*.

Please is a mean word. A word in leg irons. She doesn't say it often. Her pleases and thank-yous are per-formed in soft-focus, as they like to say in the cinema world. It has nothing to do with love, but you can imagine how it is for her, having to ask and then having to be grateful. It's too bad. Good manners had such a happy childhood, but then things got complicated. The weave of complication has brought Georgia Willow up against those she would not care to meet again, not in broad daylight anyway, and others who have extracted far more than poor Mr. Manfred at the garden fence ever dreamed of. Good manners are not always nice, not nice at all, although Mrs. Willow has a way of banishing the hard outlines of time and place, and of course she would never think of naming names. Discretion is one of her tenets.

She does a special Monday afternoon series on discretion in which she enjoins others to avoid personal inquiries and pointed judgments.

"Courtesy," concludes Georgia Willow, "is like the golden coin in the princess's silk purse. Every time it's spent worthily, another appears in its place."

Almost everyone agrees with her. However much they look into her eyes and think she is uttering mere niceties, they are sworn to that ultimate courtesy which is to believe what people want us to believe. And thus, when Mrs. Willow bids them good afternoon, they courteously rise to their feet. "Good afternoon," they smile back, shaking hands carefully, and postponing their slow, rhythmic, ominous applause and the smashing of the teacups.

THE AMERICA POEMS*

J. A. HAMILTON

*Number of Americans currently frozen in the hope of
one day coming back to life: 13*

AMARANTH

I am
stiff
as a corpse,
stiff
as a steak.
A real frigid girl.

Knock on my womb,
my ovaries clank.
My stick fingers rattle
like rosary beads.
My toes have the clatter
of crematory bones.

I am an insomniac.
I cannot sleep.
I fear death
and God and
princes.
I am cold.

How many years?
The questions dart from
my mouth in icicles.
How many years?
How much time?

The gift of frozen tongues, this,
stuck with the gift of frozen tongues, this,
and I am a porterhouse steak,
a lamb chop, a chunk of stewing beef.
I am a pot roast in plastic.
A rump roast in Ziploc.

I dare not sleep.
My eyes are crusted with ice.
Oh, how I worry, worry.
I worry about sleeping
and never waking up.
I worry about melting.

I am colorless as water.
Breathless as orgasm.
I am cold as the fires of hell
and I am licking,
licking with my dozen
tongues, licking my way
to you.

I am your fantasy,
your amanuensis,
your scheherezade.

I am the snap crackle pop
of your breakfast cereal.
I am the iceberg of time.
My tongue is a scimitar
to pierce you with longing.
I pierce you with promise.
I pierce you with immortality.

Whisper in my fossil ear.
Tell me your dreams
and your hopes and
your mother's first name.
Hear the din of a thousand winds
in my skull.

Poultice me with scented oil.
Boil me in butter.
Lift me, lift me.
My kiss is not death.

Reported cases of people bitten by rats in New York City in 1985: 311
Reported cases of people bitten by other people in New York City in
1985: 1519

MOONWALK

A maniac is loose in Manhattan.
A fat rat, a rabid rat, the latest rat
crawling up the scum holes of Harlem with
rhinestones on his goodwill tux,
a spit-shine on his dancing shoes and

a shoo-be-do-do-wah in his marble heart.
He should worry about his underarms.
No more slime-dives in the Hudson
before calling on a lady.
Rat-a-tat-tat he comes courting

with his warranties, false
passport and counterfeit tail.
He took the A train from Wall Street.
Ooee he is sharp in that top hat.
Heh heh he is cool.

His smile can charm babies. Open up.
Those little teeth? The foam is only after-shave.
This is no stiletto lover. This is solid rat-flesh
tap-dancing on your tummy, be-bop, be-bop,
moonwalking on your thighs.

Average weight of a Chinese man's testicles (in grams): 19.01
Of a Dane's: 42

FLOPPY BUSINESS

A)   who were the people measuring them what type of scale how precise was it what was the name of the airline flying the team from country to country how were the subjects chosen were there controls how much was each subject paid how big was the sampling are the results really average is it guaranteed what was the margin of error where did the funding come from what effect does size have on fertility what does it mean to an american man to an american woman are there applications in day to day life things we should know

B)   if a man has less to lug around does it mean he'll live longer less strain on his heart does it mean he's worried about exposure in country club locker rooms a chinese in a dane's locker room undressed for instance is there a scene or is it more embarrassing for danes do they believe they're over-endowed did the scale groan did a research assistant go ah in fact were women allowed on the project if a danish man marries a chinese virgin does she hide in the bathroom does he admit they were measured scientifically how does the night go are testicles that big or little according to nation what about penises what about vaginas etc

Average length of sexual intercourse for humans (in minutes): 2

J.A. HAMILTON

BEASTIE BOY

This is the two minute
warning. Number twenty-nine
is across the bed with his
pig skin, cracking his play book,
grunting signals.

This is the two minute
drill. I am the wide
receiver, tight end for
his short yardage.
No time for a huddle.

No time for fancy
plays. Straight up the middle
over tackle while I brave
my goal line stand
calling for the referee.

There isn't a penalty big enough.

Number of sexual fantasies the average person has in a day: 7

SPARK PLUGS

The fantasy is
particular and
persistent.
It involves
a pomegranate
    a soccer ball
a red wig
    a spark plug
a spatula
    my girlfriend Lydia
a cherry blossom
    the Bering Strait
three buffalos
    a used tea bag
a chicken McNugget
    the smell of Lemon Pledge
my first boyfriend
    and a hub cap.
All at once
especially on Sundays.

*Average percentage change in a man's standard of living in the year
after divorce: +43*

SUITOR

This man strings pearls
on my cucumber vines
late at night while
the moon in her hammock
spreads her legs.

This man drops money
outside my windows
late at night while
Venus is puckering
her lips in the sky.

He thinks I want it.
He believes I come out
after and gobble up the
goods. He thinks I
stuff my mouth full of

his twenties and fifties
like an excitable child.
This is how odd he is
without his wife.
This is how peculiar

he is in my garden
with his gold hoe
turning up the earth,
dropping his spare
change. He plants

rubies and opals in
disorderly rows and waters
with Mumms' champagne.
My fuchsias hang their heads
giddy and ashamed.

Such a spectacle.
They don't know where
he gets his cash. They think
it's illegal to have so
much and to do dirty things

at night. They think he
bets on the horses or does
something vague with
cheap petunias. My
fuchsias budded yesterday.

J.A. HAMILTON

Percentage decrease in the patient population of U.S. psychiatric hospitals since 1955: 79

MAD MAD

Good morning.
It is 10:06 :07 :08
in my house and in
my jungle chair.

The mad mad.
I pull wings
from my scalp
and flex them.

I served ants
at the dinner table
pinioned as cloves
in the ham.

The voices.
The children and
the husband
and the mother-in-law.
The eyes.

It is true.
I remember my hands
in the garden and
the ants' stinging bites.

Good morning.
It is 10:09 10:10 and
my jungle chair
levitates.

The mad mad.
I warble and
my red wings
beat back the night.

Percentage of Russian soldiers that God will kill at the end of the world, according to Jerry Falwell: 83

HONEY GOD

It is written.
It is hand-delivered by the angel Gabriel
to the preacher with harps in his ears
C.O.D.
Invoiced
to the minister on video waves.

Honey God
you know we are starved for justice,
yea we are thirsty
for Red blood spilling
hot on Siberia.
Honey God, you hear
and you promise
83 Russians
per one-hundred soldiers.
830 Russians
per one-thousand soldiers.
8300 Russians
per ten-thousand soldiers.
On and on.

We have kisses for your lips,
Honey God.
We have backrubs and scented tubs
and a knee to dandle you on.
To thank you
Honey God.
And yea, we have big mother breasts
in exchange for more sinners.
We have cash, we have
cash of many colors,
pens of gold
and parchment
in exchange for more
Sinners.

Percentage of nursing mothers whose milk contains traces of PCBs:
87

four a.m. feeding

i light no lamp
i go by ache
and touch
all color has been bled and it is black
here, black as iron

i light no lamp
the song of your hunger
guides me
to your hot humid nest.   my hands
curl under your arms and lift
little butterfly little moth

i light no lamp
this is instinct this gift
i give you at night
i know you
differently   when i can't see you
i smell you
like hyacinths   my little lilac
little pink bud

there are buttons to unfasten
half asleep
it is hard to work my fingers
and juggle you
but soon   i fold you
in the crook of my arm   these breasts
are pouches of stone
four hours without you
look what it does, little duck

you seek me
blindly, rooting for the source
i croon
and tell you it is there
eager hungry little rook
it is there

your caging mouth

i melt and gush
you choke break cough, little dolphin
too much
too fast
gurgling to your belly

milk splatters your face and fuzzy scalp
milk sweet and warm   such
plenty to grow on

i light no lamp
i nuzzle your head
and rock the chair
i slip my hand
under your gown
and fondle
your miniature toes

little peach little plum
i cannot imagine you
grown

Number of health professionals in Chile who specialize in treating the victims of torture: 50

PINK

This is a sensational poem.
Avoid it.

Think of a sweet pea.
There are different sorts
but this particular sweet pea is
a pink sweet pea
on a Chilean vine
in a doctor's garden.

Do you believe flowers are erotic?
Do you believe in torture?

This pink sweet pea
is the sweet pea a soldier
arresting the doctor
grinds underfoot
so it bleeds on the sole
of his boot.

Do you believe flowers ask for it?
Do you believe people die?

Percentage of Americans who believe that "some civil liberties must be suspended in the war on AIDS": 42

QUARANTINE

There are not flowers
   black enough. Nothing
comes in and
   nothing goes out.
I am furious
   and blue, roaming
in dreams like
   a dirty girl.

The sheet jabs needles into my skin
I am cuffed to the bed and
skinny with silence

I eat seeds and wait until
   autumn. A tangle
of vegetation: roots and shoots
   and thorns.
Reeds
   come up twisted. Stalks split.
My privacy is a hybrid
   everyone sees.

There are not bones
   deep enough. Something
comes in and
   something goes out.
I am rancorous. My cleft
   heart grows and
pumps red earth,
   dark flesh.

TULIPS

By J. A. HAMILTON

My mother was a junkie. We all knew this. We saw the pills. Holy moly, a pharmacopoeia. I mean, this woman couldn't afford to take time out to brush her hair there were so many pills to pop in a day, so many calls to doctors to refill her prescriptions. She was drugged. Regularly she had cigarette fires all around the house. There were three- to twelve-inch black gullies she'd burned out in all the chairs and in her bed. She just sat and we kids made out how we could; she just sat with a Cameo cigarette dangling out her mouth all the time, pulling down the corner of her bottom lip and pretty near lying on her chin. We'd bring her food, you know, stuff we'd made. "C'mon, Mom," we'd say, "you gotta eat. You gotta eat something, eat this egg." And we'd poke mouthfuls at her. "G'way," she'd say and try to focus her wobbly eyes on us. One of us would stay on duty all night — we rotated — to check she didn't burn us all up in our beds. This was in the days before smoke detectors and one or the other of us kids was always pouring water over something or mopping up smoke damage on the ceilings. We could pretty much keep our own hours, we could cut school, we could steal money out of her purse even if she was sitting a yard away.

My mother stopped going upstairs to her bedroom. She said there were memories. She'd still be sitting, lumpy and slack-jawed, when we came down in the morning for school, with the TV tuned to "Romper Room" or just lines and that high-pitched hum. She just never went upstairs to bed.

J. A. (Jena) Hamilton was born in 1954 in Hamilton and now lives outside Vancouver. She has worked as a therapist with autistic children and with children who have suffered sexual abuse. Her work has appeared in a variety of literary magazines.

Then she moved the sofa out to decay on the lawn and bought a queen-sized waterbed with a turquoise frame, no pedestal, and filled it with the garden hose and she slept there on floral sheets, on the den floor.

My father was pretty much the reason my mother was a junkie. He was one of those men who when you commented on the nice blue sky would look at you like you were hallucinating and say, "Hell, that's a cloudy sky. Those are clouds, stupid." And you'd wonder. You'd sneak in the school library at lunchtime and look up an elementary science text and see clouds identified as clouds and blue sky identified as blue sky and try to be sure. Or you'd get all twisted so you actually couldn't tell anymore if a yacht was a yacht or just a poor man's skiff. My father lived in a neighbouring town, in a sleepy seaside village where he kept his yacht. I don't know what a man of that sort is like as a husband but I'm guessing it's not too sweet. Up was down and tulips were daffodils and fidelity was infidelity. My mother managed to live with all this until he left her. After he left, everything righted itself but she was still peering out at it skewed. She couldn't handle normalcy. Somebody not correcting her every breath. I had a friend back then in a similar situation. His name was Randy and he smoked marijuana the way my mother smoked cigarettes, one joint after the other, lighting the end of the new from the roach of the old. He did this for three years until one day he quit cold turkey. He sat in the cafeteria at school and held his head and kept repeating with puzzled awe, "Everything's wrong. Everything's wrong." Well, nothing was wrong. Just he'd never felt things right. For my mother it was the same. When my father lived at home she managed to know blue was blue and chopping onions makes you cry, but when he left and onions made her weep she couldn't believe it, she sagged, she slumped, she hit the linoleum like a sack of cement.

My father became a sort of obsession with my mother. When he was with her she ignored him and his ever-present insinuations about her moral character and just went her own way with the things she liked to do, sewing and refinishing furniture. But when he left it was like she was missing a tooth and her tongue couldn't stop bothering the hole. She was on the phone to him five or six times a day, arguing and sniping. I know she was relieved he was gone, in the sort of way I was relieved when school let out for the year, she could let down her hair, but she also didn't know what to do with herself. She'd been laid off and kids weren't enough reason to get through the day. Maybe kids aren't, I don't know. We weren't, anyway. My brother basically absented him-self, took up track and field and football and barely slept at home. My sister flunked grades six and seven and eight and couldn't read a grade one primer. I kept having sex without birth control. We were not the Cleavers. We were not something for my mother to focus on. So she just sat at the kitchen table with a ring of pills a foot in diameter and a bottle of ulcer medicine and ruby patches of misapplied blush on her cheeks and stared out at nothing and stared out at nothing some more. She told me she loved my father. She wanted him back. She told me when she died I was to have her engagement ring. She told me to have her cremated. I said okay and told her I was pregnant.

My mother owned a green-and-white Comet and drove me to the town where my father had an apartment. I mean, this was in the days before tape decks and shortly before Inagodadavita and quadraphonic sound; we listened to Frank Sinatra on the staticky AM radio. Even today I have a horror for easy-listening music. My mother admired a song called "Is That All There is?" sung by Patti Page. My mother admired Engelbert Humperdinck. My mother parked on a side street that wasn't my father's and told me I was a whore.

I said I wasn't.

She told me to watch a beautiful Victorian house, a white clapboard house with marine-blue trim, and passed me a pair of binoculars. It was winter. There were a lot of chestnut trees on the street without leaves and ice gleaming in patches under the streetlights. I asked my mother where we were. She said, "That slut's house."

"Someone Dad's dating?" I asked.

My mother told me to shut my big mouth and watch. I focused the binoculars. There wasn't anything to see. There was a porch with a glider swing and a tricycle and a door with the brass numbers nine and one. I watched for a while and Tom Jones sang and I watched until my mother's bottom jaw drooped open and her head lolled and then I changed the radio station. My mother's hand rooted out and turned it back. So I asked her if she could turn on the heat. Please, I said. I asked her how long we were going to sit there. She said until I had my bastard child or she decapitated my father, whichever came first. I thought about that and watched the house again, until all the lights inside went out and my mother was asleep for real. I pulled my knees up onto the seat and blew on my hands to warm them and felt my heart miss beats, which made me cough, an inherited thing I got from Dad.

My mother fell over and slept with her head in my lap. In the morning a chic blonde woman came out of the house with two little children, got in a grey Continental, and drove off.

A few days later my mother drove me to the city for an abortion and three hours later she picked me up. She had been to the bakery and we sat in the parking lot awhile. She passed me a cinnamon bun. "I would have raised it for you," she said, trembling, and lit a cigarette.

"Yeah," I said. "Well." I ate my cinnamon bun.

"We could have been a happy family," she said, inhaling.

"Did you buy any Coke?" I asked. "Didn't you get any drinks?"

A week after this, my mother tried to kill my sister with her sewing-scissors when my sister called Dad to complain that Mom had grounded her. She threw my sister against the console stereo, where my sister's impact broke my mother's collection of Herb Alpert and the Tijuana Brass albums. My sister made for the door. Mom went after her and my sister rolled and the scissors stuck in the hardwood floor by one point, so the other point was wobbling in the air.

My mother told me that after she'd been married for four years she masturbated late one night in her marital bed and then woke up my father to exclaim over her first orgasm. My father stared at her, sat up, hit her face, and went back to sleep. My mother said their marriage wasn't the same after that day, that something else, something bad, crept in to share it with them. She told me, "That was the night you were conceived. You were such a miserable baby."

When my mother gutted the whole den with one of her fires, after the fire department left and after I flushed her pills and cigarettes down the toilet, I called my father up and said, "Dad, come and get me." I had to leave. I didn't like my father much but it was a place to go. I was seventeen and I had got my diploma three days before. My sister had dropped out of grade nine and was planning to get her beautician's licence. My brother had moved across the country. He delivered ice and grew his hair long enough to wear a ponytail. My mother tried to stop me from leaving. She scratched my arm and drew jagged lines of blood. Then she pushed me out the door and threw my stuff after me, clothes and makeup and my teddy bear, whose eyes she tore off first. She screamed about how she was keeping my electric hair-rollers and my curling-iron. I waited for my father at the end of the driveway sitting on my suitcase.

So he just showed up, and my mother, looking like she had just slipped off the pages of *Vogue*, floated from the house, across the lawn with her high heels sinking in the grass. My father gaped like he couldn't believe she was real. I couldn't believe she was real. "Get in the car," he said to me.

"Leave her alone," he shouted at my mother.

My mother drew close and smiled. She reached behind her and a second later her skirt fell to the ground. She had nothing on underneath. Another second and her blouse was unbuttoned and wafting down like a feather in the sunlight. She put her hand on her hip. The look in her eyes was defiant, and I had to admit that no matter how many drugs she stuffed in her body and how her face had gone, her body was still the shape of women in pin-up calendars.

She took one step toward my father and he grunted and fell dead at her feet. When he did that, she crossed and stood over him. She prodded him with the toe of her high heel, and when she saw he wasn't going to rise again, that down wasn't up, that dead was dead, she raised her eyebrows, turned, and tottered back across the lawn, nude.

She got to the porch steps and turned back to look at me standing like some idiot with my suitcase still in my hand, beside my father's car.

"Dinner's in ten minutes," she said.

So I picked up her clothes and went in.

DON COLES

THE EDVARD MUNCH POEMS

The poems are based on a number of paintings by the Norwegian artist Edvard Munch (1863-1944), and on his diaries. My thanks to the Director of the Munch Museum in Oslo, Arne Eggum, for permission to browse among those diaries, and to my much-younger self for coming to rest for a few years in Scandinavia, long enough to learn to read those several languages. Most of the poems share titles with the paintings they take their point of departure from; it will be understood that some of them are offered in the voice of E.M., some not. The poem-cycle should require little more explanation; I'll add only that E.M. returned obsessively throughout his working life to a very few themes from childhood or very early manhood — these include the death of his mother when he was four, the death of his sister Sophie, his love for "Fru H.", his loneliness.

Don Coles was born in Woodstock, Ontario. He teaches at York University. He is the author of five collections of poetry: *Sometimes All Over* (1975); *Anniversaries* (1979); *The Prinzhorn Collection* (1982); *Landslides* (1986); *K. in Love* (1988).

to Edvard Munch

*"det ubevidste Sjaeleliv"**

*the unknown life of the soul

THE WHITE BODIES OF THE ANGELS

When she was dying Mama asked us to
Be good and love Jesus
So she could travel up to the angels
With an easy mind.
Vil Du lovar mig det?
*Ja. **
But in Berlin each little door
Opened to a waiting white body
And the woman said, "Perhaps
You'd prefer a chubby one?", and
Yes, I said.
Human beings need to have
The things that happen to them
Explained.

Will you promise me that?
  Yes.

SICK CHILD

for Johanne Sophie Munch,
b. 1862, d. of tuberculosis, 1877

After Mother, I loved you
Best. Daddy and me
Tried to keep you but
God wouldn't answer. How
It cooked in your breast!
You haemorrhaged all the images
You could have lived towards.
When I got to your age I almost
Burst — the hand-towels crimsoned
All day long.
   Jesus help me
   I'm dying, do you think
   I'll go to Heaven if I die?
   I think you will, min kaere son.
If I had been older I'd have
Saved you. Now I've a thousand
Sketches (they believe I worried on at these
To keep you close, keep affirming you
From right in front, but that wasn't it,
I was only trying to outnumber
Death) and also that economy-size
Apotheosis of you on the gallery wall
Over there, I don't suppose you've seen it —
But more to the point, I still have
The wicker chair you're always sitting on —
Remember? No, I mean *the real chair*!
Can you believe I'm eighty?

THE ARTIST'S BROTHER

Brothers are *difficult*. Consider
The James boys (the brainy ones,
Not those others), super to everyone
Except each other — H. fled even adored Venice
When W. got too near. As for *die Gebrüder
Mann,** same story: when a reviewer
Slates Heinrich for being (on his first try,
This was) "No playwright", Thomas's
Diary notes briskly "True. And Heini's
No novelist, either." *Schlimm, so 'was.*†
But here now and pictured by his brother is
Peter Andreas Munch,
Seated before a bookcase,
Reading. Twelve years later, aged 30
And only a few months married
He will write to his family
"I can't stand life anymore," and
Die. Nobody will find out why,
Though the family never liked
His wife. It is necessary
To know this as you watch him
Read. He is eighteen years old
And what he is doing here seems
Simple, seems quiet, seems
Preferable to much else he could be up to.
I believe one or two world-religions are
Palimpsested beneath that preference.
Or here he is again, exiting
From the bedroom in which Sophie,
Eternally fifteen and pillowed
In her wicker chair is, as usual,
Dying. Typically, no fuss:
Peter Andreas has chosen for his exit
A moment when nobody's looking.
The rest of them (Inger, Laura, Edvard,
And over there Papa and Aunt Karen)
Are all present but engaged,

*the brothers Mann
†tough, that sort of thing

Heads bowed, hands clasped, this is
Grief's familiar iconography. They are
Vulgar by comparison. Not to compete
With them, to eschew as he does
This *tableau* hardly at all *vivant*,
To efface himself so, is surely
A class act. He leaves observed
By no one alive in the world then
And enters a quiet which even his brother,
Facing away in this scene (and painting it
Only years later) will forever
Deny he heard. You,
Seeing this now, in Oslo or
As a page turns, endure
The private arrow. The arrow
Privately.
        This is enough,
Almost. Just one glimpse more.
Peter Andreas's childhood drawings,
Preserved who knows why, show scores of
Single-file Red Indians, matchstick-men
In feathered headdresses, queueing across
Page after page of a schoolboy's scribbler
To attack a stockaded fort,
Their conciliatory gait and slack tomahawks
In no hurry even though
The cannonballs, black and neat and
Trailing terrific threads of wind,
Are unmistakably *en route* towards them.
This is, the gallery's pamphlet says,
"Arithmetical art . . . without value",
But I recognize
My own unpraised childish imaginings,
An identical tribe wandering there,
And feel Peter Andreas near. It reminds me
Of my chance to be like him,
To go back to where I could see myself
As I might have been
Before things showed themselves to me,
And then say
This has not happened,
Or this, or this. Back to where

I could heal all the air
I ever spoke through, and have
Nobody thinking about me, ever.
      . . . Who would
Wish for that? No one. But
All the same. To sit
Reading before the bookcase,
The one you have almost forgotten,
A long time ago,
At home. To draw Red Indians.
To leave that room without saying much.

DEATH OF MARAT

*"We travelled south, to Dresden,
drinking all day and then making
love, which weakened me still more — "*
           E.M.'s diary

Charlotte Corday stands naked
Beside a murdered man on a bed.

"Look what I've done!"

Quarts of blood but no knife.

If this is a puzzle, it is
Easily solved. She has killed him
With her nakedness. Now
Breasts, belly, all those
Good parts and
The perfunctorily painted face
Have rotated towards us. We
Understand it is our turn and
Face up to this like men.

DEATH AND THE MAIDEN

Ibsen stood beside me
A long while looking.
He seemed more interested
In the spermflowing margins
Than in Death thrusting his
Spindleshank between her thighs,
Or her ripe belly pressing
Against and apparently massaging
An everlasting absence — or
Something very hard
To guess the nature of. It
Reminded me how Fru H.'s*
Soft body would give
Way, and give way, and how
Her mouth would go down, and
Down, and I said
The world is always useless
Without just this one human being,
Isn't it. Ibsen replied
He found it painful to
Look at young girls, though
He'd be helped from now on
Remembering their smooth bodies
Were not durable. He then said
His own body had been
Silent for years.

*"Fru H." — She is usually so identified
in Munch's diaries, and although biographers
have since told us her name, I'll leave it
at that. She was a married woman and the
young E.M. had a brief affair with her. He
was probably in love with her for the rest
of his life.

SUMMER EVENING BY THE LAKE

I am painting her standing among
The white birch trees watching
The moonlight's broad track across the water.

Even from the back there is
A slight resemblance to
The unknown woman I long for.

This is partly because of what she is doing.

Naturally I have wondered about
Her face. I have gestured in the vicinity with
My loaded-up brush.

But I was frightened it would be in tears.

JEALOUSY

No, he never saw her so, his wife naked
Under her dress in trifling talk
With somebody in that dark garden
Down there — but he thought it.
If he could trade this in
For a sadder thought he would.
Now any pause by day or night
Lights it up inside, her body's gentle
Tips and declivities
Unshadow the world, he can't believe
Such bliss escapes anybody.
There must be another day somewhere,
The *real* day of which the day
This thought first occurred to him
Is the false copy, he tells himself —
When not only didn't this happen
But the guess at its possibility
Is forbidden. Now all his exciting plans
For love seem gone with her white body
Into a disordered and dark garden,
He feels his life rushing towards
Being alone, and as for the son
They used to say they were going to have,
He won't be able to carry him
On his shoulders, now, ever,
As he wanted to, will he.

PUBERTY

And here is one who is only a little part of the idea
She will become. You would like as you see her
On her enormous bed to find words that will assist her
Towards the idea she will become, or save her from it
If this is what you would rather, but your words
Will have to be very good, hardly anybody is ever
Helped or saved. They may have to be as good
As Prince Andrey's words were for Pierre Bézuhov
On that dusty road near his summer estate of Bogutcharovo
When the two men rode together all the afternoon
Of August 12, 1809, Pierre noticing the heat and dust
On the leaves of the birch trees while they rode
And remembering long afterwards how certain important words
First reached his mind only inches
Above the darkbrown, sweating and glistening motion of his
    horse
Which seemed to carry him easily forward among the important
    words,
So easily he knew he might never forget them —
Although probably she is too incomplete, this one,
To receive words like those, you cannot expect *her*
To nod and reflect and ride on slowly beside you
Knowing she is in a specially resonating seashell
Of language that cannot ever be bettered and that will
Change her life.

As for me
While I stood before her in the Munchmusé in Oslo
Feeling her incompleteness beginning to flow towards me,
A woman passing nearby paused and seemed
To fall into some thought of her own for a few minutes.
I think she was 30, of average height and build, blonde hair
In a short, straight cut, wearing grey slacks and
A red cashmere cardigan over a white small-collared shirt,
And her face was the most beautiful I have ever seen.
Not to have seen it would have changed nothing
I have done since, but some thoughts. Where the stasis
Or on the other hand the outflowings
Of art come in here is that there is nothing
In stone or bronze or on all the holy ceilings of Christendom
That will outlast that face among the images of my life,
Even though I have totally forgotten it now. I mention her here
Because I have no other way, since her thought's pause
Ended and she walked far off from me, to alter her relationship
To decay or to death.

WHAT THEY DIDN'T LIKE

What they didn't like took me years
To understand. What they *said* it was
Was the serving-maid on the conjugal bed
Or a madonna's equivocal sweating or even
Hans Jaeger's* coffeehouse rhetoric,
As if I needed smoky talk to decide
Where the paint went. But these weren't
What they really hated. It wasn't even
Those solitary ones I showed
Gazing across a salt-stirring sea
Towards something perfect they once saw —
Those horizon-aching women who were
Almost 40 now and so unused,
So quietly, quietly unused. Women
Saw them and kept just as quiet
As who they were seeing;
Men imagined, finding them new,
They could save them.
                              No, what they really
Couldn't abide, or if they could
Couldn't stand their wives'
Learning about, was *nothing. Nothing*
Was what they didn't like. What
Frightened them. That madonna, who
Could have been lying back anywhere, being
Worshipped or fucked, or Sophie dying
In her chair by the window
With its flowerpot, and then dying
Without a chair or a window or a flowerpot,
Nothing but loose brown colour
Around both their lives, all the detail
Gone, the skirting-boards, pupils
In the eyes, rubbed away, smeared over,
Dug out with the brush's butt-end,
All gone loose, even the floorboards
Unreliable — that's what was upsetting.
The framelessness of everything. All
Those things people feel confused by
Which you'd better not deprive them of.

---

* *Hans Jaeger was the leader of a so-called bohemian set in Oslo*
that the young E. M. frequented.

If the rims of our lives go imageless
Anything at all can drift in there,
A long glance for instance —
How do you cope with that? Or
You might think you want to give yourself
Completely to somebody, and if
There's no surroundings
It could all at once be hard not to —
All your trees, piano lessons, holidays, little looks
You've been on the receiving end of
Ever since you started, they'd all go
With you and there'd be nothing left
Anywhere to just wait for you, to show
A way back from this somebody
If you needed it sometime. Of course
It's frightening. And yet we all guess
It's the only place to really
Find ourselves in, don't we?
A place with no furniture? No books,
No people, no plants on the window-ledge?
All those things we never really wanted
That are always there? Oh,
We've always known this — that
Anything complicated is a lie. So
Coming now in sight of it, the lies
Pouring out of the sides of the canvases,
Must have felt contagious and worrying,
Especially to people who would be bound
To realize that others seeing this
Could understand it too. Others
Who lived with them and wished every day
They didn't. All of them together now
Falling into a place where no word
Had ever been. Like Sophie, sickening
All those months in the same room,
Her eyes taking back all the images
The room had ever had, taking them back inside
Just by looking at them so many hours. Finally
Without anything at all to look at or be safe in.
You're not supposed to admit
That this happens — especially
If you do what I do, if you make things.
But it does, you know.

SELF-PORTRAIT AT 3.15 A.M.

A skinny old party in a too-big suit
Has just turned the lights on
At a quarter past three. What
Does he do now? Where is everybody?
He is just realizing nobody has told him
How to be as old as this. Another way
Of putting it: nobody has taught old age
How to enter him. He's wondering
Why has he painted himself into this room
Which so obviously has got only
A few minutes left in it. Just inches
Below the paint's surface in that canvas
Over there the shadowy damp breasts
Of that woman remind him of something.
Was it worth her while, once, to love him?
He remembers a night-fulcrum —
Those breasts swaying close over his eyes
Again and again, half the night it seems,
Coming over like moons, his mouth too
Was continuously amazed. He always knew
Descriptions of happiness must remain illegible
But you can stay close to it if you don't move,
Can't you? No you can't. These did, though —
Glistening from his own young mouth, too;
An hour's immortal even if a life isn't.

REFLECTIONS ON FAILURE

By LOUIS DUDEK

Most writers live with failure, a haunting feeling of failure, lurking deep in the marrow of their bones. Even the best and the most famous. We eavesdrop on Shakespeare, "in disgrace with fortune and men's eyes" — "Desiring this man's art, and that man's scope,/With what I most enjoy contented least." But the youngest poet submitting to a local magazine suffers the same self-doubt and sense of failure — until he learns to hide it carefully from the world.

Louis Dudek's most recent publications are *Zembla's Rocks* (poems), *Infinite Worlds* (a selection of Dudek's poetry by Robin Blaser), and *In Defence of Art: Critical Essays and Reviews*.

The objectivity of value in books is so doubtful that even the best are shaky when brought into question. Joseph Conrad writes in an essay: "A dreadful doubt hangs over the whole achievement of literature; I mean that of its greatest and its humblest men. Wasn't it 'Papa Augier' who, being given a copy of *Hamlet*, glanced through it expertly and then dropped it with the dry remark: 'Vous appelez ça une pièce, vous?' The whole tragedy of art lies in the nutshell of this terrifying anecdote."

Or listen to Proust, the greatest novelist of our time, saying of himself: "my talent, which is negligible". Or James Joyce, in a similar vein: "My talent? I haven't any. I write with such difficulty, so slowly."

In Canada, look at the preface to Earle Birney's *Selected Poems* of 1966, where he has brought together all the inanities that critics have written about him. It is an old familiar story, but it cuts deep.

Going through several decades of my private papers and correspondence recently, I was struck by the opposite thought that anyone studying these documents, pocked with a thin rain of royalty payments and permission fees, marked by letters of congratulation, thank-yous, honours received, flowing with visits, lectures, and readings arranged, might well conclude that the writer's life is a plushy one and very gratifying to the ego. But that is not the way it was in the living of it. Most certainly not, until perhaps the last ten or fifteen years of my career.

And, as Al Purdy wrote in one of the letters in these files, when I taunted him with his success as a poet, "It doesn't come to much."

It is in fact one of the ironies of the literary life, which I have often noted in my teaching of the lives of poets, that the writer who is neglected and ignored for fifty or sixty years, and who finally receives his meed of recognition, is forever thereafter perceived as a writer who had recognition, as though he had had a great and successful career. And this is part of a phenomenon I observed in studying my own documents. We normally look about us horizontally; we see ourselves at a given point of time, harried and somewhat uncomfortable, with a past that we remember fitfully, only in so far as it bears on and supports our present feeling about ourselves. And this horizontal view, the cut through time, is so attached to the needs of the present that it is extremely unreliable. "You cannot judge the universe by how you are feeling at the moment." It is only when I see myself through my documents, letters, and papers of forty, thirty, twenty years ago that I begin to see myself somewhat objectively — that is, vertically, in the perspective of time — and then I see a different self from the one here and now to which I am accustomed.

What I see then is a very active and positive man. But nowhere, or almost nowhere, in my letters does the gnawing feeling of failure, the condition of the inner life, appear to view; nor does it appear in the letters of others, either about myself or about the writers of the letters. The subject is always specific and substantial. The general effect of the documents, for biography and for literary history, is deceptively positive, and clearly marked with a certain success, as the world knows success.

But the life of the Canadian writer is one of a perpetual and deep-rooted sense of failure. It has to be. And only those who do not face up to the truth of their inner life will deny this; only those who are ignorant of their essential misery will pretend that they are thoroughly happy.

One reason for this that immediately comes to mind is the contrast between the aspiration of any writer and his awareness of his actual achievement. We never write a poem, or a story, or even an essay, that comes anywhere near to our conception; and certainly our work as a whole, as we look back at it, is a mere foothill to the Mount Everest of art that we imagine. Quite true. And yet this is not really the source of our dejection. It is something other.

The fact is that the delight of creation is so intense, even for minor writers, that comparison with some greater work never occurs in the process of writing. The climber enjoys the climb, he does not stare at the vanishing peak. "Sometimes I envy others, fear them / a little too, if they write well," says William Carlos Williams:

> "For when I cannot write I'm a sick man
> and want to die. The cause is plain.
>
> But they have no access to my sources.
> Let them write then as they may and
> perfect it as they can they will never
> come to the secret of that form
>
> interknit with the unfathomable ground
> where we walk daily and from which
> among the rest you have sprung
> and opened flower-like to my hand."

Or, as Ken Norris wrote to me in a letter the other day,

> When I was working on the odes I was reminded of the *purity* of poetry, and how nothing can touch it. It almost seems a shame to have to come down from the mountain and have to publish it sometimes; it changes it, brings it down into the crass world, stamps a price on its ass, and we go off to the market-place. But when you're in those ethereal realms: man, there's nothing like it.

A child at play, a young girl performing a dance, a poet caught by the feverish flame, these know nothing of failure or of invidious comparisons. The act itself is the reward and the ecstasy. It is participation in the secret of creation, which is the mystery at the heart of nature — how something, everything, appears out of nothing — and which science is forever helpless to explain.

So that, although the writer is haunted by failure, it is not in the writing that he suffers self-doubt — that is the one assured happiness of his existence as an artist — nor is it the comparison with greater writers that bothers him. They are in fact his inspiration, his silent companions, a constant encouragement. His rankling doubt has some other cause.

All human living is directed toward some perceived good, and the greater the good the greater the passion of our desire and our devotion. The admired writers of the past and the present define that high goal for us. They are not a cause of our discouragement, but, on the contrary, they are the very source of our confidence and our belief in the power of art.

The canker of defeat has nothing to do with the writing itself, which is our only solace, the sole joy of our miserable existence: it has to do with the world outside, as Ken Norris says, with "the marketplace".

For somehow the work written, the work finished, is not quite complete in itself. It wants to be brought before people. I have noticed that the itch to "show" is most intense, almost irresistible, and dangerously so, immediately after a new work has been completed. Dangerous because when the work cools, a few weeks later, it may need to be revised, or cancelled entirely, and you may be ashamed of your hasty mailings. (I sent parts of *Continuation II* to friends, editors, even to virtual strangers, as the work was being written. I now can't remember where some of them are lodged, those first copies, though corrections have been few.)

This desire to propagate, in the literal sense, is perhaps the key to both our sense of failure and our sense of mission. It has to do with our relation to the "other", the public — to mankind. For there is, in writing, a kind of need to love, and to be loved. It is a surrogate for the love relationship.

Every human being alive suffers from deprivation. He (she) has been torn from his mother's breast and thrown into the world. Our understanding of this, in psychological terms, is that mother love is eventually replaced by marital love, and that the fund is hoarded, and then richly dispensed in the marital bed. But for the artist there is a diversion of the primal energy. Some damming, or frustration, in the maternal or familial circle — a neurosis, an early crisis, a trauma — or a fortunate fall from narrow innocence, causes him (her) to seek help in a wider field, some desperate love in the wilderness: the love of mankind, or the tribe, to replace the love of the mother.

This desire to win the love of the generality, to win fame, as a substitute for love in the personal and fulfilling sense, is obviously a delusion, and many ancient writers, and moderns, have remarked upon its deceptions and its folly. "Wealth is like sea water; the more we drink, the thirstier we become; and the same is true of fame," says Schopenhauer. And LaBruyère: "We seek our happiness outside ourselves, and in the opinion of men whom we know to be flatterers, insincere, unjust, full of envy, caprice and prejudice. How absurd!" Or Thomas Mann, in whose essays I read: "Ambition must not come at the beginning, it must not stand *before* the work. It must grow with the work and belong more to it than to the ego of the artist."

Many writers have also remarked upon their craft as a demanding mistress, the bane of marriage, and their wives have ruefully concurred. For marital love and public acclaim are in competition: they are two forms of the same profound need, the need for love and acceptance, one at the personal level, the other public and generalized.

Worse still, however, there is no satisfaction to be had from the demanding mistress called art as a worldly temptress; and the source of our secret discontents, the sense of failure, lies in this inability of the social muse to satisfy. We enter here into the realm of history and the sociology of literature, a subject that has preoccupied me all my life, and that has its own very peculiar conditions of stress and discomfort in our time.

We have said that the writer is profoundly motivated to reach a public, to find an audience for his work. His motive is a need for love; he wants a response from the public that corresponds to that of the lover who answers the call of a loved one. ("To you, Milton, with Love" reads the memorial tribute to Milton Acorn in the *Writer's Quarterly*. A similar affection for Margaret Laurence, and for Gwendolyn MacEwen, has come a bit tardily after their deaths.) In fact the common response to an artist we truly admire is love: "I love her," we say of Emily Dickinson. "I love you, it's a great book," I wrote to Harry Howith in one of my letters when he sent me a good manuscript. We see this phenomenon also in popular entertainments and stage performances where the stars "throw kisses" to their audiences — give love, and get love in return, since the popularity of mass celebrities most nearly approaches the complete fulfilment of the love-dream of fame.

But this fame is no piece of cake. Too many of the truly famous — though not "truly great" — end in suicide, or in personal tragedy. Joseph Heller has etched it in acid in his comment on modern success: "Success and failure are both difficult to endure. Along with success come drugs, divorce, fornication, bullying, travel, medication, depression, neurosis and suicide. With failure comes failure."

There must be a general reason for this. To my thinking, the sudden experience of popular fame induces something like a state of hysteria, which can be toxic and lethal. The individual has embraced an illusion, the fulfilment of all his (or her) dreams, but it is a spectre and an unreality, some inconceivable mass of people who are more terrifying than desirable at close quarters, and so he or she cracks up, or at best holds together against an impending crack-up.

For most of us, however, the celebrity experience is mercifully not the issue. (The one most successful writer in Canada who is a celebrity, Leonard Cohen, is also, to judge from his work, the one most afflicted with the canker as defined here: there is no escape from the dilemma.) Most poets achieve no fame at all, and very little recognition. This is a result of the void in modern culture, in which the arts of the past have been wiped out by the entertainment and communications industry, where the educated middle class has been displaced by a moneyed *barbarie*, and where poetry and literature must be subsidized merely to lie on the library shelves. (These subsidies are actually an act of nostalgia; they have not even the twitches of protest of a living culture.)

In this situation, as we know, most writers live and write without an audience, and have little hope of ever finding one. Success is a matter of chance. "Certainly anybody whose experience has been gained in the literary field," Rebecca West writes, "cannot believe that merit alone decides the success or failure of a writer." And Kathleen O'Brien has said, "There is probably no other trade in which there is so little relationship between profits and actual value, or into which sheer chance so largely enters." The result is a chronic sense of failure, hidden from the world's view, but inescapable as part of the writer's consciousness. (The most extravagant account of artists' lives as modern tragedy is to be found in Malcolm Lowry's "Strange Comfort Afforded by the Profession", originally published in *Partisan Review,* reprinted in Klinck and Watters' *Canadian Anthology.* It is a somewhat hysterical account; but the hysteria is expected and unavoidable, for love perpetually denied leads by definition to a potential hysteria — the Werther syndrome.

What, then, is the answer? "Prepare for failure" is the best advice one can give to any young writer. "Take it as part of your destiny, as your vocation." Since you have chosen to pursue a phantom, a ghoul — an amorphous, fickle, undefinable mob — for favours, do not demand or expect substance from the empty air. But there are also a few counsels of hope one might give, and small communities where the alienation of the writer might be partly relieved.

I love to attend small readings in bookstores in Montreal, where thirty or forty young people sit quietly and listen to a poet read his (or her) sensitive, ironic, reflective, invariably honest and personal poems of contemporary life. Honesty is so rare, in the media, or in the bombast of conversation, that these readings, at The Word bookstore on Milton Street, at the Librairie sur le Parc, facing Girouard Park on Sherbrooke, or at the Yellow Door Coffee House on Aylmer, are like an oasis in the modern wasteland. But, most important of all, there is an obvious affection — love — among the young poets for those who read, and for one another among those who listen. In a small way, therefore, this is a public, created by poets for poetry, where the audience, which does not exist in modern society, since none of their books are reviewed in the local papers or on radio, comes into being for a while as a small community (like that of the early Christians), for agape, to love and to be loved.

I say it in many a poem:

> I like to be at a meeting of poets
>   where they read
> Each proud of his art, stands up
> and works his high effect
>
> different from any other
>   strange, separate
> as the grasses, or the species
>
> Some declaim, others jest
> some seem to suffer — for the sake of the game
>   (as all do in fact)
> some in the very clouds, some in dirt
> but all devotional in their secular praise
>
> of the actual and the endless ways
> their syllables turn and return to contain themselves.

But of course the early Christians were the beginnings of a great Christian society. We can say this also about poetry and good writing — that it foreshadows a great literate society; for poetry never dies, and enlightenment, whatever the setbacks and regressions, is the destiny of mankind. It may start with the few, in a mass society, as if starting all over again in a dark age, but it will continue again to its great successes. In Canada especially, which is still a country of beginnings, it has always been the few — a handful of poets, writers, painters — who have pioneered the first settlements of art and book culture.

My favourite painting in the National Gallery, of which we have a print hanging in our house, is that by Robert Harris, *A Meeting of the School Trustees*, which shows a schoolteacher in a country schoolhouse facing a group of hard-bitten farmers — one sympathetic, three less so — arguing the case for more books, for better schooling. This is a theme common in Canadian novels and stories, the arrival of the disturbing schoolteacher. It is our beginning. The beginning of a culture.

In the 1940s, when my generation was just beginning, and we felt that modernism was opening up in Canada, the poets were filled with anger and indignation toward the limitations and philistine prejudices of this country, but they were also filled with confidence and hope for the coming future of the modernist renewal. "Give us five hundred readers," we used to say, "and we will give you a literature."

Today, a half-century later, these five hundred readers are still the fond hope of many bright, determined poets, good poets, writing and publishing quietly (if somewhat bitterly), in a noisy world indifferent to poetry. They suffer secretly from the curse of failure, although on the face of it they may show no sign of it. Read their poetry, however; there you will find evidence of "the invisible worm" — the lack of human response — "that flies in the night, through the howling storm". It is endemic to all creative work, but it is perhaps more particular and more crippling in our time than at any other in history, despite our "mass audiences" and mass entertainments — or perhaps because of them.

SIMPLE SUFFERINGS

By THOMAS KING

Thomas King is a professor in the Native Studies Department at the University of Lethbridge. His fiction has appeared in *The Malahat Review, Canadian Fiction Magazine,* and *Whetstone.* He co-edited *The Native in Literature* and edited a special issue of *Canadian Fiction Magazine* which featured the short fiction of Native writers in Canada. His first novel, *Medicine River,* is to be published by Penguin. He is currently working on a collection of stories, a second novel, and an anthology of Native literature.

W e all suffer. I say this to myself. Sometimes I share it with others. For my birthday, Rachael bought me a stop-watch and paid for a three-month membership at the Trim-Tone Health Club.

"It's for checking your heart when you exercise," she said.

I have not been to the Trim-Tone Health Club. I have tied the watch to my rear-view mirror and am timing the commute to and from work.

"This button turns the watch on. The red one."

I get in the car.

I start the watch.

"It has this other button . . . right here, that lets you time your pulse."

Forty-seven minutes to work, seventy-three minutes home. That is an average, mind you, and it may change as I collect more data.

"Obesity is a real danger as you get older," Rachael tells me. "Vaginas outlive penises by fifteen years and part of the reason is obesity."

I love Rachael. I hate exercise. All the penises at work exercise. Jerry jogs. Bob swims. Fred plays baseball for a community league.

I do not like to sweat. Sweat is sticky. You have to wash it off. It smells. You have to take a shower and then get dressed again.

The deodorants the companies manufacture are supposed to keep you from sweating, and you have to do your part. I tell Rachael this.

"Come on, honey," Rachael says. "All you penises like to sweat. It's macho to sweat."

She does not believe this completely, but she is worried that I will get fatter. Rachael was a cheerleader in high school. She twirled the baton and did the splits on the thick grass in front of the bleachers, while the football players crashed into one another.

When we were first married, Rachael brought home a jock-strap and had me put it on. I have not mentioned this to anyone. It was too large and too new, a great gaping cup, and I jiggled in it when I walked. Whenever Rachael was interested, she would whisper in my ear, "Put on the jock."

Rachael is worried about my health. My shirts work their way out of my pants. The waistband on my slacks folds over. I wear my sports coats open.

"Harold Rogers had a heart attack last month. Edna says he's going to take up swimming and doesn't know why he didn't do it sooner."

Rachael has stopped making her apple pies. I have begun to find carrots in my lunch and slices of uncooked cauliflower and broccoli. I eat these first, out of love. Nevertheless, I need new slacks. For bowling.

I go to Sheldon's Penis Store. They carry big and tall clothing. I am under six feet tall. I have perfectly good slacks at home in my closet. I will be able to wear them soon.

Jake Armando smiles and opens his arms. "Mr. Lincoln." He gives me a hug. "Wonderful health!" He beats my shoulders and pats my stomach, though we are only acquaintances. "What will it be for you today? A suit? A nice sports coat?"

Armando likes to start with the expensive things.

"Shirts . . . shoes . . . underwear . . . ties?"

Armando likes to tell jokes.

"There's this travelling salespenis and his car breaks down. So he goes to this farm house . . . "

It is the way he warms his customers to a sale. I tell him I need slacks. For bowling. He puts the tape around my waist.

I tell him I am now a thirty-eight, maybe a thirty-seven.

Armando smiles at me and pulls several pairs of black slacks off the rack.

"Here," he says, "try these."

He is fast, but I can see he gets them from the forty section.

"They look big."

"They're Italian."

Rachael and her sisters are slender. I tell her it all has to do with genes. My father was large. His father was large. You cannot fight genes.

The slacks are tight.

"Maybe one size larger?" says Armando.

"These are fine," I say, standing up straight. "They are for bowling."

These are the kinds of things that are at the heart of the suffering in the world. We bear up under the catastrophes well enough, the death of a relative or a friend, a terminal illness, a traffic accident, war, natural disasters. Perhaps it is because these are rare, and they encourage in us a strength we do not normally have.

I have told Armando this. He does not understand. He thinks the problem lies elsewhere.

"Vaginas," Armando always tells me when I visit his shop. "You can't live with them; you can't live without them."

We manage disaster rather well. The sufferings that most of us bear, the sufferings that destroy us, are simpler and less dramatic. Marriage, for example. Divorce. Children. Obesity, middle age, indigestion, bad breath. Baldness, varicose veins, yellow teeth, wrinkles, lower-back strain. Irregularity. Warts.

"Vaginas," Armando says. "You can't live with them; you can't live without them."

Armando stands in his shop, his tape measure draped over his shoulders like a priest's stole, and measures people and tells his jokes. He smiles (his teeth are very white). He laughs. It is not Armando's fault. His father showed him the trick. Armando will show his sons.

"Good wool, this," says Armando. He lowers himself to his knees. He pushes the tape into my crotch. "You want cuffs?"

"No cuffs," I say.

Armando walks me to the door.

I get in the car.

I start the watch.

Two years ago on our anniversary, I came out of the bathroom in just the jock-strap.

"Surprise!" I said.

Rachael pulled the covers over her head and kicked her feet and laughed and laughed and laughed.

"You are a sweetheart," she said, tears running down her face. "What a precious. God, we used to do that too, didn't we. Honey . . . God . . . take it off." And she began laughing again. "The children . . . what if the children came in . . ." More laughing. "What a silly penis you are."

"Come to bed," she said, and she held out her arms. I remember Rachael's breasts hanging out over the covers. The mole near the nipple had a long hair growing out of it. "What a sweetheart you are for remembering."

The next morning, I put the jock-strap in the trash and tied the ends of the black plastic bag together.

From Armando's to home is twenty-three minutes.

By the time I arrive, I have forgiven Rachael and am full of love for her. We will make love tonight, and I will play the big bear and growl the way she likes me to do. When we play the big bear, I get to roll her around on the bed and put my nose in her armpits and her crotch. I snort and growl, and we wallow about in one another like two great pigs in a puddle.

Rachael is setting the table. She is beautiful.

"Honey," she says. "Come here. . . . I've got something for you."

I growl.

"Here," she says. "Try it on; see if it fits. Don't be silly."

She hands me a box.

"I have to get ready. Helen and Joan and Betty are coming by tonight. We're supposed to plan that fundraiser for Tommy's school."

It is a running-suit. It is blue and maroon. It says "Nike" across the front.

"I saw it when I was shopping the other day. It was on sale. Try it on."

The bathroom is dark and cold. I can smell stale urine and perfume. I stand there with the lights off for ten minutes. I come out.

"It fits perfectly."

"Oh, honey . . . you're supposed to let me see it. You should have left it on." Rachael takes a cake out of the refrigerator. It is chocolate. "Listen, when you come home from bowling, could you stop off at the store. We need milk."

"Bowling is tomorrow night," I say.

"Oh . . . honey. It is, isn't it? I forgot. Well, what am I going to do with you." She puts her arms around me.

"I know," she says and gives me a kiss. "Go to the club and try out the new suit." She puts her hand on my crotch. "Run a few laps and get nice and sweaty. When you get home, I'll have a piece of cake for you." She squeezes me gently. "Who knows . . .

"But don't come home before ten."

I kiss her goodbye.

I get in the car.

I start the watch.

ORANGES AND APPLES

By ALICE MUNRO

"I hired a looker from out Shawtown," Murray's father said. "She's a Delaney, but so far she doesn't seem to have any bad habits. I put her in Men's Wear."

This was in the spring of 1955. Murray was just out of college. He'd come home and seen at once what fate was waiting for him. Anybody could see it, written on his father's darkened, scooped-out face, rising almost daily in his father's stomach — the hard loaf that would kill before winter. In six months Murray would be in charge, sitting in the little lookout office that hung like a cage at the back of the store, over Linoleum.

Zeigler's then was still called Zeigler's Department Store. It was about the same age as the town itself. The present building — three stories high, red brick, the name in angled gray brick letters that had always looked, to Murray, puzzlingly jaunty and Oriental — had gone up in 1880, replacing an earlier building of wood. The store did not deal in groceries or hardware anymore, but they still had Men's, Ladies', and Children's Wear, Dry Goods, Boots and Shoes, Draperies, Housewares, Furniture.

Murray strolled by to have a look at the looker. He found her penned behind rows of cellophaned shirts. Barbara. She was tall and well developed, as his father in a lowered and regretful voice had said. Her thick black hair did not curl or lie flat — it sprang up like a

Alice Munro's most recent book was *The Progress of Love*. She is working on a new story collection and hopes to write further memoirs.

crest from her wide white forehead. Her eyebrows were thick and black as well, and glossy. Murray found out later that she put Vaseline on them, and plucked out the hairs that would have met above her nose.

Barbara's mother had been the mainstay of a marginal farm. When she died, the family migrated to Shawtown, which was a rackety half-rural settlement on the edge of Walley. Barbara's father did odd jobs, and her two brothers had got into trouble with cars and breaking and entering. One later disappeared. The other married a managing sort of girl and settled down. It was that one who was coming into the store at this time and hanging around, on the pretext of visiting Barbara.

"Watch out for him," Barbara told the other clerks. "He's a jerk, but he knows how to stick things to his fingers."

Hearing about this, Murray was impressed by her lack of family feeling. He was an only child, not spoiled but favored, and he felt himself bound by many ties of obligation, decency, and love. As soon as he got home from college, he had to go around greeting all the people who worked in the store, most of whom he'd known since childhood. He had to chat and smile on the streets of Walley, affable as a crown prince.

Barbara's brother was caught with a pair of socks in one pocket and a package of curtain hooks in the other.

"What do you think he wanted the curtain hooks for?" Murray asked Barbara. He was anxious to make a joke of this, showing her how nothing was held against her on her brother's account.

"How should I know?" said Barbara.

"Maybe he needs counselling," said Murray. He had taken some sociology courses, because he had hoped at one time to become a United Church minister.

Barbara said indifferently, "Maybe he needs to be hanged."

Murray fell in love with her then, if he was not in love already. Here is a noble girl, he thought. A bold black-and-white lily out of the Swamp Irish — Lorna Doone with a rougher tongue and a stronger spine. Mother won't like her, he thought. (About that he was entirely right.) He was happier than he'd been at any time since he lost his faith. (That was an unsatisfactory way of putting it. It was more as if he'd come into a closed-off room or opened a drawer and found that his faith had dried up, turned to a mound of dust in the corner.)

He always said that he made up his mind at once to get Barbara, but he used no tactics beyond an open display of worship. A capacity for worship had been noticeable in him all through his school days, along with his good nature and a tendency to befriend underdogs. But he was sturdy enough — he had enough advantages of his own — that it hadn't got him any serious squelching. Minor squelches he was able to absorb.

Barbara refused to ride on a float as the Downtown Merchants' contestant for the Queen of the Dominion Day Parade.

"I absolutely agree with you," said Murray sympathetically. "Beauty contests are degrading."

"It's the paper flowers," said Barbara. "They make me sneeze."

Murray and Barbara live now at Zeigler's Resort, twenty-five miles or so northeast of Walley. The land here is rough and hilly. The farmers abandoned it around the turn of the century and let it go back to bush. Murray's father bought two hundred acres of it and built a primitive cabin and called the place his hunting camp. When Murray lost the store in Walley, and the big house and the little house on the lot behind the store, he came up here, with Barbara and their two small children. He drove a school bus to get some cash income, and worked all the rest of the time building eight new cabins and renovating the one that was there, to serve as the lodge and as living quarters for his family. He learned carpentry, masonry, wiring, plumbing. He cut down trees and dammed the creek and cleaned the creek bed and trucked in sand, to make a swimming pond and a beach. For obvious reasons (as he says), Barbara handled the finances.

Murray says that his is a common story. Does it deserve to be called a classic? "My great-grandfather got the business going. My grandfather established it in all its glory. My father preserved it. And I lost it."

He doesn't mind telling people. Not that he waylays them and unburdens himself immediately. Guests are used to seeing him always at work. Repairing the dock, painting the rowboat, hauling in groceries, digging up drains, he looks so competent and unfrazzled, so cheerfully committed to whatever job he's doing, that they take him for a farmer turned to resort-keeping. He has the kind of patience and uninquisitive friendliness, the unathletic but toughened and serviceable body, the sunburned face, the graying boyishness that they might expect of a country man. But the same guests come back year after year, and sometimes they become friends who are invited on their last night to eat dinner at the family table. (It is considered an achievement, among the regulars, to become friends with stately Barbara. Some never manage it.) Then they may get to hear Murray's story.

"My grandfather used to go up on the roof of our building in Walley," Murray says. "He went up on the roof and he threw down money. Every Saturday afternoon. Quarters, dimes, nickels — five-cent pieces, I guess you called them then. It drew the crowds. The men who started Walley were flashy fellows. They weren't well educated. They weren't genteel. They thought they were building Chicago."

Then something different happened, he says. In came the ladies and the rectors and the grammar school. Out with the saloons and in with the garden parties. Murray's father was an elder of St. Andrew's; he stood for the Conservative Party.

"Funny — we used to say 'stood for' instead of 'ran for.' The store was an institution by that time. Nothing changed for decades. The old display cases with curved glass tops, and the change zinging overhead in those metal cylinders. The whole town was like that, into the fifties. The elm trees weren't dead yet. They'd started. In the summer there were the old cloth awnings all around the square."

When Murray decided to modernize he went all out. It was 1965. He had the whole building covered in white stucco, the windows blocked in. Just little, classy, eye-level windows left along the street, as if intended to display the Crown jewels. The name "Zeigler's" — just that — written across the stucco in flowing script, pink neon. He chucked the waist-high counters and carpeted the varnished floors and put in indirect lighting and lots of mirrors. A great skylight over the staircase. (It leaked, had to be repaired, was taken out before the second winter.) Indoor trees and bits of pools and a kind of fountain in the ladies' room.

Insanity.

Meanwhile the mall had opened south of town. Should Murray have gone out there? He was too mired in debt to move. Also, he had become a downtown promoter. He had not only changed the image of Zeigler's, he had changed himself, becoming a busy loudmouth on the municipal scene. He served on committees. He was on the building committee. That was how he discovered that a man from Logan, a dealer and developer, was getting government money for restoring old buildings when the fact of the matter was that he was tearing the old buildings down and preserving only a remnant of the foundation to incorporate into his new, ugly, badly built, profitable apartment blocks.

"Aha — corruption," says Murray when he recalls this. "Let the people know! I ranted to the newspaper. I practically ranted on the street corners. What did I think? Did I think the people *didn't* know? It must have been a death wish. It was a death wish. I got to be such a ranter and public entertainment that I was turfed off the committee. I'd lost credibility. They said so. I'd also lost the store. I'd lost it to the bank. Plus the big house my grandfather built and the little house on the same lot, where Barbara and I and the kids were living. The bank couldn't get at them, but I sold them off, to get square — that was the way I wanted to do it. Lucky thing my mother died before the crash came."

Sometimes Barbara excuses herself while Murray is talking. She could be going to get more coffee, she might come back in a moment. Or she might take the dog, Sadie, and go for a walk down to the pond, in among the pale trunks of the birch and poplar trees and under the droopy hemlocks. Murray doesn't bother explaining, though he listens, without appearing to do so, to hear her come back. Anybody who becomes their friend has to understand how Barbara balances contact with absences, just as they have to understand that Barbara doesn't want to *do* anything. She does plenty, of course. She does the cooking, she manages the resort. But when people find out how much she has read, and that she's never been to college, they sometimes suggest that she should go, she should get a degree.

"What for?" says Barbara.

And it turns out that she doesn't want to be a teacher, or a scholar, or a librarian, or an editor, or to make television documentaries, or review books, or write articles. The list of things that Barbara doesn't want to do is as long as your arm. Apparently she wants to do what she does — read, and go for walks, eat and drink with pleasure, tolerate some company. And unless people can value this about her — her withdrawals, her severe indolence (she has an air of indolence even when she's cooking an excellent dinner for thirty people) — they don't remain among the company she tolerates.

When Murray was busy renovating and borrowing money and involving himself in municipal life, Barbara was reading. She had always read, but now she let it take up more and more of her time. The children had started to school. Some days Barbara never left the house. There was always a coffee cup by her chair, and a pile of fat dusty books from the library. *Remembrance of Things Past*, *Joseph and His Brothers*, books by lesser Russians whom Murray had never heard of. Barbara has a real mania for reading, his mother said — isn't she worried about bringing all those books from the library into the house? You never know who has been handling them.

Reading such heavy books, Barbara grew heavier herself. She did not get really fat, but she put on twenty or twenty-five pounds, well distributed over her tall, never delicate frame. Her face changed, too — flesh blurred its firm lines, making her look softer and in a way younger. Her cheeks puffed out and her mouth looked more secretive. Sometimes she had — she still has — the expression of a self-absorbed and rather willful little girl. Nowadays she reads skimpy-looking books by Czechs or Japanese or Rumanians, but she is still heavy. Her hair is still long, too, and black, except around the face, where it has gone white, as if a piece of veiling had been thrown over it.

Murray and Barbara are driving down out of the hills, from twisting, hilly roads to the flat, straight grid of the farmland. They are driving to Walley, for a special reason.

Two weeks ago Barbara discovered a lump in the flesh of one of her buttocks. She was drying herself after coming out of the pond — it was the last swim, the last spurt of warm weather of the year. The lump was about the size of a marble. "If I wasn't so fat I'd probably have found it sooner," she said, without particular regret or alarm. She and Murray spoke of the lump as they would of a bad tooth — a nuisance that had to be dealt with. She had it removed in the hospital in Walley. Then there had to be a biopsy.

"Is it possible to have cancer of the buttock?" she asked the doctor. "What an undignified thing!"

The doctor said that the lump could be a floater — malignant cells that had their origin somewhere else in the body. A sealed message. And they could remain a mystery — bad cells whose home base could never be found. If indeed they proved to be bad cells at all. "The future is unclear till we know," said the doctor.

Yesterday the doctor's receptionist phoned and said that the results were in. She made an appointment for Barbara to see the doctor in his office in Walley that afternoon.

"Is that all?" Murray said.

"All what?"

"Is that all she said?"

"She's just the receptionist. That's all she's supposed to say."

They are driving between walls of corn. The stalks are eight or nine feet high. Any day now the farmers will start to cut them. The sun is low enough even by midafternoon to shine through the cornstalks and turn them to coppery gold. They drive through an orderly radiance, mile after mile.

Last night they stayed up late; they watched an old, old movie, *The Trail of the Lonesome Pine*. Murray had seen it when he was a child, in the Roxy Theatre, in Walley. All he had remembered was the part about Buddy getting killed and Henry Fonda chipping out the pine-tree coffin.

Thinking about that, he starts to sing. "'Oh, they cut down the old pine tree, and they hauled it away to the mill.' I always thought," he says, interrupting himself, "that that song came from that movie."

Barbara continues singing. "'To make a coffin of

pine, for that sweetheart of mine.'" Then she says, "Don't be squeamish."

"I wasn't," says Murray. "I forgot what came next."

"Don't come and sit in the waiting room. It's awful. Go down to the beach and wait for me. I'll come down the Sunset Steps."

They have to drive past the farm where Beatrice Sawicky used to keep horses. At one time she had a riding school. That didn't last very long. She boarded horses then, and she must have made a living out of that, because she kept at it, she stayed there, until four or five years ago, when she sold out and, presumably, moved away. They didn't know where she would go; they had seen her a few times in town but never talked to her. When they used to drive past, and saw the horses in the fields, one or the other of them would say, "I wonder what happened to Victor." Not every time they passed, but about once a year, one of them would say that, and the other would answer, "God knows," or something of the sort. But they haven't bothered saying it since Beatrice and the horses left.

The first time that Victor Sawicky came into the store, he scattered the clerks — so Murray said to Barbara — like a cat among the pigeons. And, in fact, many of the clerks whom Murray had inherited with the store did look like pigeons — they were gray-haired maiden ladies whom maidenhood had not kept from growing stout and bosomy. It was easy to imagine a clammy dew of alarm between those bosoms at the sight of Victor. One of the women came pattering up the ramp to Murray's little office to tell him that there was a foreigner and that none of them could make out what it was he wanted.

He wanted work clothes. It wasn't so difficult to tell what he was saying. (After all, he had lived for several years in England.) It was not the Polish accent that dismayed the clerks in Zeigler's store, it was Victor's looks. Murray put Victor immediately into the same class of human beings as Barbara, but of the two he found Victor far the more splendid and disturbing. He had been able to look at Barbara and think, "That is a rare girl," but she was still a girl, and he wanted to sleep with her. (He had been married to her now for seven years.) Victor drew his attention as a sleek and princely animal might — say, a golden palomino, bold but high-strung, shy about the stir he created. You'd try to say something soothing but deferential and stroke his shining neck, if he'd let you.

Murray said, "Work clothes."

Victor was tall and light-boned and looked polished. In the coffee shop of the British Exchange Hotel, where he and Murray got in the habit of going, a waitress said to him one day, "You mind telling me? Because we kind of have a bet going on? How tall are you?"

"I am six feet and five inches," said Victor.

"Is that all? We had you going up as high as seven feet."

His skin was a pale-olive color, his hair a dark blond, his eyes a light, bright blue. The eyes protruded a little, and the eyelids never lifted quite all the way. His teeth were large and stained, like his fingers, from nicotine. He smoked all the time. He was smoking while he gave his puzzled consideration to the overalls in Zeigler's store. They were all too short in the legs.

He said that he and his wife, who was English, had bought a farm just on the edge of town. Murray wanted to talk to him without the clerks hanging around in amazement, so he took him along the street, for the first time, to the British Exchange. He knew the farm Victor was talking about, and he didn't think much of it. But Victor said that they were not intending to farm it. They were going to keep horses and run a riding school. Victor asked Murray's opinion about whether or not this would be a success. Were there enough little rich girls around? "I think if you have a riding school you must have the little rich girls. They are the ones for the horse riding."

"You could advertise in the city papers, and they could come in the summers," Murray said.

"Of course. To the camp. To the horse camp. Here and in the United States they always go in summer to the camp, isn't that so?"

Victor seemed delighted with this idea. Everything was absurd to him, everything acceptable. The winters — is it true that there is frost from October to May? Does the snow actually reach to the windowsills? Can one drink the well water without boiling, or is there a danger of catching typhoid fever? What kind of trees, cut down, will provide the best heat in the stove?

Murray could not remember afterward which questions came the first day, or if there was ever a boundary between the practical questions and the more general or personal. He didn't think there was — they came all mixed up together. When Victor wondered about anything, he asked. When were those buildings put up? What is the people's main religion and are they very serious about it? Who is that important-looking man, that sad-looking woman? What do the people work at? Are there agitators, freethinkers, very rich people, Communists? What sort of crimes are committed, when was the last time there was a murder, is there a certain amount of adultery? Did Murray play golf, did he own a pleasure boat, did his employees call him sir? (Not much, and no, and no.) Victor's blue eyes continued to shine with pleasure, whatever the question, whatever the answer. He stretched his long legs out of the coffee-shop booth and clasped his hands behind his head. He luxuriated, taking everything in. Soon Murray was telling him about how his grandfather threw coins down into the street, and about his father's dark suits and silk-backed vests, and his own notions of becoming a minister.

"But you did not?"

"I lost my faith." Murray always felt he had to grin when he said this. "That is — "

"I know what it is."

When he came to find Murray at the store, Victor would not ask any of the clerks if he could see him but would go straight up to the office, up the ramp to the little cage. It had wrought-iron walls around it, about as high as Murray was — about five-nine. Victor would try to come up stealthily, but of course his presence would have already disturbed the store, stirring up ripples of attention, misgiving, excitement. Murray usually knew when he was coming but pretended not to. Then Victor, for a surprise, would rest his gleaming head on the top of the wall, his neck held between two of the pointed, decorative spikes. He grinned at the idiotic effect.

Murray found this inexpressibly flattering.

Victor had a history of his own, of course. He was ten years older than Murray; he had been nineteen when the war broke out. He was a student then, in Warsaw. He had been taking flying lessons, but did not yet have his pilot's license. Nevertheless he went out to the airstrip where the planes of the Polish Air Force were sitting — he and some of his friends went out there almost as a prank, on the morning of the German invasion, and almost as a prank they took some of the planes into the air, and then they flew them to Sweden. After that, he got to England and joined the Polish Air Force, which was attached to the Royal Air Force. He flew on many raids, and was shot down over France. He bailed out; he hid in the woods, he ate raw potatoes from the fields, he was helped by the French Underground and made his way to the Spanish border. He got back to England. And he found to his great disappointment that he was not to be allowed to fly again. He knew too much. If he should be shot down again and captured and interrogated, he knew too much. He was so disappointed, so restless, he made such a nuisance of himself, that he was given another job — he was sent to Turkey, on a more or less secret mission, to be part of a network that helped Poles, and others, who were escaping through the Balkans.

That was what he had been doing while Murray and his friends had been building model airplanes and fixing up a kind of cockpit in the bicycle shed at school, so that they could pretend to be bombing Germany.

"But do you believe all that stuff really?" Barbara said.

"They did fly Polish planes to Sweden before the Germans could get them," Murray said stubbornly. "And people did get shot down over France and escape."

"Do you think anybody as conspicuous as Victor could escape? Do you think anybody that conspicuous would ever get sent on a secret mission? You have to look more like Alec Guinness to get sent on a secret mission."

"Maybe he's so conspicuous he looks innocent," Murray said. "Maybe he'd look like the last person on earth to be sent on a secret mission and that would be the very reason nobody would suspect."

Perhaps for the first time, he thought that Barbara's cynicism was automatic and irritating. It was like a quirk she had, a tic.

They had this conversation after Victor and Beatrice had come to dinner. Murray had been anxious for Victor and Barbara to meet. He wanted to present them to each other, almost to show them off to each other. But when the opportunity arrived they were not at their best. Each seemed standoffish, lukewarm, nervous, ironical.

The day of the dinner party, in late May, had been freakishly cold and rainy. The children — Felicity was five then, and Adam three — had been playing indoors all day, getting in Barbara's way, messing up the living room, which she had cleaned, and by bedtime they weren't tired enough to settle down. The long, light evening was no help. There were many calls for drinks of water, reports of a stomach ache, complaints about a dog that had almost bitten Felicity last week. Finally Adam raced into the living room wearing only his pajama top, shouting, "I want a bicky, I want a bicky." "Bicky" was a baby word for "biscuit" which he didn't normally use anymore. It seemed very likely that he had been inspired to this performance and probably rehearsed in it by Felicity. Murray scooped him up and carried him into the children's room and whacked his conveniently bare bottom. Then he whacked Felicity's once for good measure and returned to the dining room rubbing his hands together, playing a role he detested, that of the hearty disciplinarian. The bedroom door stayed shut after that, but it could not shut out a prolonged and vengeful howling.

Everything had gone wrong from the start with this visit. Murray had opened the door and said expansively, "'The chestnut casts his flambeaux, and the flowers stream from the hawthorn on the wind away!,'" referring to the weather, and thinking that Beatrice would appreciate an English poem. Victor, smiling distractedly, said, "What? What do you say?" and Beatrice said, "It's a poem," just as if somebody had asked, "What's that running across the road?" and she had replied, "It's a groundhog."

Victor's gaiety remained muted. His large, bright-eyed grin, his laughter seemed misplaced and forced, without energy. Even his skin looked dull and putty-colored. He was like the statue of a prince in a story Murray remembered, a children's story. The prince has his jewel eyes plucked out to be sold to help the poor, and finally gives all his gold-leaf skin to serve the same purpose. A little swallow helps him when he is blind, and remains his only friend.

The whole house smelled of the cooking. Barbara

had done a pork roast. She had made the potatoes accord-ing to a new recipe, slicing them and cooking them in the oven in a buttered dish. They seemed greasy to Murray, and slightly on the raw side. The other vegetables were overcooked, because she had been so harassed in the kitchen, distracted by the children. The pecan pie was too rich a dessert for the meal, and the crust was too brown. Beatrice did not even try it. Beatrice did not finish the potatoes on her plate. She did not laugh when Adam made his disastrous sortie. She probably felt that children should be trained and kept in line as strictly as horses.

Murray reflected that he had never met a woman who was crazy about horses whom he had liked. They were narrow, righteous, humorless women, and usually not good-looking. Beatrice had a rosy, almost raw-looking complexion. Her hair was dull and graying and cut with no style. She wore no lipstick — an eccentricity that was a declaration of piety or contemptuous carelessness in a woman at that time. Her loosely belted mushroom-colored dress announced that she had no hopes of this dinner party and made no concessions to it.

Barbara, by way of contrast, was wearing a polished-cotton skirt of yellow and orange and copper colors, a tight black belt, a low-necked black blouse, and large, cheap hoop earrings. One of the things about Barbara that Mur-ray did not understand and was not proud of — as opposed to the things he did not understand but was proud of — would have to be this taste she had for cheaply provocative clothes. Low necklines, cinch belts, tight tore-ador pants. She would go out into the streets of Walley showing off her body, which was lavish, in the style of the time — or one of the styles of the time, the style not of Audrey Hepburn but of Tina Louise — and the embarrass-ment Murray felt about this was complex and unmention-able. He felt that she was doing something that didn't fit in with her seriousness and aloofness, her caustic tone. She was behaving in a way that his mother might have pre-dicted. ("I'm sure she is really a nice girl, but I'm not sure she has been very well educated," his mother had said, and even Murray understood that she was not referring to the books Barbara might have read or the marks she had got at school.) What was more troubling was that she was behaving in a way that didn't even tie in with her sexual nature, or what Murray knew of it — and he had to assume he knew everything. She was not really very passionate. Sometimes he thought that she pretended to be more passionate than she was. That was what these clothes reminded him of and why he couldn't mention them to her. There was something unsure, risky, excessive about them. He was willing to see all sorts of difficult things about Barbara — her uncharitableness, perhaps, or intransigence — but nothing that made her seem a little foolish, or sad.

There was a bouquet of lilacs in the center of the table. They got in the way of the serving dishes and dropped their messy flowers on the tablecloth. Murray became more and more irritated at the sight of them, and at last he said, "Barbara — do we really have to have those flowers on the table?" (The fed-up voice of a proper husband.) "We can't even see around them to talk."

At the moment, nobody was talking.

Barbara bent forward, shamelessly showing cleavage. She lifted the bouquet without a word, creating a shower of lilac blossoms onto the cloth and the meat platter. One of her earrings fell off and landed in the applesauce.

They should have laughed then. But nobody was able to. Barbara gave Murray a look of doom. He thought that they might as well get up now, they might as well get up from the table and abandon the unwanted food and inert conversation. They might as well go their own ways.

Victor picked the earring out of the applesauce with a spoon. He wiped it on his napkin and, bowing slightly to Barbara, laid it beside her plate. He said, "I have been trying to think who it is that is the heroine of a book, that you remind me of."

Barbara clipped the earring back onto her ear. Beatrice looked past or through her husband's head at the tasteful but inexpensive wallpaper — cream medallions on an ivory ground — that Murray's mother had chosen for the gardener's cottage.

"It is Katerina Ivanovna Verkhovtsev," said Victor. "She is the fiancée — "

"I know who she is," said Barbara. "I think she's a pain."

Murray knew by the abrupt halt of her words that she had been about to say "pain in the arse."

"It's Beatrice," Murray said to Barbara as he helped her do the dishes. He had apologized about the lilacs. He said that it was Beatrice who had unnerved him, who had blighted the evening for them all. "He isn't himself with her," he said. "He had his light hidden under a bushel." He thought of Beatrice descending on Victor, to extinguish him. Her jabbing bones. Her damp skirts.

"I could do without either one," said Barbara, and it was then that they had the exchange about conspicuous people and secret missions. But they ended up finishing the wine and laughing about the behavior of Adam and Felicity.

Victor began to come around in the evenings. Apparently the dinner party had not signalled for him any break or difficulty in the friendship. In fact, it seemed to have brought him a greater ease. He was able now to say something about his marriage — not a complaint or an explanation, just something like "Beatrice wants . . ." or "Beatrice believes . . ." — and be sure that a good deal would be understood.

And after a while he said more.

"Beatrice is impatient that I do not have the barn ready for the horses, but I have to first deal with the drainage problems and the tiles have not come. So it is not a very fine atmosphere on the farm. But a beautiful summer. I am happy here."

Finally he said, "Beatrice has the money. You know that? So she is obliged to call the piper. No — have I got that wrong?"

It was as Murray had suspected.

"He married her for her money and now he has to work for it," said Barbara. "But he gets time for visiting."

"He can't work till midnight," Murray said. "He doesn't come by for coffee in the daytime anymore."

This was the way they continued to talk about Victor — Barbara sniping, Murray defending. It had become a game. Murray was relieved to see that Barbara didn't make Victor feel unwelcome; she didn't seem displeased when he showed up in the evenings.

He usually arrived around the time that Murray was putting the lawnmower away or picking up some of the children's toys or draining the wading pool or moving the sprinkler on his mother's lawn. (His mother, as usual, was spending part of the summer far away, in the Okanagan Valley.) Victor would try to help, bending to these tasks like a bemused and gentle robot. Then they moved the two wooden lawn chairs to the middle of the yard and sat down. They could hear Barbara working in the kitchen, without turning the lights on, because, she said, they made her hot. When she had finished, she would take a shower and come out into the yard barefoot, barelegged, her long hair wet, smelling of lemon soap. Murray went into the house and made three drinks, with gin and tonic and ice and limes. Usually he forgot that Barbara didn't keep the limes in the refrigerator, and had to call out demanding to know where they were or if she had forgotten to buy any. Victor vacated his chair and stretched out on the grass, his cigarette glowing in the half-dark. They looked up and tried to see a satellite — still a rare and amazing thing to see. They could hear sprinklers, and sometimes distant shrieks, police sirens, laughter. That was the sound of television programs, coming through the open windows and screen doors along the street. Sometimes there was the slap of screen doors closing as people left those programs behind for a moment, and boisterous but uncertain voices calling into the back yards where people sat drinking, as they did, or watching the sky. There was a sense of people's lives audible but solitary, floating free of each other under the roof of beech and maple branches in front of the houses, and in the cleared spaces behind, just as people in the same room, talking, float free on the edge of sleep. The sound of ice cubes tinkling unseen was meditative, comforting.

Sometimes the three of them played a game that Barbara had invented or adapted from something else. It was called Oranges and Apples, and she used it to keep the children occupied on car trips. It was a game of choices, going from very easy to very hard. Peanut butter or oatmeal porridge was where you might start, going on to peanut butter or applesauce, which was harder. The really hard choices could be between two things you liked very much or two things you disliked very much or between things that were for some reason almost impossible to compare. There was no way to win. The pleasure was in thinking up tormenting choices or in being tormented by them, and the end came only when somebody cried, "I give up. I can't stand it. It's too stupid. I don't want to think about it anymore!"

Would you rather eat fresh corn on the cob or homemade strawberry ice cream?

Would you sooner dive into a cool lake on a blistering hot day or enter a warm kitchen where there is fresh bread baking after you've walked through a bog in a snowstorm?

Would you prefer to make love to Mrs. Khrushchev or Mrs. Eisenhower?

Would you rather eat a piece of cold pork fat or listen to a speech at the Kiwanis luncheon?

Things were going badly at the farm. The well water was not safe to drink. The tops of the potatoes wilted from a blight. Insects of many sorts invaded the house, and the drains were still not completed. But it seemed that this was nothing compared to the human malevolence. One evening before Barbara came out to join them, Victor said to Murray, "I cannot eat any longer at the farm. I must eat all my meals at the coffee shop."

"Is it as unpleasant as all that?" said Murray.

"No, no. It is always unpleasant, but what I have discovered now is worse than the unpleasantness by many degrees."

Poison. Victor said that he had found a bottle of prussic acid. He did not know how long Beatrice had had it but he did not think very long. There was no use for it on the farm. There was only the one use, that he could think of.

"Surely not," said Murray. "She wouldn't do that. She isn't crazy. She isn't a poisoning sort of person."

"But you have no idea. You have no idea what sort of person she is or what she might do. You think she would not poison, she is an English lady. But England is full of murders and often it is the ladies and gentlemen and the husbands and wives. I cannot eat in her house. I wonder if I am safe even to sleep there. Last night I lay awake beside her, and in her sleep she was as cold as a snake. I got up and lay on the floor in the other room."

Murray remembered then the caretaker's apartment, empty now for years. It was on the third floor of the store building, at the back.

"Well, if you really think so," he said. "If you really want to move out . . ." And after Victor had accepted, with surprise, relief, and gratitude, Murray said, "Barbara will get it cleaned up for you."

It did not occur to him at that time that he himself or Victor might be capable of sweeping out and scrubbing some dirty rooms. It did not occur to Barbara, either. She cleaned out the apartment the next day, and provided sheets and towels and a few pots and dishes, though of course she was skeptical about the danger of poisoning. "What good would he be to her dead?"

Victor got a job immediately. He became the night watchman at the surface installation of the salt mine. He liked working at night. He didn't have the use of a car anymore, so he walked to work at midnight and back to the apartment in the morning. If Murray was in the store before eight-thirty, he would hear Victor climbing the back stairs. How did he sleep, in the bright daylight in that little box of a room under the hot flat roof?

"I sleep beautifully," Victor said, "I cook, I eat, I sleep. I have relief. It is all of a sudden peace."

And one day Murray came home unexpectedly, in the middle of the afternoon.

Those words took shape in his mind afterward. They were so trite and sombre. *One day I came home unexpectedly . . .* Is there ever a story of a man who comes home unexpectedly and finds a delightful surprise?

He came home unexpectedly, and he found — not Victor and Barbara in bed together. Victor was not in the house at all — nobody was in the house. Victor was not in the yard. Adam was in the yard, splashing in the plastic pool. Not far away from the pool Barbara was lying on the faded quilt, stained with suntan oil, that they used when they went to the beach. She was wearing her strapless black bathing suit, a garment that resembled a corset and would not be considered at all attractive in a few years' time. It cut straight across the thighs, and pushed them together; it tightly confined the waist and stomach and hips, and uplifted and thrust out the breasts so that they appeared to be made of something at least as firm as

Styrofoam. Her arms, legs, chest, and shoulders looked white in the sun, though they would show a tan when she came indoors. She was not reading, though she had a book open beside her. She was lying on her back with her arms loose at her sides. Murray was just about to call to her through the screen door, but he didn't.

Why not? He saw her lift one arm, to shield her eyes. Then she lifted her hips, she changed her position slightly. The movement might have been seen as entirely natural, casual — one of those nearly involuntary adjustments that our bodies make. What told Murray that it wasn't? Some pause or deliberateness, a self-consciousness, about that slight swelling and settling of the flesh made it clear to him — a man who knew this woman's body — that the woman wasn't alone. In her thoughts, at least, she wasn't alone.

Murray moved to the window over the sink. The yard was hidden from the back alley and the delivery platform at the back of the store by a high cedar hedge. But it was possible to see the back yard — the part of the back yard where Barbara lay — from the apartment window of the third floor. Barbara had not put up any curtains in the apartment. And Murray saw Victor sitting there, in that window. Victor had brought a chair over so that he could sit and look out at his ease. There was something odd about his face, as if he had a gas mask on.

Murray went to the bedroom and got the binoculars that he had bought recently. (He had thought of going for country walks and teaching the children to know the birds.) He moved very quietly through the house. Adam was making quite a lot of distracting noise outside.

When he looked at Victor through the binoculars, he saw a face like his own — a face partly hidden by binoculars. Victor had them, too. Victor was looking through binoculars at Barbara.

It appeared that he was naked — at least, what you could see of him was naked — sitting on a straight-backed chair at the window in his hot room. Murray could feel the heat of the room and the sweat-slicked hard seat of the chair and the man's powerful but controlled and concentrated excitement. And looking at Barbara he could feel the glow along the surface of her body, the energy all collected at the skin, as she gave herself up to this assault.

She lay not quite still — there was a constant ripple passing over her, with little turns and twitches. Stirrings, shiftings. It was unbearable to watch. In the presence of her child in the middle of the day, in her own back yard, she lay on the grass inviting him. Promising — no, she was already providing — the most exquisite co-operation. It was obscene, enthralling, unbearable.

Murray could see himself — a man with binoculars watching a man with binoculars watching a woman. It was a scene from a movie. A comedy.

He did not know where to go. He could not go out into the yard and put a stop to this. He could not go back to the store and be aware of what was going on over his head. He left the house and got out the car, which he kept in his mother's garage, and went for a drive. Now he had another set of words to add to *One day I came home unexpectedly:*

I understood that my life had changed.

But he did not understand it. He said, My life has changed, my life has been changed, but he did not understand it.

He drove around the back streets of Walley and over a railway crossing, out into the country. Everything looked as usual and yet like a spiteful imitation of itself. He drove with the windows down, trying to get a breeze, but he was going too slowly. He was driving at the town speed outside the town limits. A truck honked, to get by him. This was in front of the brickyard. The noise of the truck's horn and the sunlight glaring off the bricks hit him all at once, banged him on the head so that he whimpered, as if he had a hangover.

Daily life continued, ringed by disaster as by a jubilant line of fire. He felt his house transparent, his life transparent — but still standing — himself a stranger, soft-footed and maliciously observant. What more would be revealed to him? At supper his daughter said, "Mommy, how come we never go to the beach this summer?" and it was hard to believe she didn't know everything.

"You do go," said Barbara. "You go with Heather's mother."

"But how come you and me and Adam don't go?"

"Adam and I like it here." Very smug and secure

Barbara sounds — creamy. "I got tired of talking to the Other Mothers."

"Don't you like Heather's mother?"

"Sure."

"You don't."

"I do. I'm just lazy, Felicity. I'm unsociable."

"You don't," said Felicity with satisfaction. She left the table, and Barbara began to describe, as if for Murray's entertainment, the beach encampment set up by the Other Mothers. Their folding chairs and umbrellas, inflatable toys and mattresses, towels and changes of clothing, lotions, oils, antiseptic, Band-Aids, sun hats, lemonade, Kool-Aid, home-frozen popsicles, and healthful goodies. "Which are supposed to keep the little brutes from whining for French fries," said Barbara. "They never look at the lake unless one of their kids is in it. They talk about their kids' asthma or where they get the cheapest T-shirts."

Victor still came to visit in the evenings. They still sat in the back yard and drank gin. Now it seemed that in the games and the aimless conversations both Victor and Barbara deferred to Murray, laughed appreciatively, applauded any joke or his sighting of a falling star. He often left them alone together. He went into the kitchen to get more gin or ice, he went to check on the children, pretending that he had heard one of them cry out. He imagined then that Victor's long bare foot would slide out of its sandal and would graze, then knead, Barbara's offered calf, her outstretched thigh. Their hands would slide over whatever parts of each other they could reach. For a risky instant they might touch tongues. But when he came clattering out they were always prudently separated, talking some treacherous ordinary talk.

Victor had to leave earlier than he used to, to get to work at the salt mine. "Off to the salt mine," he would say — the same thing so many people said around here, the joke that was literally true.

Murray made love to Barbara then. He had never been so rough with her, or so free. He had a sense of despair and corruption. This is destruction, he thought. Another sentence in his head: *This is the destruction of love.* He fell asleep at once and woke up and had her again. She was full of a new compliance and passivity and she kissed him goodbye at breakfast with what seemed to him a strange, new, glistening sympathy. The sun shone every day, and in the mornings, particularly, it hurt his eyes. They were drinking more — three or four drinks now, instead of two — in the evenings, and he was putting more gin in them.

There came a time every afternoon when he couldn't stay in the store any longer, so he drove out into the country. He drove through the inland towns — Logan, Carstairs, Dalby Hill. Sometimes he drove as far as the hunting camp that had belonged to his father and now belonged to him. There he got out and walked, or sat on the steps of the neglected, boarded-up cabin. Sometimes he felt in all his trouble a terrible elation. He was being robbed. He was being freed of his life.

That summer, as in other summers, there came a Sunday when they spent the day picking blackberries along the country roads. Murray and Barbara and Adam and Felicity picked blackberries, and on the way home they bought sweet corn at a farmer's stand. Barbara made the annual supper of the first corn on the cob with the first fresh-blackberry pie. The weather had changed even as they were picking the berries, and when they bought the corn the farmer's wife was putting up the shutters on her stand and had loaded what she hadn't sold into the back of a truck. They were her last customers. The clouds were dark, and the kind of wind they hadn't felt for months was lifting the boughs of the trees and tearing off the dry leaves. A few drops of rain slapped the windshield, and by the time they reached Walley they were driving through a full-blown rainstorm. The house was so chilly that Murray turned on the furnace, and with the first wave of heat a cellar smell was driven through the house — that forgotten cave smell of roots, earth, damp concrete.

Murray went out in the rain and picked up the sprinkler, the plastic pool. He shoved the lawn chairs under the eaves.

"Is our summer over?" he said to Barbara, shaking the rain off his head.

The children watched "Walt Disney," and the boiling of the corn clouded the windows. They ate the supper. Barbara washed the dishes while Murray put the children to bed. When he shut the door on them and came out to the kitchen, he found Barbara sitting at the table in the near dark, drinking coffee. She was wearing one of last winter's sweaters.

"What about Victor?" Murray said. He turned on the lights. "Did you leave any blankets for him over in the apartment?"

"No," said Barbara.

"Then he'll be cold tonight. There's no heat on in the building."

"He can come and get some blankets if he's cold," said Barbara.

"He wouldn't come and ask," Murray said.

"Why not?"

"He just wouldn't."

Murray went to the hall closet and found two heavy blankets. He carried them into the kitchen.

"Don't you think you better take these over?" He laid them on the table, in front of her.

"Why not you?" said Barbara. "How do you even know he's there?"

Murray went to the window over the sink. "His light's on. He's there."

Barbara got up stiffly. She shuddered, as if she'd been holding herself tightly and now felt a chill.

"Is that sweater going to be enough?" said Murray. "Don't you need a coat? Aren't you going to comb your hair?"

She went into the bedroom. When she came out she was wearing her white satin blouse and black pants. She had combed her hair and put on some new, very pale lipstick. Her mouth looked bleached-out, perverse, in her summer-tanned face.

Murray said, "No coat?"

"I won't have time to get cold."

He laid the blankets on her arms. He opened the door for her.

"It's Sunday," she said. "The doors'll be locked."

"Right," said Murray, and got the spare keys from the kitchen hook. He made sure she knew which one of them opened the side door of the building.

He watched the glimmer of her blouse until it vanished, and then he walked all through the house very quickly, taking noisy breaths. He stopped in the bedroom and picked up the clothes she had taken off. Her jeans and shirt and sweater. He held them up to his face and smelled them and thought, This is like a play. He wanted to see if she had changed her underpants. He shook out her jeans but the pants weren't there. He looked in the clothes hamper but he didn't see them. Could she have been sly enough to slip them under the children's things? What was the use of being sly now?

Her jeans had the smell jeans get when they've been worn a while without being washed — a smell not just of the body but of its labors. He could smell cleaning powder in them, and old cooking. And there was flour that she'd brushed off on them tonight, making the pastry for the pie. The smell of the shirt was of soap and sweat and perhaps of smoke. Was it smoke — was it cigarette smoke? He wasn't sure, as he sniffed again, that it was smoke at all. He thought of his mother saying that Barbara was not well educated. His mother's clothes would never smell this way, of her body and her life. She had meant that Barbara was not well-mannered, but couldn't she also have meant — *loose*? A loose woman. When he heard people say that, he'd always thought of an unbuttoned blouse, clothes slipping off the body, to indicate its appetite and availability. Now he thought that it could mean just that — loose. A woman who could get loose, who wasn't fastened down, who was not reliable, who could roll away.

She had got loose from her own family. She had left them completely. Shouldn't he have understood by that how she could leave him?

Hadn't he understood, all the time?

He had understood that there would be surprises.

He went back to the kitchen. (*He stumbles into the kitchen.*) He poured himself half a tumbler of gin, without tonic or ice. (*He pours half a tumbler of gin.*) He thought of further humiliations. His mother would get a new lease on life. She would take over the children. He and the children would move into his mother's house. Or perhaps the children would move and he would remain here, drinking gin. Barbara and Victor might come to see him, wanting to be friends. They might establish a household and ask him over in the evenings, and he might go.

No. They would not think of him. They would banish the thought of him, they would go away.

As a child Murray had seldom got into fights. He was diplomatic and good-humored. But eventually he had been in a fight and had been knocked to the ground of the Walley schoolyard, knocked out, probably, for half a minute. He lay on his back in a daze, and saw the leaves on a bough above him turn into birds — black, then bright as the sun poked through and the wind stirred them. He was knocked into a free, breezy space where every shape was light and changeable and he himself the same. He lay there and thought, *It has happened to me.*

The flight of seventy-eight steps from the beach to the park on top of the cliffs is called the Sunset Steps. Beside these steps there is a sign on which the time of the sunset is posted for every day from the beginning of June to the end of September. "SEE THE SUN SET TWICE," the sign says, with an arrow pointing to the steps. The idea is that if you run very quickly from the bottom to the top of the steps you can see the last arc of the sun disappear a second time. Visitors think that this notion, and the custom of posting the sunset time, must be an old Walley tradition. Actually, it is a new wrinkle dreamed up by the Chamber of Commerce.

The boardwalk is new as well. The old-fashioned bandstand in the park is new. There was never a bandstand there before. All this charm and contrivance pleases visitors — Murray can hardly be against it; he is in the tourist business himself — and nowadays it pleases the townspeople as well. During that summer in the sixties, when Murray spent so much time driving around the country, it looked as if everything from an earlier time were being torn up, swept away, left to rot, disregarded. The new machinery was destroying the design of the farms, trees were cut down for wider roads, village stores and schools and houses were being abandoned. Everybody alive seemed to be yearning toward parking lots and shopping centers and suburban lawns as smooth as paint. Murray had to face up to being out of step, to having valued, as if they were final, things that were only accidental and temporary.

Out of such facing up, no doubt, came the orgy of smashing and renovating, which he was to get into a few months later.

And now it looks as if the world has come round to Murray's old way of thinking. People are restoring old houses and building new houses with old-style verandas. It is hard to find anybody who is not in favor of shade trees and general stores, pumps, barns, swings, nooks and crannies. But Murray himself can't quite recall the pleasure he took in these things, or find much shelter.

When he has walked beyond the end of the boardwalk to where the cedar trees crowd onto the beach, he sits on a boulder. First he noticed what a strange, beautiful boulder this was, with a line through it as if it had been split diagonally and the halves fitted together again not quite accurately — the pattern was jagged. He knew enough geology to understand that the line was a fault, and that the boulder must have come from the Precambrian shield that was a hundred miles away from here. It was rock formed before the last Ice Age; it was far older than the shore on which it sat. Look at the way it had been folded, as well as split — the layer on top hardened in waves like lapping cream.

He stopped being interested in the boulder and sat down on it. Now he sits looking at the lake. A line of turquoise blue at the horizon, fine as if drawn with turquoise ink, then a clear blue to the breakwater, shading into waves of green and silver breaking on the sand. La Mer Douce the French had called this lake. But of course it could change color in an hour; it could turn ugly, according to the wind and what was stirred up from the bottom.

People will sit and watch this lake as they'd never watch a field of waving grass or grain. Why is that, when the motion is the same? It must be the washing away, the wearing away, that compels them. The water all the time returning — eating, altering, the shore.

A similar thing happens to a person dying that kind of death. He has seen his father, he has seen others. A washing away, a vanishing — one fine layer after another down to the lighted bone.

He isn't looking in that direction, but he knows when Barbara comes into sight. He turns and sees her at the top of the steps. Tall Barbara, in her fall wrap of handwoven wheat-colored wool, starting down with no particular hurry or hesitation, not holding on to the rail — her usual deliberate yet indifferent air. He can't tell anything from the way she moves.

When Barbara opened the back door, her hair was wet from the rain — stringy — and her satin blouse ruinously spotted.

"What are you doing?" she said. "What are you drinking? Is that straight gin?"

Then Murray said what neither of them ever mentioned or forgot. "Didn't he want you?" he said.

Barbara came over to the table and pushed his head against the wet satin and the cruel little buttons, pushed it mercilessly between her hard breasts. "We are never going to talk about it," she said. "We never will. O.K.?" He could smell the cigarette smoke on her now, and the smell of the foreign skin. She held him till he echoed her.

"O.K."

And she held to what she'd said, even when he told her that Victor had gone away on the morning bus and had left a note addressed to both of them. She didn't ask to see or touch the note, she didn't ask what was in it.

("I am full of gratitude and now I have enough money that I think it is time for me to follow my life elsewhere. I think of going to Montreal where I will enjoy speaking French.")

At the bottom of the steps Barbara bends down and picks up something white. She and Murray walk toward each other along the boardwalk, and in a minute Murray can see what it is: a white balloon, looking somewhat weakened and puckered.

"Look at this," Barbara says as she comes up to him. She reads from a card attached to the string of the balloon. "'Anthony Burler. Twelve years old. Joliet Elementary School. Crompton, Illinois. October 15th.' That's three days ago. Could it have flown over here in just three days?

"I'm O.K.," she says then. "It wasn't anything. It wasn't anything bad. There isn't anything to worry about."

"No," says Murray. He holds her arms, he breathes the leafy, kitchen smell of her black-and-white hair.

"Are you shaking?" she says.

He doesn't think that he is.

Easily, without guilt, in the long-married way, he cancels out the message that flashed out when he saw her at the top of the steps — a message that he didn't try to understand:

Don't disappoint me again.

He looks at the card in her hand and says, "There's more. 'Favorite book — *The Last of the Mohicans*.'"

"Oh, that's for the teacher," Barbara says, with the familiar little snort of laughter in her voice, dismissing and promising. "That's a lie."

OH, WHAT AVAILS

BY *ALICE MUNRO*

I — DEADEYE DICK

They are in the dining room. The varnished floor is bare except for the rug in front of the china cabinet. There is not much furniture — a long table, some chairs, the piano, the china cabinet. On the inside of the windows, all the wooden shutters are closed. These shutters are painted a dull blue, a grayish blue. Some of the paint on them, and on the window frames, has flaked away. Some of it Joan has encouraged to flake away, using her fingernails.

This is a very hot day in Logan. The world beyond the shutters is swimming in white light; the distant trees and hills have turned transparent; the town is floating in the midst of cornfields under the still leaves, and dogs seek the vicinity of pumps and the puddles round the drinking fountains.

Some woman friend of their mother's is there. Is it the schoolteacher, Gussie Toll, or the station agent's wife? Their mother's friends are lively women, often transient — adrift and independent in attitude if not in fact.

On the table, under the fan, the two women have spread out cards and are telling their fortunes. Morris is lying on the floor, writing in a notebook. He is writing down how many copies of *New Liberty* magazine he sold that week, and who has paid and who still owes money. He is a solid-looking twelve-year-old boy, jovial but reserved, wearing glasses with one dark lens.

W hen Morris was four years old, he was roaming around in the long grass at the foot of the yard, near the creek, and he tripped over a rake that had been left lying there, prongs up. He tripped, he fell on the prongs, his brow and eyelid were badly cut and his eyeball was grazed. As long as Joan can remember — she was a baby when it happened — he has had a scar, and been blind in one eye, and worn glasses with a smoky lens.

A tramp left the rake there. So their mother said. She told the tramp she would give him a sandwich if he raked up the leaves under the walnut trees. She gave him the rake, and the next time she looked he was gone. He got tired of raking, she guessed, or he was mad at her for asking him to work first. She forgot to go and look for the rake. She had no man to help her with anything. Within a little more than half a year, she had to sustain these three things: Joan's birth, the death of her husband in a car accident (he had been drinking, she believed, but he wasn't drunk), and Morris's falling on the rake.

She never took Morris to a Toronto doctor, a specialist, to have a better job done fixing up the scar or to get advice about the eye. She had no money. But couldn't she have borrowed some (Joan, once she was grown up, wondered this), couldn't she have gone to the Lions Club and asked them to help her, as they sometimes did help poor people in an emergency? No. No, she couldn't. She did not believe that she and her children were poor in the way that people helped by the Lions Club were poor. They lived in a large house. They were landlords, collecting rent from three small houses across the street. They still owned the lumberyard, though they were sometimes down to one employee. (Their mother liked to call herself Ma Fordyce, after a widow on a radio soap opera, Ma Perkins, who also owned a lumberyard.) They had not the leeway of people who were properly poor.

What is harder for Joan to understand is why Morris himself has never done anything. Morris has plenty of money now. And it wouldn't even be a question of money anymore. Morris pays his premiums on the government health-insurance plan, just the way everybody else does. He has what seem to Joan very right-wing notions about mollycoddling and individual responsibility and the impropriety of most taxes, but he pays. Wouldn't it make sense to him to try to get something back? A neater job on the eyelid? One of those new, realistic, artificial eyes, whose magic sensitivity enables them to move in unison with the other, real eye? All that would entail is a trip to a clinic, a bit of inconvenience, some fussing and fiddling.

All it would entail is Morris's admission that he'd like a change. That it isn't shameful to try to turn in the badge misfortune has hung on you.

Their mother and her friend are drinking rum-and-Coke. There is a laxity in that house that might surprise most people Joan and Morris go to school with. Their mother smokes, and drinks rum-and-Coke on hot summer days, and she allows Morris to smoke and to drive the car by the time he's twelve years old. (He doesn't like rum.) Their mother doesn't mention misfortune. She tells about the tramp and the rake, but Morris's eye now might as well be some special decoration. She does give them the idea of being part of something special. Not because their grandfather started the lumberyard — she laughs at that, she says he was just a woodcutter who got lucky, and she herself was nobody, she came to town as a bank clerk — and not because of their large, cold, unmanageable house, but because of something private, enclosed, in their small family. It has to do with the way they joke, and talk about people. They have private names — their mother has made up most of them — for almost everybody in town. And she knows a lot of poetry, from school or somewhere. She will fix a couple of lines on somebody, summing them up in an absurd and unforgettable way. She looks out the window and says a bit of poetry and they know who has gone by. Sometimes she comes out with it as she stirs the porridge they eat now and then for supper as well as for breakfast, because it is cheap.

Morris's jokes are puns. He is dogged and sly-faced about this, and their mother pretends to be driven crazy. Once she told him that if he didn't stop she would empty the sugar bowl over his mashed potatoes. He didn't, and she did.

There is a smell in the Fordyce house, and it comes from the plaster and wallpaper in the rooms that have been shut off, and the dead birds in the unused chimneys, or the mice whose seedlike turds they find in the linen cupboard. The wooden doors in the archway between the dining room and living room are closed, and only the dining room is used. A cheap partition shuts off the side hall from the front hall. They don't buy coal or repair the ailing furnace. They heat the rooms they live in with two stoves, burning ends from the lumberyard. None of this is important, none of their privations and difficulties and economies are important. What is important? Jokes and luck. They are lucky to be the products of a marriage whose happiness lasted for five years and proclaimed itself at parties and dances and on wonderful escapades. Reminders are all around — gramophone records, and fragile, shapeless dresses made of such materials as apricot georgette and emerald silk moiré, and a picnic hamper with a silver flask. Such happiness was not of the quiet kind; it entailed lots of drinking, and dressing up, with friends — mostly from other places, even from Toronto — who had now faded away, many of them, too, smitten by tragedy, the sudden poverty of those years, the complications.

They hear the knocker banging on the front door, the way no caller of decent manners would bang it.

"I know, I know who that'll be," says their mother. "It'll be Mrs. Loony Buttler, what do you want to bet?" She slips out of her canvas shoes and slides the archway doors open carefully, without a creak. She tiptoes to the front window of the no longer used living room, from which she can squint through the shutters and see the front veranda. "Oh, shoot," she says. "It is."

Mrs. Buttler lives in one of the three cement-block houses across the road. She is a tenant. She has white hair, but she pushes it up under a turban made of different-colored pieces of velvet. She wears a long black coat. She has a habit of stopping children on the street and asking them things. Are you just getting home from school now — did you have to stay in? Does your mother know you chew gum? Did you throw bottle caps in my yard?

"Oh, shoot," their mother says. "There isn't anybody I'd sooner not see."

Mrs. Buttler isn't a constant visitor. She arrives irregularly, with some long rigmarole of complaint, some urgent awful news. Many lies. Then, for the next several weeks, she passes the house without a glance, with the long quick strides and forward-thrust head that take away all the dignity of her black outfit. She is preoccupied and affronted, muttering to herself.

The knocker sounds again, and their mother walks softly to the doorway into the front hall. There she stops. On the one side of the big front door is a pane of colored glass with a design so intricate that it's hard to see through, and on the other, where a pane of colored glass has been broken (one night when we partied a bit too hard, their mother has said), is a sheet of wood. Their mother stands in the doorway barking. *Yap-yap-yap*, she barks, like an angry little dog shut up alone in the house. Mrs. Buttler's turbanned head presses against the glass as she tries to see in. She can't. The little dog barks louder. A frenzy of barking — angry excitement — into which their mother works the words *go away, go away, go away*. And *loony lady, loony lady, loony lady. Go away, loony lady, go away.*

Mrs. Buttler on her next visit says, "I never knew you had a dog."

"We don't," their mother says. "We've never had a dog. Often I think I'd like a dog. But we never had one."

"Well, I came over here one day, and there was nobody home. Nobody came to the door, and, I could swear to it, I heard a dog barking."

"It may be a disturbance in your inner ear, Mrs. Buttler," their mother says next. "You should ask the doctor."

"I think I could turn into a dog quite easily," their mother says later. "I think my name would be Skippy."

They got a name for Mrs. Buttler. Mrs. Buncler, Mrs. Buncle, and finally Mrs. Carbuncle. It suited. Without knowing exactly what a carbuncle was, Joan understood how the name fitted, attaching itself memorably to something knobby, deadened, awkward, intractable in their neighbor's face and character.

Mrs. Carbuncle had a daughter, Matilda. No husband, just this daughter. When the Fordyces sat out on the side veranda after supper — their mother smoking and Morris smoking, too, like the man of the house — they might see Matilda going around the corner on her way to the confectionery that stayed open late, or to get a book out of the library before it closed. She never had a friend with her. Who would bring a friend to a house ruled by Mrs. Carbuncle? But Matilda didn't seem lonely or shy or unhappy. She was beautifully dressed. Mrs. Carbuncle could sew — in fact, that was how she made what money she made, doing tailoring, and alterations for Gillespie's Ladies' and Men's Wear. She dressed Matilda in pale colors, often with long white stockings.

"Rapunzel, Rapunzel, let down thy gold hair," their mother says softly, seeing Matilda pass by. "How can she be Mrs. Carbuncle's daughter? You tell me!" She says there is something fishy. She wouldn't be at all surprised — she wouldn't be at *all* surprised — to find out that Matilda is really some rich girl's child, or the child of some adulterous passion, whom Mrs. Carbuncle is being paid to raise. Perhaps, on the other hand, Matilda was kidnapped as a baby, and knows nothing about it. "Such things happen," their mother says.

The beauty of Matilda, which prompted this talk, was truly of the captive-princess kind. It was the beauty of storybook illustrations. Long, waving, floating light-brown hair with golden lights in it, which was called blond hair in the days before there were any but the most brazen artificial blonds. Pink-and-white skin, large, mild blue eyes. "The milk of human kindness" was an expression that came mysteriously into Joan's head when she thought of Matilda. And there was something milky about the blue of Matilda's eyes, and her skin, and her looks altogether. Something milky and cool and kind — something stupid, possibly. Don't all those storybook princesses have a tender blur, a veil of stupidity over their blond beauty, an air of unwitting sacrifice, helpless benevolence? All this appeared in Matilda at the age of twelve or thirteen. Morris's age, in Morris's room at school. But she did quite well there, so it seemed she wasn't stupid at all. She was known as a champion speller.

Joan collected every piece of information about Matilda that she could find and became familiar with every outfit that Matilda wore. She schemed to meet her, and because they lived in the same block she often did. Faint with love, Joan noted every variation in Matilda's appearance. Did her hair fall forward over her shoulders today or was it pushed back from her cheeks? Had she put a clear polish on her fingernails? Was she wearing the pale-blue rayon blouse with the tiny edging of lace around the collar, which gave her a soft and whimsical look, or the starched white cotton shirt, which turned her into a dedicated student? Matilda owned a string of glass beads, clear pink, the sight of which, on Matilda's perfect white neck, caused a delicate sweat to break out along the insides of Joan's arms.

At one time Joan invented other names for her. "Matilda" brought to mind dingy curtains, gray tent flaps, a slack-skinned old woman. How about Sharon? Lilliane? Elizabeth? Then, Joan didn't know how, the name Matilda became transformed. It started shining like silver. The "il" in it was silver. But not metallic. In Joan's mind the name gleamed now like a fold of satin.

The matter of greetings was intensely important, and a pulse fluttered in Joan's neck as she waited. Matilda of course must speak first. She might say "Hi," which was lighthearted, comradely, or "Hello," which was gentler and more personal. Once in a while she said "Hello, Joan," which indicated such special notice and teasing regard that it immediately filled Joan's eyes with tears and laid on her a shameful, exquisite burden of happiness.

This love dwindled, of course. Like other trials and excitements, it passed away, and Joan's interest in Matilda Buttler returned to normal. Matilda changed too. By the time Joan was in high school Matilda was already working. She got a job in a lawyer's office; she was a junior clerk. Now that she was making her own money, and was partway out of her mother's control — only partway, because she still lived at home — she changed her style. It seemed that she wanted to be much less of a princess and much more like everybody else. She got her hair cut short, and wore it in the trim fashion of the time. She started wearing makeup, bright-red lipstick that hardened the shape of her mouth. She dressed the way other girls did — in long, tight slit skirts, and blouses with floppy bows at the neck, and ballerina shoes. She lost her pallor and aloofness. Joan, who was planning to get a scholarship and study art and archeology at the University of Toronto, greeted this Matilda with composure. And the last shred of her worship vanished when Matilda began appearing with a boyfriend.

The boyfriend was a good-looking man about ten years older than Matilda. He had thinning dark hair and a pencil mustache and a rather unfriendly, suspicious, determined expression. He was very tall, and he bent toward Matilda, with his arm around her waist, as they walked along the streets. They walked on the streets so much because Mrs. Carbuncle had taken a huge dislike to him and would not let him inside the house. At first he didn't have a car. Later he did. He was said to be either an airplane pilot or a waiter in a posh restaurant, and it was now known where Matilda had met him. When they walked, his arm was actually below Matilda's waist — his spread fingers rested securely on her hipbone. It seemed to Joan that this bold, settled hand had something to do with his gloomy and challenging expression.

But before this, before Matilda got a job, or cut her hair, something happened that showed Joan — by then long past being in love — an aspect, or effect, of Matilda's beauty that she hadn't suspected. She saw that such beauty marked you — in Logan, anyway — as a limp might, or a speech impediment. It isolated you — more severely, perhaps, than a mild deformity would have done, because it could be seen as a reproach. After she realized that, it wasn't so surprising to Joan, though it was still disappointing, to see that Matilda would do her best to get rid of or camouflage that beauty as soon as she could.

Mrs. Buttler, Mrs. Carbuncle, invading their kitchen as she does every so often, never removes her black coat and her multicolored velvet turban. That is to keep your hopes up, their mother says. Hopes that she's about to leave, that you're going to get free of her in under three hours. Also to cover up whatever god-awful outfit she's got on underneath. Because she's got that coat, and is willing to wear it every day of the year, Mrs. Carbuncle never has to change her dress. A smell issues from her — camphorated, stuffy.

She arrives in mid-spiel, charging ahead in her talk — about something that has happened to her, some person who has outraged her, as if you were certain to know what it was or who. As if her life were on the news and you had just failed to catch the last couple of bulletins. Joan is always eager to listen to the first half hour or so of this report, or tirade, preferably from outside the room, so that she can slip away when things start getting repetitious. If you try to slip away from where Mrs. Carbuncle can see you, she's apt to ask sarcastically where you're off to in such a hurry, or accuse you of not believing her.

Joan is doing that — listening from the dining room, while pretending to practice her piano piece for the public-school Christmas concert. Joan is in her last year at the public grade school, and Matilda is in her last year at high school. (Morris will drop out, after Christmas, to take over the lumberyard.) It's a Saturday morning in mid-December — gray sky and an iron frost. Tonight the high-school Christmas Dance, the only formal dance of the year, is to be held in the town armory.

It's the high-school principal who has got into Mrs. Carbuncle's bad books. This is an unexceptionable man named Archibald Moore, who is routinely called by his students Archie Balls, or Archie Balls More, or Archie More Balls. Mrs. Carbuncle says he isn't fit for his job. She says he can be bought and everybody knows it; you'll never pass out of high school unless you slip him the money.

"But the exams are marked in Toronto," says Joan's mother, as if genuinely puzzled. For a while, she enjoys pushing things along, with mild objections and queries.

"He's in cahoots with them, too," says Mrs. Carbuncle. "Them, too." She goes on to say that if money hadn't changed hands he'd never have got out of high school himself. He's very stupid. An ignoramus. He can't solve the problems on the blackboard or translate the Latin. He has to have a book with the English words all written in on top. Also, a few years ago, he made a girl pregnant.

"Oh, I never heard that!" says Joan's mother, utterly genteel.

"It was hushed up. He had to pay."

"Did it take all the profits he made on the examinations?"

"He ought to have been horsewhipped."

Joan plays the piano softly — "Jesu, Joy of Man's Desiring" is her piece, and very difficult — because she hopes to hear the name of the girl, or perhaps how the baby was disposed of. (One time, Mrs. Carbuncle described the way a certain doctor in town disposed of babies, the products of his own licentious outbursts.) But Mrs. Carbuncle is swinging around to the root of her grievance, and it seems to be something about the dance. Archibald Moore has not managed the dance in the right way. He should make them all draw names for partners to take. Or else he should make them all go without partners. Either one or the other. That way, Matilda could go. Matilda hasn't got a partner — no boy has asked her — and she says she won't go alone. Mrs. Carbuncle says she will. She says she will make her. The reason she will make her is that her dress cost so much. Mrs. Carbuncle enumerates. The cost of the net, the taffeta, the sequins, the boning in the midriff (it's strapless), the twenty-two-inch zipper. She made this dress herself, putting in countless hours of labor, and Matilda wore it once. She wore it last night in the high-school play on the stage in the town hall, and that's all. She says she won't wear it tonight; she won't go to the dance, because nobody has asked her. It is all the fault of Archibald Moore, the cheater, the fornicator, the ignoramus.

Joan and her mother saw Matilda last night. Morris didn't go — he doesn't want to go out with them anymore in the evenings. He would sooner listen to the radio or scribble figures, probably having to do with the lumberyard, in a special notebook. Matilda played the role of a mannequin a young man falls in love with. Their mother told Morris when she came home that he was smart to stay away — it was an infinitely silly play. Matilda did not speak, of course, but she did hold herself still for a long time, showing a lovely profile. The dress was wonderful — a snow cloud with silver sequins glinting on it like frost.

Mrs. Carbuncle has told Matilda that she has to go. Partner or not, she has to go. She has to get dressed in her dress and put on a coat and be out of the door by nine o'clock. The door will be locked till eleven, when Mrs. Carbuncle goes to bed.

But Matilda still says she won't go. She says she will just sit in the coal shed at the back of the yard. It isn't a coal shed anymore, it's just a shed. Mrs. Carbuncle can't buy coal any more than the Fordyces can.

"She'll freeze," says Joan's mother, really concerned with the conversation for the first time.

"Serve her right," Mrs. Carbuncle says.

Joan's mother looks at the clock and says she is sorry to be rude but she has just remembered an appointment she has uptown. She has to get a tooth filled, and she has to hurry — she has to ask to be excused.

So Mrs. Carbuncle is turned out — saying that it's the first time she heard of filling teeth on a Saturday — and Joan's mother immediately phones the lumberyard to tell Morris to come home.

Now there is the first argument — the first real argument — that Joan has ever heard between Morris and their mother. Morris keeps saying no. What his mother wants him to do he won't do. He sounds as if there were no convincing him, no ordering him. He sounds not like a boy talking to his mother but like a man talking to a woman. A man who knows better than she does, and is ready for all the tricks she will use to make him give in.

"Well, I think you're very selfish," their mother says. "I think you can't think of anybody but yourself. I am very disappointed in you. How would you like to be that poor girl with her loony mother? Sitting in the *coal shed*? There are things a gentleman will do, you know. Your father would have known what to do."

Morris doesn't answer.

"It's not like proposing marriage or anything. What will it cost you?" their mother says scornfully. "Two dollars each?"

Morris says in a low voice that it isn't that.

"Do I very often ask you to do anything you don't want to do? Do I? I treat you like a grown man. You have all kinds of freedom. Well, now I ask you to do something to show that you really can act like a grownup and deserve your freedom, and what do I hear from you?"

This goes on a while longer, and Morris resists. Joan does not see how their mother is going to win and wonders that she doesn't give up. She doesn't.

"You don't need to try making the excuse that you can't dance, either, because you can, and I taught you myself. You're an elegant dancer!"

Then, of all things, Morris must have agreed, because the next thing Joan hears is their mother saying, "Go and put on a clean sweater." Morris's boots sound heavily on the back stairs, and their mother calls after him, "You'll be glad you did this! You won't regret it!"

She opens the dining-room door and says to Joan, "I don't hear an awful lot of piano-playing in here. Are you so good you can give up practicing already? The last time I heard you play that piece through, it was terrible."

Joan starts again from the beginning. But she doesn't keep it up after Morris comes down the stairs and slams the door and their mother, in the kitchen, turns on the radio, opens the cupboards, begins putting together something for lunch. Joan gets up from the piano bench and goes quietly across the dining room, through the door into the hall, right up to the front door. She puts her face against the colored glass. You can't see in through this glass, because the hall is dark, but if you get your eye in the right place you can see out. There is more red than any other color, so she chooses a red view — though she has managed every color in her time — blue and gold and green; even if there's just a tiny leaf of it, she has figured a way to squint through.

The gray cement-block house across the street is turned to lavender. Morris stands at the door. The door opens, and Joan can't see who has opened it. Is it Matilda or is it Mrs. Carbuncle? The stiff, bare trees and the lilac bush by the door of that house are a dark red, like blood. Morris's good yellow sweater is a blob of golden red, a stoplight, at the door.

Far back in the house, Joan's mother is singing along with the radio. She doesn't know of any danger. Between the front door, the scene outside, and their mother singing in the kitchen, Joan feels the dimness, the chilliness, the frailty and impermanence of these high half-bare rooms — of their house. It is just a place to be judged like other places — it's nothing special. It is no protection. She feels this because it occurs to her that their mother may be mistaken. In this instance — and further, as far as her faith and suppositions reach — she may be mistaken.

It is Mrs. Carbuncle. Morris has turned away and is coming down the walk and she is coming after him. Morris walks down the two steps to the sidewalk, he walks across the street very quickly without looking around. He doesn't run, he keeps his hands in his pockets, and his pink, blood-eyed face smiles to show that nothing that is happening has taken him by surprise. Mrs. Carbuncle is wearing her loose and tattery seldom-seen housedress, her pink hair is wild as a banshee's; at the top of her steps she halts and shrieks after him, so that Joan can hear her through the door, "We're not so bad off we need some Deadeye Dick to take my daughter to a dance!"

II - FRAZIL ICE

Morris looks to Joan like the caretaker when she sees him out in front of the apartment building, cutting the grass. He is wearing dull-green work pants and a plaid shirt, and, of course, his glasses, with the dark lens. He looks like a man who is competent, even authoritative, but responsible to someone else. Seeing him with a gang of his own workmen, at a construction site, you'd probably take him for the foreman — a sharp-eyed, fair-minded foreman with a solid but limited ambition. Not the boss. Not the owner of the apartment building. He is round-faced and partly bald, with a recent tan and new freckles showing on the front of his scalp. Sturdy but getting round-shouldered, or is that just the way he looks when pushing the mower? Is there a look bachelors get, bachelor sons — bachelor sons who have cared for old parents, particularly mothers? A closed-in, patient look that verges on humility? She thinks that it's almost as if she were coming to visit an uncle.

This is 1972, and Joan herself looks younger than she did ten years ago. She wears her dark hair long, tucked back behind her ears; she makes up her eyes but not her mouth; she dresses in voluminous soft, bright cottons or brisk little tunics that cover only a couple of inches of her thighs. She can get away with this — she hopes she can get away with it — because she is a tall, slim-waisted woman with long, well-shaped legs.

Their mother is dead. Morris has sold the house and bought an apartment building. His own apartment is there. The people who bought the house are making it into a nursing home. Joan has told her husband that she wants to go home — that is, back to Logan — to help Morris get settled, but she knows, in fact, that he will be settled; with his grasp of things Morris always seemed settled. All he needs Joan to help him with is the sorting out of some boxes and a trunk, full of clothes, books, dishes, pictures, curtains, that he doesn't want or doesn't have space for and has stored temporarily in the basement of his building.

Joan has been married for years. Her husband is a journalist. They live in Ottawa. People know his name — they even know what he looks like, or what he looked like five years ago, from his picture at the top of a back-page column in a magazine. Joan is used to being identified as his wife, here and elsewhere. But in Logan this identification carries a special pride. Most people here do not care for the journalist's wit, which they think cynical, or for his opinions, but they are pleased that a girl from this town has got herself attached to a famous, or semi-famous, person.

Joan has a daughter and a son, thirteen and ten years old.

She has told her husband that she will be staying here for a week. It's Sunday evening when she arrives, a Sunday late in May, with Morris cutting the first grass of the year. She plans to leave on Friday, spending Saturday and Sunday in Toronto. If her husband should find out that she has not spent the entire week with Morris, she has a story ready — about having decided, when Morris no longer needed her, to visit a woman friend she has known since college. Perhaps she should tell that story anyway — it would be safer. She worries about whether she should take the friend into her confidence.

It is the first time she has ever managed anything of this sort.

The apartment building runs deep into the lot, its windows looking out on parking space or on the Baptist church. A driving shed once stood here, for the farmers to leave their horses in during the church service. It's a red brick building. No balconies. Plain, plain.

Joan hugs Morris. She smells cigarettes, gasoline, soft, worn, sweaty shirt, along with the fresh-cut grass. "Oh, Morris, you know what you should do?" she shouts over the sound of the lawnmower. "You should get an eyepatch. Then you'd look just like Moshe Dayan!"

Every morning Joan walks to the post office. She is waiting for a letter from a man in Toronto, whose name is John Brolier. She wrote to him and told him Morris's name, the name of Logan, the number of Morris's post-office box. Logan has grown, but it is still too small to have home delivery.

On Monday morning she hardly hopes for a letter. On Tuesday she does hope for one. On Wednesday she feels she should have every reasonable expectation. Each day she is disappointed. Each day a suspicion that she has made a fool of herself — a feeling of being isolated and unwanted — rises closer to the surface. She has taken a man at his word when he didn't mean it. He has thought again.

The post office she goes to is a new, low pinkish brick building. The old one, which used to make her think of a castle, has been torn down. The look of the town has greatly changed. Not many houses have been pulled down, but most have been improved. Aluminum siding, sandblasted brick, bright roofs, wide double-glazed windows, verandas demolished or enclosed as porches. And the wide, wild yards have disappeared — they were really double lots — and the extra lots have been sold and built on. New houses crowd in between the old houses. These are all suburban in style, long and low, or split-level. The yards are tidy and properly planned, with nests of ornamental shrubs, round and crescent-shaped flower beds. The old habit of growing flowers like vegetables, in a row beside the beans or potatoes, seems to have been forgotten. Many of the great shade trees have been cut down. They were probably getting old and dangerous. The shabby houses, the long grass, the cracked sidewalks, the deep shade, the unpaved streets full of dust or puddles — all of this which Joan remembers is not to be found. The town seems crowded, diminished, with so many spruced-up properties, so much deliberate arrangement. The town of her childhood — that dim, haphazard, dreamy Logan — was just Logan going through a phase. Its leaning board fences and sun-blistered walls and flowering weeds were no permanent expression of what the town could be. And people like Mrs. Buttler — costumed, obsessed — seemed to be bound to that old town and not to be possible anymore.

Morris's apartment has one bedroom, which he has given to Joan. He sleeps on the living-room sofa. A two-bedroom apartment would surely have been more convenient for the times when he has visitors. But he probably doesn't intend to have visitors, very many of them, or very often. And he wouldn't want to lose out on the rent from the larger apartment. He must have considered taking one of the bachelor apartments in the basement, so that he'd be getting the rent from the one-bedroom place as well, but he must have decided that that would be going too far. It would look mingy, it would call attention. It would be a kind of self-indulgence better avoided.

The furniture in the apartment comes from the house, where Morris lived with their mother, but not much of it dates from the days when Joan lived at home. Anything that looked like an antique has been sold, and replaced with fairly durable, fairly comfortable furniture that Morris has been able to buy in quantity. (He rents out some furnished apartments in this building, and also some over stores on the main street.) Joan sees some things she sent as birthday presents, Christmas presents. They don't fit in quite as well, or liven things up as much, as she had hoped they would.

A print of St. Giles Church recalls the year she and her husband spent in Britain — her own embarrassing postgraduate homesickness and transatlantic affection. And here on the glass tray on top of the coffee table, politely and prominently displayed, is a book she sent to Morris. It's a history of machinery. There are sketches of machines in it, and plans of machines, from the days before photography, from Greek and Egyptian times. Then photographs from the nineteenth century to the present day — road machines, farm machines, factory machines, sometimes shot from a distance, sometimes on the horizon, sometimes seen from close up and low down. Some photographs stress the workings of the machines, both minute and prodigious; others strive to make machines look as splendid as castles or as thrilling as monsters. "What a wonderful book for my brother!" Joan remembers saying to the friend who was with her in the bookstore. "My brother is crazy about machinery." *Crazy about machinery* — that was what she said.

Now she wonders what Morris really thought of this book. Would he like it at all? He wouldn't actually dislike it. He might be puzzled by it, he might discount it. For it wasn't true that he was crazy about machinery. He used machinery — that was what machinery was for.

Morris takes her on drives in the long spring evenings. He takes her around town and out into the countryside, where she can see what enormous fields, what vistas of corn or beans or wheat or clover, those machines have enabled the farmers to create, what vast and parklike lawns the power mowers have brought into being. Clumps of lilacs bloom over the cellars of abandoned farmhouses. Farms have been consolidated, Morris tells her. He knows the value. Not just houses and buildings but fields and trees, woodlots and hills appear in his mind with a cash value and a history of cash value attached to them, just as every person he mentions is defined as someone who has got ahead or has not got ahead. Such a way of looking at things is not at all in favor at this time — it is thought to be unimaginative and old-fashioned and callous and destructive. Morris is not aware of this, and his talk of money rambles on with a calm enjoyment. He throws in a pun here and there. He chuckles as he tells of certain chancy transactions or extravagant debacles.

While Joan listens to Morris, and talks a little, her thoughts drift on a familiar, irresistible underground stream. She thinks about John Brolier. He is a geologist, who once worked for an oil company, and now teaches (science and drama) at what is called an alternate school. He used to be a person who was getting ahead, and now he is not getting ahead. Joan met him at a dinner party in Ottawa a couple of months ago. He was visiting friends who were also friends of hers. He was not accompanied by his wife, but he had brought two of his children. He told Joan that if she got up early enough the next morning he would take her to see something called frazil ice on the Ottawa River.

She thinks of his face and his voice and wonders what could compel her at this time to want this man. It does not seem to have much to do with her marriage. Her marriage seems to her commodious enough — she and her husband have twined together, developing a language, a history, a way of looking at things. They talk all the time. But they leave each other alone, too. The miseries and nastiness that surfaced during the early years have eased or diminished.

What she wants from John Brolier appears to be something that a person not heard from in her marriage, and perhaps not previously heard from in her life, might want. What is it about him? She doesn't think that he is particularly intelligent and she isn't sure that he is trustworthy. (Her husband is both intelligent and trustworthy.) He is not as good-looking as her husband, not as "attractive" a man. Yet he attracts Joan, and she already has a suspicion that he has attracted other women. Because of his intensity, a kind of severity, a deep seriousness — all focussed on sex. His interest won't be too quickly satisfied, too lightly turned aside. She feels this, feels the promise of it, though so far she is not sure of anything.

Her husband was included in the invitation to look at the frazil ice. But it was only Joan who got up and drove to the riverbank. There she met John Brolier and his two children and his hosts' two children in the freezing, pink, snowbound winter dawn. And he really did tell her about frazil ice, about how it forms over the rapids without ever quite getting a chance to freeze solid, and how when it is swept over a deep spot it mounts up immediately, magnificently. He said that this was how they had discovered where the deep holes were in the riverbed. And he said, "Look, if you can ever get away — if it's possible — will you let me know? I really want to see you. You know I do. I want to, very much."

He gave her a piece of paper that he must have had ready. A box number written on it, of a postal station in Toronto. He didn't even touch her fingers. His children were capering around, trying to get his attention. When can we go skating? Can we go to the warplanes museum?

Can we go and see the Lancaster Bomber? (Joan saved this up to tell her husband, who would enjoy it, in view of John Brolier's pacifism.)

She did tell her husband, and he teased her. "I think that jerk with the monk's haircut has taken a shine to you," he said. How could her husband believe that she could fall in love with a man who wore a fringe of thinning hair combed down over his forehead, who had rather narrow shoulders and a gap between his front teeth, five children from two wives, an inadequate income, an excitable and pedantic way of talking, and a proclaimed interest in the writings of Alan Watts? (Even when the time came when he had to believe it, he couldn't.)

When she wrote, she mentioned lunch, a drink, or coffee. She did not tell him how much time she had left open. Perhaps that was all that would happen, she thinks. She would go to see her woman friend after all. She has put herself, though cautiously, at this man's disposal. Walking to the post office, checking her looks in shop-windows, she feels herself loosed, in jeopardy. She has done this, she hardly knows why. She only knows that she cannot go back to the life she was living or to the person she was before she went out that Sunday morning to the river. Her life of shopping and housekeeping and married lovemaking and part-time work in the art-gallery bookstore, and dinner parties and holidays and ski out-ings at Camp Fortune — she cannot accept that as her only life, she cannot continue it without her sustaining secret. She believes that she does mean to continue it, and in order to continue it she must have this other. This other what? This investigation — to herself she still thinks of it as an investigation.

Put like that, what she was up to might sound cold-hearted indeed. But how can a person be called cold-hearted who walks to the post office every morning in such a fainthearted condition, who trembles and holds her breath as she turns the key in the lock, and walks back to Morris's apartment feeling so drained, bewildered, deserted? Unless this, too, is part of what she is investigat-ing?

Of course she has to stop and talk to people about her son and daughter and her husband and her life in Ottawa. She has to recognize high-school friends and recall her childhood, and all this seems tedious and irritating to her. The houses themselves, as she walks past — their tidy yards and bright poppies and peonies in bloom — seem tedious to the point of being disgusting. The voices of people who talk to her strike her as harsh and stupid and self-satisfied. She feels as if she had been shunted off to some corner of the world where the real life and thoughts, the uproar and energy of the last few years, have not penetrated at all. They have not very effectively penetrated Ottawa, either, but there, at least, people have heard rumors, they have tried imitations, they have got wind of what might be called profound, as well as trivial, changes of fashion. (Joan and her husband, in fact, make fun of some of these people — those who showily take up trends, go to encounter groups and holistic healers, and give up drink for dope.) Here even the trivial changes have hardly been heard of. Back in Ottawa next week, and feeling especially benevolent toward her husband, eager to fill up their time together with chat, Joan will say, "I'd have given thanks if somebody had even handed me an alfalfa-sprout sandwich. Really. It was that bad."

"No, I haven't room" is what Joan keeps saying as she and Morris go through the boxes. There are things here she would have thought she'd want, but she doesn't. "No. I can't think where I'd put it." No, she says, to their mother's dance dresses, the fragile silk and cobwebby georgette. They'd fall apart the first time anybody put them on, and Claire, her daughter, will never be interested in that kind of thing — she wants to be a horse trainer. No to the five wineglasses that didn't get broken, and no to the leatherette-bound copies of Lever and Lover, George Borrow, A. S. M. Hutchinson. "I have too much stuff now," she says sadly as Morris adds all this to the pile to go to the auction rooms. He shakes out the little rug that used to lie on the floor in front of the china cabinet, out of the sun, and that they were not supposed to walk on, because it was valuable.

"I saw one exactly like that a couple of months ago," she says. "It was in a secondhand store, not even an antique store. I was in there looking for old comics and posters for Rob's birthday. I saw one just the same. At first I didn't even know where I'd seen it before. Then I felt quite shocked. As if there were only supposed to be one of them in the world."

"How much did they want for it?" says Morris.

"I don't know. It was in better condition."

She doesn't understand yet that she doesn't want to take anything back to Ottawa because she herself won't be staying in the house there for much longer. The time of accumulation, of acquiring and arranging, of padding up the corners of her life, has come to an end. (It will return years later, and she will wish she had saved at least the wineglasses.) In Ottawa, in September, her husband will ask her if she still wants to buy wicker furniture for the sunroom, and if she would like to go to the wicker store, where they're having a sale on summer stock. A thrill of distaste will go through her then — at the very thought of looking for chairs and tables, paying for them, arranging them in the room — and she will finally know what is the matter.

On Friday morning, there is a letter in the box with Joan's name typed on it. She doesn't look at the postmark; she tears the envelope open gratefully, runs her eyes over it greedily, reads without understanding. It seems to be a chain letter. A parody of a chain letter, a joke. If she breaks the chain it says, DIRE CALAMITY will befall her. Her finger-nails will rot and her teeth will grow moss. Warts as big as cauliflowers will sprout on her chin, and her friends will avoid her. What can this be, thinks Joan. A code in which John Brolier has seen fit to write to her? Then it occurs to her to look at the postmark, and she does, and she sees that the letter comes from Ottawa. It comes from her son, obviously. Rob loves this sort of joke. His father would have typed the envelope for him.

She thinks of her child's delight when he sealed up the envelope and her own state of mind when she tore it open.

Treachery and confusion.

Late that afternoon, she and Morris open the trunk, which they have left till the last. She takes out a suit of evening clothes — a man's evening clothes, still in a plastic sheath, as if they had not been worn since being cleaned. "This must be Father's," she says. "Look, Father's old evening clothes."

"No, that's mine," says Morris. He takes the suit from her, shakes down the plastic, stands holding it out in front of him over both arms. "That's my old soup-and-fish — it ought to be hanging up in the closet."

"What did you get it for?" Joan says. "A wedding?" Some of Morris's workmen lead lives much more showy and ceremonious than his, and they invite him to elaborate weddings.

"That, and some things I have to go to with Matilda," Morris says. "Dinner dances, big dress-up kinds of things."

"With Matilda?" says Joan. "Matilda *Buttler*?"

"That's right. She doesn't use her married name." Morris seems to be answering a slightly different question, not the one Joan meant to ask. "Strictly speaking, I guess she doesn't have a married name."

Joan hears again the story she just now remembers having heard before — or read before, in their mother's overlong, lively letters. Matilda Buttler ran off to marry her boyfriend. The expression "ran off" is their mother's, and Morris seems to use it with unconscious emphasis, a son's respect — it's as if the only way he can properly talk about this, or have the right to talk about it, were in his mother's language. Matilda ran off and married that man with the mustache, and it turned out that her mother's suspicions, her extravagant accusations, had for once some grounds. The boyfriend turned out to be a bigamist. He had a wife in England, which was where he came from. After he had been with Matilda three or four years — fortunately, there were no children — the other wife, the real wife, tracked him down. The marriage to Matilda was annulled; Matilda came back to Logan, came back to live with her mother, and got a job in the courthouse.

"How could she?" says Joan. "Of all the stupid things to do."

"Well. She was young," says Morris, with a trace of stubbornness or discomfort in his voice.

"I don't mean *that*. I mean coming back."

"Well, she had her mother," Morris says, apparently without irony. "I guess she didn't have anybody else."

Looming above Joan, with his dark-lensed eye, and the suit laid like a body over his arms, he looks gloomy and troubled. His face and neck are unevenly flushed, mottled. His chin trembles slightly and he bites down on his lower lip. Does he know how his looks give him away? When he starts to talk again, it's in a reasonable, explanatory tone. He says that he guesses it didn't much matter to Matilda where she lived. In a way, according to her, her life was over. And that was where he, Morris, came into the picture. Because every once in a while Matilda had to go to functions. Political banquets. Retirement banquets. Functions. It was a part of her job, and it would be awkward if she didn't go. But it was also awkward for her to go alone — she needed an escort. And she couldn't go with a man who might get ideas, not understanding how things stood. Not understanding that Matilda's life, or that certain part of Matilda's life, was over. She needed somebody who understood the whole business and didn't need explanations. "Which is me," says Morris.

"Why does she think that way?" says Joan. "She's not so old. I bet she's still good-looking. It wasn't her fault. Is she still in love with him?"

"I don't think it's my place to ask her any questions."

"Oh, Morris!" Joan says, in a fond dismissive voice that surprises her, it sounds so much like her mother's. "I bet she is. In love with him still."

Morris goes off to hang his evening clothes in a closet in the apartment, where they can wait for his next summons to be Matilda's escort.

In bed that night, lying awake, looking out at the street light shining through the fresh leaves on the square, squat tower of the Baptist church, Joan has something to think about besides her own plight. (She thinks of that, too, of course.) She thinks of Morris and Matilda dancing. She sees them in Holiday Inn ballrooms, on golf-club dance floors, wherever it is that the functions are held. In their unfashionable formal clothes, Matilda's hair in a perfect sprayed bouffant, Morris's face glistening with the sweat of courteous effort. But it probably isn't an effort; they probably dance very well together. They are so terribly perfectly balanced, each with stubbornly preserved, and wholeheartedly accepted, flaws. Flaws they could quite easily disregard or repair. But they would never do that. Morris in love with Matilda — in that stern, unfulfilled, lifelong way — and she in love with her bigamist, stubbornly obsessed with her own mistake and disgrace.

They dance in Joan's mind's eye — sedate, absurd, romantic. Who but Morris after all, with his head full of mortgages and contracts, could turn out to be such a romantic?

She envies him. She envies them.

She has been in the habit of putting herself to sleep with a memory of John Brolier's voice — his hasty, lowered, private voice when he said "I want to, very much." Or she pictured his face; it was a medieval face, she thought — long and pale and bony, with the smile she dismissed as tactical, the sober, glowing, not dismissible dark eyes. Her imagining won't work tonight; it won't open the gates for her, into foggy, tender, familiar territory. She isn't able to place herself anywhere but here, on the hard single bed in Morris's apartment — in her real and apparent life. And nothing that works for Morris and Maltida is going to work for her. Not self-denial, the exaltation of balked desires, no kind of high-flown helplessness. She is not to be so satisfied.

She knows that, and she knows what she will have to do. She casts her mind ahead — inadmissibly, tentatively, shamefully, she casts her mind ahead, fumbling for the shape of the next lover.

T hat won't be necessary.

What Joan has forgotten altogether is that mail comes to small-town post offices on Saturday. Saturday isn't a mail-less day here. Morris has gone to see what's in his box; he hands her the letter. The letter sets up a time and place. It is very brief, and signed only with John Brolier's initials. This is wise, of course. Such brevity, such caution, is not altogether pleasing to Joan, but in her relief, her transformation, she doesn't dwell on it.

She tells Morris the story she meant to tell him had the letter come earlier. She has been summoned by her college friend, who got word that she was here. While she washes her hair and packs her things, Morris takes her car to the cut-rate gas bar north of town and fills up the tank.

Waving goodbye to Morris, she doesn't see any suspicion on his face but perhaps a little disappointment. He has two days less to be with someone now, two days more to be alone. He wouldn't admit to such a feeling. Maybe she imagines it. She imagines it because she has a feeling that she's waving to her husband and her children as well, to everybody who knows her, except the man she's going to meet. All so easily, flawlessly deceived. And she feels compunction, certainly. She is smitten by their innocence; she recognizes an irreparable tear in her life. This is genuine — her grief and guilt at this moment are genuine, and they'll never altogether vanish. But they won't get in her way, either. She is more than glad; she feels that she is right to be going.

III — ROSE MATILDA

Ruth Ann Leatherby is going with Joan and Morris to the cemetery. Joan is a little surprised about this, but Morris and Ruth Ann seem to take it for granted. Ruth Ann is Morris's bookkeeper. Joan has known of her for years, and may even have met her before. Ruth Ann is the sort of pleasant-looking, middle-sized, middle-aged woman whose looks you don't remember. She lives now in one of the bachelor apartments in the basement of Morris's building. She is married, but her husband hasn't been around for a long time. She is a Catholic, so has not thought about getting a divorce. There is some tragedy in her background — a house fire, a child? — but it has been thoroughly absorbed and is not mentioned. Ruth Ann seems to be a woman who can absorb things and keep track of things at the same time.

It is Ruth Ann who got the hyacinth bulbs to plant on their parents' graves. She had heard Morris say it would be nice to have something growing there, and when she saw the bulbs on sale at the supermarket she bought some. A wife-woman, thinks Joan, observing her. Wife-women are attentive yet self-possessed, they are dedicated but cool. What is it that they are dedicated to?

Joan lives in Toronto now. She has been divorced for twelve years. She has a job managing a bookstore that specializes in art books. It's a good job, though it doesn't pay much; she has been lucky. She is also lucky (she knows that people say she is lucky, for a woman of her age) in having a lover, a friend-lover — Geoffrey. They don't live together; they see each other on weekends and two or three times during the week. Geoffrey is an actor. He is talented, cheerful, adaptable, poor. One weekend a month he spends in Montreal with a woman he used to live with and their child. On these weekends Joan goes to see her children, who are grown up and have forgiven her. (Her son, too, is an actor — in fact, that's how she met Geoffrey. Her daughter is a journalist, like her father.) And what is there to forgive? Many parents got divorced, most of them shipwrecked by affairs, at about the same time. It seems that all sorts of marriages begun in the fifties without misgivings, or without misgivings that anybody could know about, blew up in the early seventies, with a lot of spectacular — and, it seems now, unnecessary, extravagant — complications. Joan thinks of her own history of love with no regret but some amazement. It's as if she had once gone in for skydiving.

And sometimes she comes to see Morris. Sometimes she gets Morris to talk about the very things that used to seem incomprehensible and boring and sad to her. The bizarre structure of earnings and pensions and mortgages and loans and investments and legacies which Morris sees underlying every human life — that interests her. It's still more or less incomprehensible to her, but its existence no longer seems to be a sorry delusion. It reassures her in some way. She's curious about how people believe in it.

This lucky woman, Joan, with her job and her lover and her striking looks — more remarked upon now than ever before in her life (she is as thin as she was at fourteen and has a wing, a foxtail, of silver white in her very short hair) — is aware of a new danger, a threat that she could not have imagined when she was younger. She couldn't have imagined it even if somebody described it to her. And it's hard to describe. The threat is of a change, but it's not the sort of change one has been warned about. It's just this — that suddenly, without warning, Joan is apt to think: *Rubble.* Rubble. You can look down a street, and you can see the shadows, the light, the brick walls, the truck parked under a tree, the dog lying on the sidewalk, the dark summer awning, or the grayed snowdrift — you can see all these things in their temporary separateness, all connected underneath in such a troubling, satisfying, necessary, indescribable way. Or you can see rubble. Passing states, a useless variety of passing states. Rubble.

Joan wants to keep this idea of rubble at bay, naturally. She pays attention now to all the ways in which people seem to do that. Acting is an excellent way — she has learned that from being with Geoffrey. Though there are gaps in acting. In Morris's sort of life or way of looking at things, there seems to be less chance of gaps.

As they drive through the streets, she notices that many of the old houses are re-emerging; doors and porches that were proud modern alterations fifteen or twenty years ago are giving way to traditional verandas and fanlights. A good thing, surely. Ruth Ann points out this feature and that, and Joan approves but thinks there is something here that is strained, meticulous.

Morris stops the car at an intersection. An old woman crosses the street in the middle of the block ahead of them. She strides across the street diagonally, not looking to see if there's anything coming. A determined, oblivious, even contemptuous stride, in some way familiar. The old woman is not in any danger; there is not another car on the street, and nobody else walking, just a couple of young girls on bicycles. The old woman is not so old, really. Joan is constantly revising her impressions these days of whether people are old or not so old. This woman has white hair down to her shoulders and is wearing a loose shirt and gray slacks. Hardly enough for the day, which is bright but cold.

"There goes Matilda," says Ruth Ann. The way that she says "Matilda" — without a surname, in a tolerant, amused, and distant tone — announces that Matilda is a character.

"Matilda!" says Joan, turning toward Morris. "Is that Matilda? What ever happened to her?"

It's Ruth Ann who answers, from the back seat. "She just started getting weird. When was it? A couple of years ago? She started dressing sloppy, and she thought people were taking things off her desk at work, and you'd say something perfectly decent to her and she'd be rude back. It could have been in her makeup."

"Her *makeup*?" says Joan.

"Heredity," Morris says, and they laugh.

"That's what I meant," says Ruth Ann. "Her mother was across the street in the nursing home for years — she was completely round the bend. Anyway, Matilda got a little pension when they let her go at the courthouse. Why work if you don't have to? She just walks around. Sometimes she talks to you as friendly as anything, other times not a word. And she never fixes up. She used to look so nice."

Joan shouldn't be so surprised, so taken aback. People change. They disappear, and they don't all die to do it. Some die — John Brolier has died. When Joan heard that, several months after the fact, she felt a pang, but not so sharp a pang as when she once heard a woman say at a party, "Oh, John Brolier, yes. Wasn't he the one who was always trying to seduce you by dragging you out to look at some natural marvel? God, it was uncomfortable!"

"She owns her house," Morris says. "I sold it to her about five years ago. And she's got that bit of pension. If she can hold on till she's sixty-five she'll be O.K."

Morris digs up the earth in front of the headstone; Joan and Ruth Ann plant the bulbs. The earth is cold, but there hasn't been a frost. Long bars of sunlight fall between the clipped cedar trees and the rustling poplars, which still hold many gold leaves, on the rich, green grass.

"Listen to that," says Joan, looking up at the leaves. "It's like water."

"People like it," says Morris. "Very pop'lar sound."

Joan and Ruth Ann groan together, and Joan says, "I didn't know you still did that, Morris."

Ruth Ann says, "He never stops."

They wash their hands at an outdoor tap and read a few names on the stones.

"Rose Matilda," Morris says.

For a moment Joan thinks that's another name he's read; then she realizes he's still thinking of Matilda Buttler.

"That poem Mother used to say about her," he says. "Rose Matilda."

"Rapunzel," Joan says. "That was what Mother used to call her. 'Rapunzel, Rapunzel, let down thy gold hair.'"

"I know she used to say that. She said 'Rose Matilda,' too. It was the start of a poem."

"It sounds like a lotion," Ruth Ann says. "Isn't that a skin lotion? Rose Emulsion?"

"'Oh, what avails,'" says Morris firmly. "That was the start of it. 'Oh, what avails.'"

"Of course, I don't know hardly any poems," says Ruth Ann — apologetic, versatile, unabashed. She says to Joan, "Does it ring a bell with you?"

She has really pretty eyes, Joan thinks — brown eyes that can look soft and shrewd at once.

"It does," says Joan. "But I can't think what comes next."

Morris has cheated them all a little bit, these three women. Joan, Ruth Ann, Matilda. Morris isn't habitually dishonest — he's not foolish that way — but he will cut a corner now and then. He cheated Joan a long time ago, when the house was sold. She got about a thousand dollars less out of that than she should have. He thought she would make it up in the things she chose to take back to her house in Ottawa. Then she didn't choose anything. Later on, when she and her husband had parted, and she was on her own, Morris considered sending her a check, with an explanation that there had been a mistake. But she got a job, she didn't seem short of money. She has very little idea of what to do with money anyway — how to make it work. He let the idea drop.

The way he cheated Ruth Ann was more complicated, and had to do with persuading her to declare herself a part-time employee of his when she wasn't. This got him out of paying certain benefits to her. He wouldn't be surprised if she had figured all that out, and had made a few little adjustments of her own. That was what she would do — never say anything, never argue, but quietly get her own back. And as long as she just got her own back — he'd soon notice if it was any more — he wouldn't say anything, either. She and he both believe that if people don't look out for themselves what they lose is their own fault. He means to take care of Ruth Ann eventually anyway.

If Joan found out what he had done, she probably wouldn't say anything, either. The interesting part, to her, would not be the money. She has some instinct lacking in that regard. The interesting part would be: why? She'd worry that around and get her curious pleasure out of it. This fact about her brother would lodge in her mind like a hard crystal — a strange, small, light-refracting object, a bit of alien treasure.

He didn't cheat Matilda when he sold her the house. She got that at a very good price. But he told her that the hot-water heater he had put in a year or so before was new, and of course it wasn't. He never bought new appliances or new materials when he was fixing up the places he owned. And three years ago last June, at a dinner dance in the Valhalla Inn, Matilda said to him, "My hot-water heater gave out. I had to replace it."

They were not dancing at the time. They were sitting at a round table, with some other people, under a canopy of floating balloons. They were drinking whiskey.

"It shouldn't have done that," Morris said.

"Not after you'd put it in new," said Matilda, smiling. "You know what I think?"

He kept looking at her, waiting.

"I think we should have another dance before we drink any more!"

They danced. They had always danced easily together, and often with some special flourish. But this time Morris felt that Matilda's body was heavier and stiffer than it had been — her responses were tardy, then overdone. It was odd that her body should seem unwilling when she was smiling and talking to him with such animation, and moving her head and shoulders with every sign of flirtatious charm. This, too, was new — not at all what he was used to from her. Year after year she had danced with him with a dreamy pliancy and a serious face, hardly talking at all. Then, after she had had a few drinks, she would speak to him about her secret concerns. Her concern. Which was always the same. It was Ron, the Englishman. She hoped to hear from him. She stayed here, she had come back here, so that he would know where to find her. She hoped, she doubted, that he would divorce his wife. He had promised, but she had no faith in him. She heard from him eventually. He said he was on the move, he would write again. And he did. He said that he was going to look her up. The letters were posted in Canada, from different, distant cities. Then she didn't hear. She wondered if he was alive; she thought of detective agencies. She said she didn't speak of this to anybody but Morris. Her love was her affliction, which nobody else was permitted to see.

Morris never offered advice, he never laid a comforting hand on her except as was proper, in dancing. He knew exactly how he must absorb what she said. He didn't pity her, either. He had respect for all the choices she had made.

It was true that the tone had changed before the night at the Valhalla Inn. It had taken on a tartness, a sarcastic edge, which pained him and didn't suit her. But this was the night he felt it all broken — their long complicity, the settled harmony of their dancing. They were like some other middle-aged couple, pretending to move lightly and with pleasure, anxious not to let the moment sag. She didn't mention Ron, and Morris, of course, did not ask. A thought started forming in his mind that she had seen him finally. She had seen Ron or heard that he was dead. Seen him, more likely.

"I know how you could pay me back for that heater," she teased him. "You could put in a lawn for me! When has that lawn of mine ever been seeded? It looks terrible; it's riddled with creeping Charlie. I wouldn't mind having a decent lawn. I'm thinking of fixing up the house. I'd like to put burgundy shutters on it to counter the effect of all that gray. I'd like a big window in the side. I'm sick of looking out at the nursing home. Oh, Morris, do you know they've cut down your walnut trees! They've levelled out the yard, they've fenced off the creek!"

She was wearing a long, rustling peacock-blue dress. Blue stones in silver disks hung from her ears. Her hair was stiff and pale, like spun taffy. There were dents in the flesh of her upper arms; her breath smelled of whiskey. Her perfume and her makeup and her smile all spoke to him of falsehood, determination, and misery. She had lost interest in her affliction. She had lost her nerve to continue as she was. And in her simple, dazzling folly she had lost his love.

"If you come around next week with some grass seed and show me how to do it, I'll give you a drink," she said. "I'll even make you supper. It embarrasses me to think that all these years you've never sat down at my table."

"You'd have to plow it all up and start fresh."

"Plow it all up, then! Why don't you come Wednesday? Or is that your evening with Ruth Ann Leatherby?"

She was drunk. Her head had dropped against his

shoulder, and he felt the hard lump of her earring pressing through his jacket and shirt into his flesh.

The next week he sent one of his workmen to plow up and seed Matilda's lawn, for nothing. The man didn't stay long. According to him, Matilda came out and yelled at him to get off her property, what did he think he was doing there, she could take care of her own yard. You better scram, she said to him.

Scram. That was a word Morris could remember his own mother using. And Matilda's mother had used it, too, in her old days of vigor and ill will. Mrs. Buttler, Mrs. Carbuncle. *Scram out of here.* Deadeye Dick.

He did not see Matilda for some time after that. He didn't run into her. If some business had to be done at the courthouse, he sent Ruth Ann. He got word of changes that were happening, and they were not in the direction of burgundy shutters or house renovations.

"Oh, what avails the sceptred race!" says Joan suddenly when they are driving back to the apartment. And as soon as they get there she goes to the bookcase — it's the same old glass-fronted bookcase. Morris didn't sell that, though it's almost too high for this living room. She finds their mother's *Anthology of English Verse.*

"First lines," she says, going to the back of the book.

"Sit down and be comfortable, why don't you?" says Ruth Ann, coming in with the late-afternoon drinks. Morris gets whiskey-and-water, Joan and Ruth Ann white-rum-and-soda. A liking for this drink has become a joke, a hopeful bond, between the two women, who understand that they are going to need something.

Joan sits and drinks, pleased. She runs her finger down the page. "Oh what, oh what — " she murmurs.

"Oh, what the form divine!" says Morris, with a great sigh of retrieval and satisfaction.

They were taught specialness, Joan thinks, without particular regret. The tag of poetry, the first sip of alcohol, the late light of an October afternoon may be what's making her feel peaceful, indulgent. They were taught a delicate, special regard for themselves, which made them go out and grab what they wanted, whether love or money. But that's not altogether true, is it? Morris has been quite disciplined about love, and abstemious. So has she been about money — in money matters she has remained clumsy, virginal, superior.

There's a problem, though, a hitch in her unexpected pleasure. She can't find the line. "It's not in here," she says. "How can it not be in here? Everything Mother knew was in here." She takes another, businesslike drink and stares at the page. Then she says, "I know! I know!" And in a few moments she has it; she is reading to them, in a voice full of playful emotion:

Ah what avails the sceptred race,
Ah what the form divine!
What every virtue, every grace,
Rose Aylmer — Rose *Matilda* — all were thine!

Morris has taken off his glasses. He'll do that now in front of Joan. Maybe he started doing it sooner in front of Ruth Ann. He rubs at the scar as if it were itchy. His eye is dark, veined with gray. It isn't hard to look at. Under its wrapping of scar tissue it's as harmless as a prune or a stone.

"So that's it," Morris says. "So I wasn't wrong."

PATRICIA YOUNG

FORECAST

Last night, Jane, the psychic masseuse,
had a baby boy. And Clare,
who turns six tomorrow
and sounds as though she's from the Bronx
moved in
three houses down.
These are only two
of the happiest occurrences.
Also, school's out.
So I went to the bookstore and spent all our money.
Then, a wagon ride down the hill with Clare.
It's more complicated for Jane.
There are three men in her life
and each claims he's the father.
She won't answer the phone
and when they come calling
she shoos them away.
On this side of the street
our son leans out the bay window,
whistles and croons,
at 11 p.m. he must invent
Clare on the front lawn.
This love song
is better than all the new books
money can buy.
Yesterday we stood around admiring
the snow-covered mountains
when Jane placed a hand
on her large stomach, made
some predictions — earthquakes and
election results. I have
a portentous dream
now and then but that doesn't
mean I want to know the future.
Couldn't we just sail into summer
on a hunch or in the wrap of
each other's arms?

Patricia Young was born in 1954 in Victoria. She is an assistant editor of *The Malahat Review* and teaches writing at the University of Victoria. She has published four books of poetry, most recently a sequence of poems about Jean Rhys called *All I Ever Needed Was a Beautiful Room*.

THE MAD AND BEAUTIFUL MOTHERS

We are the children of the fifties
with the mad and beautiful mothers.
In the forties they went to movies in toeless
high-heels, smoked cigarettes and danced
with Leslie Howard, their madness occurring
some time later.

Perhaps it struck the night we were born
or that day at the park, swinging from our knees
we slipped from the bars. After that,
clotheslines collapsed in every backyard,
and children fell through the air
like bombs in September.

We left for school
and they barricaded the doors
with livingroom furniture. Later,
we climbed in through basement windows,
twisted and jived to rock'n'roll
while upstairs our mothers
bent their heads over sinks
unable to wash their hair.

We hid our mothers from our friends,
our friends from our mothers. Thunder
and lightning and some disappeared
into closets or hospitals from which they
never emerged. Perhaps madness first struck
on that flight from Amsterdam, London, Glasgow,
the cabin hot and crowded,
and rain seeping in.

We learned to shift our lives
around and through them where they sat
at the diningroom table staring through doors
in the wallpaper for days at a time.
We are the children who survived
the fifties and their mothers, even
their conversations with God.

It has taken us years to forgive them
their madness, though they loved us
despite it. Years to go back
to the muggy afternoons
the whole world reeked of spice
and sweat and vinegar.

It is late August
and our mothers are in the kitchen
pickling beets and cucumbers.
Like fiends they are pickling
silver-skinned onions
and anything else
that gets in their way.

ALL THE TEN YEAR OLD GIRLS IN THE WORLD

all the ten year old girls in the world are washing
their hair they are sudsing it up with soap
that smells of green apples they are kneeling

in bathtubs and rivers they are washing their
blonde or black or auburn hair sculpting the stuff
into spikes and curls they are laughing and calling

their mothers from gardens or books or the youngest
child helmets and crowns whip like cream on top
of their heads all over the world mothers are seeing

their daughters as never before thinking perhaps
this is the last time these girls will be perfect as
long-stemmed lilies all arms and legs and beautiful

eyes the mothers are standing in doorways or
crouching on sand banks all over the world the sun
drops behind mountains or sky-lights or violet clouds

and the mothers turn back to their other concerns
thinking about these girls whose hair smells of green
apples where in the world will they go from here?

DRIVING IN FROM THE FERRY

And I'm thinking there's only so much
a person deserves and I've had more
than my share, take this man
beside me, how he makes me laugh,
I'm thinking especially of how
he makes me laugh.
The boy and girl in the back seat
are counting the miles
because home is where the,
I won't say it, but it's true for them,
and for us, and for lots of people
we've never met. He's driving

too fast, all the cars
speeding past the next guy and racing
into curves. *This isn't the western speedway,*
I say and close my eyes tight, knowing
I've had more than my share
of love and cilantro, the exotic taste of it
still on my tongue, and all week
my favorite weather, sunny
and hot when

suddenly we turn into the driveway,
the unmown lawn hitting me in the face.
How long and green the grass
but everything else looks the same,
looks just fine. I leap

up the stairs, three at a time, up
to our bedrooms where
the faint smell of ocean and our lives
blows through an open window.
On the bed I collapse delirious to be
alive alive O and where the sometimes lonely
heart is.

CHASTE WINDS OF PARADISE

For my birthday
you gave me fan earrings.

Now I sit in the rocking chair
wearing white lace.

Chaste
like your grandmother?
             *
I never thought I could be
cruel, I never thought
I could be
         translucent.
Hard.

Would you really prefer
a fool's paradise?

Today the world is a cold desert.
And the wind, more honest
than white.
             *
Last night you slept alone.

You'd disagree.
You'd say the earth's deserts expand yearly,
the possibility of paradise
shrinks each day.

Would you love me less if:

I dropped the coffee pot, burned the soup,
shrank your clothes (forgive me,
particularly, the green cashmere
sweater).
             *
My left eye twitches
though I no longer notice.

I live with its peculiar vision
like a cripple lives
with his limp.

But happily?

I adjust my head, contort my face, squint.

In this way I can See.
In this way I can Read.

Even a child knows
hallelujah and confession
are good for the soul.

*

In and out of your nightmares I sally forth.

Each morning you itemize
my latest shenanigans.

Nothing, you say, is worth the dreams.

I agree *(nothing, nothing)*.
Rock in the chair *(is worth)*.
Grim, in white lace *(the dreams)*.

*

Can we begin to open the curtains

to paradise?
Parakeets on my shoulders,
fans on my ears?

Foolish, I hobble toward you,

Twitching.

*

The chaste winds of paradise
rustle the curtains and I am stunned
by what I see — the fans of the desert
open, purple butterflies!

With you I would sally forth all the days of my life.

Sometimes
I am even amused
by our latest shenanigans.
Almost believe we have come this far

to alight in the green garden
of now and here.

IN MY BEST HANDWRITING I WROTE SIX WORDS

Because for days they'd been groping
round in my head, orphans
demanding a mother.

I sharpened my pencil, made a phone call, a pot of tea.
Passed the window three times, waited
while the sun sank in the west,
an orange, half peeled.

I returned to the table.
Added cream, stirred in honey.
Picked up the pencil and stared
for some time, the loops and curves —
CHILDREN FROM MY FLIGHT OF DREAMS.

But the idea was locked in, a seed
trapped too long in a shrivelled up shell.
It would not blossom
into the deeds or misdeeds of children
whose flight was fabulous,
perfect. Not even

the image of a dodo
entered my brain, not even this clumsy bird
waddled toward me through mud
flapping its goddamned
rudimentary
        wings.

WINSOME

Something tells me there's a horse in this neighbourhood
and it's not
the smell of lilac.

Lilac is no clue
though it does make me optimistic
about a future on this planet.
You move down its sunny side in a luxury coach,
but who's that beside you, laughing
at your jokes?

Somewhere in this neighbourhood
a horse wants out. I've heard that neigh before:
winsome, broken-hearted.

I could say
I miss you like a horse would miss
the taste of summer hay but.
Where would that leave me?
Pawing the ground?

I watched T.V. late and alone tonight
White light flooding into the room
with bad and ominous news.
The oceans have had it.
The forests/air/rivers/ozone layer
too.

You lean forward in your reclining seat, and love?
On top of her head, a little coconut tree.

Out of time and out of turn, O my best companion

just when the day was beginning
to smell so sweet.

BANFF WRITING/ BANFF WRITERS

Every year in May, a few poets and prose writers come to the Banff Centre to work with editors on the revision of book-length manuscripts. The program offers them individual attention, uninterrupted time and space to work, and the beauty of the Rocky Mountains. In 1988 ten such writers came to the May Studio to work with Don Coles and Jennifer Glossop and other writers and editors on novels and on collections of poems and short stories. A second program, Writing Plus, brought in another complement of writers at an advanced stage in their careers. Assisting the resident editors last summer, in a resource capacity, were a variety of artists and editors, among them Sylvia Fraser, William Stafford, Leon Rooke, and Rachel Wyatt.

The May Studio was begun by W. O. Mitchell in 1980. For the past two years the Writing Program at Banff has been headed by Adele Wiseman. Writers interested in applying should write The Writing Program, The Banff Centre, Box 1020, Banff, Alberta, T0L 0C0.

In the following pages are works from four writers from the May Studio.

UNACCEPTABLE PEOPLE

BY GREG HOLLINGSHEAD

The first thing I noticed about Cary Dean Griffith was his left hand, because it was stroking my wife's leg. It was a big hand with soft fingers and you could tell that somebody was being paid to take care of the nails. The tiny hairs on the back were silky and colourless, and the light played on them as the hand worked the flesh.

This was a black-tie function at the home of a guy called Alan Ignatius: white broadloom, gold chandeliers, old masters, framed weed arrangements. The weed arrangements were the work of Alan's girlfriend, Thomasina. She dried them and then she glazed them. They were what first caught my eye when I walked in. Second, the guards, like bouncers, in shiny suits; Ignatius made his money on both sides of the burglar-alarm business, so he only trusted blue-jaws. Third, at the Steinway, the celebrated Brenda Popescue, my wife, with her magnificent smile. Fourth, that big soft hand.

Later I walked through French doors onto a vast lawn. I found a rack of croquet mallets out there and hit balls around. They made a nice click. By the time I came in, Brenda Popescue and Cary Dean Griffith were long gone.

Six weeks later I ran into my wife at a bar, and she did not look well. It came out that she had been left by Cary Dean, or the other way around — it was not clear. At closing I begged her to come back. I did this because I thought I was depressed without her, but in retrospect I would say that after all the crises a woman like that will put you through, my life had levelled out into a quiet recuperative trough, and I was just bored.

Greg Hollingshead was born in Toronto in 1947. He teaches English at the University of Alberta. His stories have appeared in many Canadian literary magazines and he has published a collection called *Famous Players.*

It did not work out. Before it did not we were sitting around drinking one night and I asked her about this Cary Dean Griffith because I had started to hear some funny things about him. In fact I had been hearing funny things about him for years, but it was only after he borrowed my wife that I had started to put them together.

Brenda thought for a couple of minutes and said, "Jack? You know the saddest single thing Cary ever said to me?"

"No, what."

I stood up, my hand out for her glass, which was empty.

"He said his father told him that a man should have a goal, but he never told him what it should be."

"That is sad."

"Now, somebody like you, Jack — " Brenda rolled up her eyes to show me how carefully she was framing the delicate point she would make next. I flopped down on the chesterfield and spread my arms along the back to show her I was waiting. "You don't think anything about things your father told you, do you?"

"*My* father? No. Would you?"

"I didn't think you did." Brenda had her chin on her knees and was hugging them, rocking a little.

A week later, on short notice, I flew out to the west coast to set up a club for a guy who called himself Bob S. Lee. Bob S. had payroll problems, it took eight months, and I did not get around to calling. By the time I arrived back Brenda also had moved past all the crises into a sort of peace. But she was dead.

Here are three funny things I had heard about Cary Dean Griffith.

One, the biggest problem in his life was spending the interest on the interest. On family fur-trade money. And some of us thought all that was over with the coureurs de bois.

Two, Cary Dean Griffith was a drinker who really did have the perfect control we all pretend we do. Hours, days, probably weeks ahead he would plan major bouts, including quantities. Even at home, where his daily beverage was coconut fenny — Goan mescal — I never saw him lose it.

Three, in an expensive restaurant once he shot a pork chop; that's right: the chop was too tough, so he pulled out a .38 and shot it three times.

It happened that Brenda died two days after I got back, and I never saw her. Since nobody stepped forward to pay for her funeral, I sold the Plymouth. You know when you marry someone like that you are taking on a big responsibility. Anyway, who needs a car in a city like ours with its marvellous transport system?

Ten people came to the funeral; none of them was Cary Dean Griffith. Afterwards we went to her favourite bar, and there he was, with that horse face, white shoes, and mohair jacket, in a booth, in profile.

A few drinks and it could have been Happy Hour, but not for Cary Dean — who paid us no attention — and not for me. The others kept saying they didn't know her all that well. This made me wonder. After eighteen years I sure knew certain old patterns she had with me, but as for a woman who once had never had a pattern with me and if she had lived might one day not have one any more, I was lost. Another thing everybody kept saying was how she looked just like she was asleep, but whatever it was in that box it did not even look like her dead. Why can't people understand that the point of a funeral, where you pay a man good money to make a corpse look like something done in soap, is that the person is dead? There is a big difference between being dead and being asleep. Those too dumb to grasp the difference should not be allowed at funerals.

In my hand I am holding a mug of black coffee. We are still at the bar, in the back. If I open my eyes I can see Cary Dean Griffith, as close to the floor as myself, in a chair exactly the same colour, drinking coconut fenny from a crystal tumbler etched with dancing loons. His deep tan gives him the look of a man being scorched by a hot blast of unhappiness. His long nose seems to be crushed and fallen, his eyes and ears and soft mouth are sagging.

Is he thinking she died from the same thing that had her with men like us? But how are we supposed to talk about that? More to the point: who are men like us?

"She was a wonderful woman, Jack." He reaches out his big hand flat on the table and I look at it.

These foolish breaks in the wall.

Cary tells me, "Know what I am, Jack? A player. If I couldn't be a player I'd be a junkie."

Brenda Popescue and her magnificent, inconvincible lovers.

It never ends, it is never enough.

"A player at what game, Cary?"

He smiles with his long teeth. "Life," he tells me. "Lived to the hilt."

Brenda looked thirty forever and she was beautiful, but she had a hard, hard mouth.

This adversary attraction. What is it instead of?

The light comes through and it's the wrong light. Pathos and sentiment have never made anybody a nice guy. They make him do and say sad things.

I throw back my head and finish my coffee.

These people come into your life and it is such chance and they are such a puzzle or such a drag that you almost think they are not really in your life at all. They are not people you feel you need to be other than yourself with; in fact you are a little surly about being no more than yourself, and so it ends up easy. Even though they are often boring or difficult, over the months or years you spend a lot of time with them because with them you do not have to worry about yourself. If it's a woman and she looks good enough you might even marry her. What I am saying is, you think you know these people better than you want to and you think you do not know them at all, but it is all the same. In the end it is a simple matter of a lack of regard, and it cuts both ways. They were the stuff of your life, and now they are nothing but memories, and not loving them is suddenly no protection against their pain.

HEART TO HEART

BY ELIZA CLARK

aylou had sat on the plane to Florida next to Renee Louisianna Harp, a fatty with a heart of gold. Renee Louisianna had done herself up for the plane ride and kept rearranging to show her best side. She was wearing a silky rayon blouse with a tropical-fruit theme patterned on it. In no time at all she had pulled out snapshots of her only son, Pernell, a big-headed boy with bright eyes and a side part lying almost on top of his left ear.

"This here's Pernell eating a sloppy joe," she said. Maylou took the dog-eared photograph and studied it for a minute before passing it back.

"Pernell can sometimes eat three of those at a sitting, if you can believe that, with two cream puffs for dessert afterwards. That's when he's feeling like himself. He's still in mourning at the present time though." Renee L. was fishing through her handbag for some talc, which she found and sprinkled generously on her wrists and palms.

"Sweaty palms," she said, "like my mother and my grandmother before me. You know what they say, 'cold hands warm heart', but they never say anything about hot hands. Lord knows I'm not cold-hearted if that follows, not in the least. Unless I'm provoked. When I'm provoked I change my colors altogether, like a chameleon. You wouldn't even know it was me you were looking at."

"Why is Pernell in mourning?" Maylou asked, thinking maybe they had something in common, she and the boy.

"Oh, it's sad that story. Pernell's daddy bought him this baby cockatiel for his birthday,

Eliza Clark studied writing at York University under Don Coles. Until recently, she hosted a movie-review show on one of the Toronto TV stations, an occupation she gave up to concentrate on her novel-in-progress *Saving Graces,* from which our excerpt is taken.

'cause Pernell had been going on and on about getting a bird and how he'd look after it and all, and so we thought it might be a good idea. Teach him some responsibility for another living creature. But this bird was born crippled with a busted foot. It just came out with its foot twisted almost right around on itself, and Pernell took it to the vet and the vet broke the foot and set it back the way it should've been from the start. It had a dressing of white gauze wrapped around and around its tiny ankle that Pernell had to change every morning. Well we, Basil, my husband and I, thought it was important to leave Pernell alone to do the doctoring; we made sure he had enough gauze and all, but we let him be. Anyway, a week goes by and I happen to be in Pernell's room making up his bed when he's changing the dressing. And I smell this horrible smell. It was like . . ." Renee searched.

"Rotten eggs," Maylou offered.

"Yeah," said Renee L. nodding slowly, "but worse, kind of like . . ." Maylou waited, trying to think of something else, some worse smell. "Like a chili fart," Renee Louisianna said and paused to let the full horror of that particular smell come to Maylou's memory.

"And I dropped the bedsheet and went and looked at that poor bird's crippled foot. Well, I can't tell you how swollen and puffed it was, blue and yellow and inflamed. I almost screamed, the poor sad little creature. I whacked Pernell good, I don't know what he could have been thinking of. But I guess he honestly didn't know any better. He'd never seen infection before. So I wrapped the foot up loosely and put the bird, Birdy he was called, in the back seat and Pernell rode up front with me, to the vet's. But here's where the tragedy comes. On the way there, Birdy chewed off his own sore foot and when Pernell turned around, there was Birdy still pecking at the bloody stump and the infected foot lying clear across on the other side of the cage where he'd pitched it. Pernell was scarred for life. He choked and started pulling at my arm while I was driving till I thought for sure we'd run off into the ditch. I had no idea what had happened. Who would've thought that Birdy would maim himself in such a brutal way. But then I guess that's nature in the raw, taking care of itself. It was something that Pernell had to learn the hard way, I guess." Renee L. was shaking her head and trying to pry off her high-heeled pumps with the toe of one put to the heel of the other, but due to the air pressure her feet had swollen and the shoes could only be pulled off by hand.

"Honey, I hate to bother you this way, but my shoes just won't come unstuck, would you reach down there and . . ."

"Surely," Maylou said and undid her safety belt and pulled off the shiny black pumps, half expecting the fat feet to come off in them.

"So what happened to that bird, Birdy? Did it die on the way to the vet's after all?" Maylou asked, drying off her palms discreetly, sticky from the wet nylons.

"No ma'am, it did not die. In fact the vet said it was the best thing that could of happened. Here take this," Renee L. said, handing Maylou a Kleenex. "No, no Birdy still hops around on one foot, you hear it at night on the bottom of the tin cage. Tap, tap, tap. Tap, tap, tap." Renee L. used her index finger to charade the one-legged bird hopping.

"So why is Pernell in mourning then if his bird didn't die?"

"We're not sure exactly why. We think maybe he's just mourning after what might have been. A perfect world where all birds have enough feet. You know kids. They get these notions."

Just then the stewardess brought them their in-flight meal of filet mignon wrapped in bacon, carrots, and mashed potatoes. There was also a cole-slaw salad and a jelly roll for dessert, and a cup for tea or coffee. Renee Louisianna took a good look at her portion of meat which she got first, then at Maylou's, but since Maylou's filet looked smaller, substantially smaller, Renee L. seemed satisfied and started in.

"I'm ready for this," she said, tucking in. "That'll be Kentucky bluegrass down there," she said, waving a fork over Maylou as she looked out the window. Maylou had the window seat, but since they were seated directly on the wing, there was nothing to see anyway. Unless the plane tilted on a real angle, which made Maylou so nervous that she wouldn't look out.

"You know it's green, not blue, that grass. My Lord, I'm feeling like particular hell today," she said. "Look at my complexion all pasty and bumped," she said rubbing her fingertips across her cheek and sticking out her chin. Maylou looked but didn't notice too much wrong with Renee L.'s face, except for the roll of fat making another chin under the primary one. "Do you know that ninety per cent or so of household dust is skin? Just dead skin that's fallen off and covers the top of the TV and the lampshades. I didn't know that until quite recently. It changes the way you look at things, knowing that. It makes you wonder what else, what other things you don't know about. Day-to-day things that you should have some information on." Renee L. took a huge forkful of cole slaw then, some of which fell off into her lap, which made her laugh a bit in shame.

"First thing I'm going to do is settle myself into a roomette in Tampa–St. Pete. I'm going to strip down and lie naked on the bed and let the air conditioning make me shiver. I might sleep that way for an hour or so."

Maylou was picking at her jelly roll when the plane lurched in such a way as to make her tray slide across in front of Renee L., who stopped it by putting a finger on the jelly roll and pushing it back to Maylou that way. Maylou had her hair back off her face in a long braid, and she looked wrung out. It wasn't until Renee L. stopped the jelly roll that she took her first good look at Maylou and right away got the feeling that something wasn't quite right.

"Maylou, where are you off to, I never did ask," Renee L. said and put down her napkin to listen intently. She could be so self-centered.

"Largo," Maylou said. "My mama just died there and I've got to drive my father back home and take care of things."

"Um-hm, like the cremation and all. Florida State law. I know all about it. I had to have my Uncle Castor done not even a year ago this coming Christmas. Let me just advise you one thing if I may — don't feel like you've got to spend a lot of money on the urn for your dear mama's ashes. Only a fool is money-proud. Remember that. Those urns are more costly than you'd think. My Lord, are they ever. Just choose wisely, your sweet mama will understand. What happened to her anyway?"

"Heart rot, I guess. She was playing cards and they thought she was laughing because she won, but she wasn't, she was gasping for breath."

"Too much excitement, I suppose. Who was she playing up against?"

"My father and Doris and Vern Morris." Maylou could feel herself tightening.

"Doris Morris? Good God, what the hell kind of name is that for a human being."

"I don't know, I never met her. They're going to drive my father to the airport to meet me. I guess you'll see her then too."

"I'll keep my eye out, I'd hate to miss that one." And then Renee Louisianna settled back to nap and Maylou got back to the book she was reading called *The Elvis Murders.*

Maylou had always read. She was raised by her nana, who smelled of cinnamon sticks and vanilla, and loved Lawrence Welk as much as reading and storytelling. Maylou used to sit either on her nana's lap or curled up on the floor between her legs, most of the time. She would tell Maylou stories that she'd made up herself from scratch and others that she'd added to, to suit Maylou's special tastes. "Beauty and the Beast" was Maylou's favourite, the Beast being a kind of kangaroo with teeth like a piranha. Maylou always had a thing about teeth and she liked the idea of being hopped around in a kangaroo's pouch. Most of the time, the stories ended badly, with Maylou, as Beauty, being chewed and left scarred or limbless to hobble off behind a white rose bush and pine away. Maylou liked this better, preferred it to a rosy-hued Harlequin ending, as did her nana herself, if the truth be known. Maylou's nana spent her last years in a nursing home, and died while having her hair done by the in-house hairdresser at the Golden Age Coiffure Hut they had set up on the main floor. You could tell when it was she died because there was one section of hair, at the nape of her neck, that was straight as a pin, where the hairdresser hadn't bothered to finish.

As they got off the plane the heat hit like a towel being whipped from the dryer. Renee L. was carrying a large over-the-shoulder bag and a straw hat and there was already perspiration across her top lip. Maylou was feeling apprehensive about seeing her father and the unknown Morrises, Doris and Vern. Though she did hope Oscar would be there. Oscar was her wiener dog of seventeen years. Just after Maylou had married Zak, Oscar had packed up camp and left. He'd sensed a certain coldness and disdain coming from Zak, not unfounded, that had made the hairs on the back of his neck bristle. And one day, when Maylou's father was over, Oscar had seized the moment and followed him into his car and wouldn't come out again, even for a plate of cold beans. Maylou could understand it in a way. Her choice of Zak didn't necessarily have to suit anyone else, but still she missed Oscar and the fun they'd had.

"God, it's hotter than hell, isn't it, Maylou?" Renee Louisianna said, fanning herself with her hat as they waited for their bags to come.

"I don't guess that it is, after all," said Maylou thinking that fatties always sweat more and feel hotter.

"I guess you're right, Sweetie Pie, I'm always stretching the truth like an elastic band. If I wasn't so fat, I'd be cool as a cucumber now I bet," Renee L. said.

"You're not fat," said Maylou falsely and soft.

"No, you're right, Honey Bunch," she stepped in, "I'm not

fat. I'm just fluffy." And Renee Louisianna got a good laugh at that. Maylou had this image of the rhyming woman, Doris Morris, waiting for her behind the barrier, and couldn't laugh herself.

Once through the gates, Renee Louisianna gave Maylou a big hug and pinched her arm.

"You take care now, Sugar Loaf," she said. "I took the liberty of scribbling my sister's phone number on the back cover of that Elvis book you were reading. She'll know how to get hold of me when you want. Call me up and we'll have a heart to heart sometime soon. I feel like we're already that close."

And as she walked away, Maylou checked the back jacket of her book and there it was:

Renee Louisianna Harp
c/o Carolina Rosetta Harp (her Sister)
(813) 499-2376   CALL ME !!

all in this flowery print, except for the exclamation marks at the end, which were threats, reinforced with double lines. Maylou carefully tore off the back jacket of her book and ripped it in half. She'd intended to throw both halves into a nearby garbage container, but she missed, and only one half made it into the can, the other half fell onto the floor behind it. That half read: (813) 499-2376 CALL ME !! Later that night, the message would be found by a lonely janitor who would call up the number that seemed so anxious to be called and would, not long after, end up marrying the fatty sister spinster called Carolina Rosetta Harp. But Maylou would have no way of knowing this, as in her opinion Renee Louisianna Harp was a raisin-brained stump-head and her sister likewise and she wanted nothing to do with them. Life had a way of coming round to bite its own tail if you let it.

THE MARRIAGEABLE DAUGHTER — *an excerpt from a novel by* DANIEL GAGNON

I

O Phyllis, you are my dear sister in Medicine Hat, Alberta, Canada, aren't you? do you understand me well, excuse my so bad English, mister Smith mon professeur d'anglais gave me your precious name and now I have my kindred soul. I am twelve and I believe it is immoral for a woman not to give herself completely to a man she loves unless she has had the poor judgment to fall in love with a man who's bad for her (mother and father), then she should run a mile from him, do you, Phyllis, on the quiet, secretly read the book series of blacklist in the library room of your parents, at night with a flashlight, in your pyjama, to have the shivers, to make you shudder, to be thrilled with delight, to have a tickle in your organism? I will talk to you about a boyfriend in my class, one can't help liking him, did you ever read on orgasm?, it is a great mystery, I did not ask my mother, I walk on the street, I prick up my ears, the question is why deny oneself all pleasure, O Phyllis, I don't know you well, but I know you profoundly, deeply, I have no doubt, I shall see him before long, do you want to hear a good deal about him? everyone is talking about orgasm, it is common gossip, we divided a cake into portions at my birthday anniversary, my parents slipped quietly away, he took my third finger, my ring finger, Phyllis, no mister Paragraph Smith, mon professeur d'anglais, will not see this letter to sub-edit my heart, just to be a stickler for etiquette and to get on his high horse, I address this

Daniel Gagnon was born in 1946 in Quebec. He attended the University of Montreal and completed a Licence ès Lettres in French studies. More than fifty of his short stories have been published in France and Canada, and seven novels and a story collection have appeared (*Surtout à cause,* 1972; *Loulou,* 1976; *King Wellington,* 1978; *La Fille à marier,* 1985; *Mon Mari le Docteur,* 1986; *La Fée calcinée,* 1987; *Le Péril amoureux,* 1986; and *O ma source!,* 1988). He received Le Prix Molson de l'Académie canadienne-française in 1986 for *La Fille à marier.* This excerpt is from his novel *The Marriageable Daughter,* composed originally in English, and forthcoming from Oolichan Books. He lives in Montreal.

letter to you personally, if you keep quiet, no one will be any wiser, do you know what an erection is, did you read about it or did you ever do see one, Phyllis, did you do? what is it exactly, I asked my big sister on the sidewalk, now if you are groaning that I'm taking all the romance out of sex and turning it into something mechanical and inhuman, you couldn't be more wrong, she said to me, so obviously there are a thousand things to say and there is not going to be a time to say most of them, it is difficult to know where to begin, I am almost completely in the dark, do you like the poetess Anne Wilkinson? she writes: "She met a lion face to face, As she went walking, Up to her lips in grass, On the wild savannah", also this: "Then two in one the lovers lie And peel the skin of summer, With their teeth, And suck its marrow from a kiss So charged with grace, the tongue, all knowing, Holds the sap of June, Aloof from season, flowing," it is nice, Phyllis, my tongue, may sap aloff on the wild savannah two in one face to face lovers and suck their marrow from a kiss . . . such is life, do you love life, Phyllis? Did a boy ever touch you somewhere on your corpse Phyllis?

II

O Phyllis, do you think I should go to my gynecologist, do you have problems, if you are not overweight but just flabby or poorly proportioned, then exercise, do you wear parfum, he tells me that I smell heavenly, who could advise me how to apply make-up, what foundation is right for my skin tone, mother has several magazines which have monthly articles on make-up, do you know what colors are flattering to you Phyllis, during your periods be sure you change your sanitary napkins and tampons often enough so there is no chance of odor build-up (said mother), smelling in love area is not sexy, keep your fingernails and toenails clean and shampoo your hair until it squeaks, I want to read a book I found secretly in mother's room, it is called *Rapport Hite*, it is about sexual pleasure, la jouissance sexuelle, they are supposed to say that the one area of body that women forget to touch is the clitoris because of its shape and curves deep in the flesh and it remains hidden from view, I put my legs to flight, the right and the wrong side of me, reversible material in a mirror, and it is hidden from view like the princess living in a tower as if spellbound, but it is described when I touch by touch the touchstone, cursory glance, in hydroplane, babbling and purling, no I will not show my letter to mister le professeur d'anglais Smith, o Phyllis, il me semble que je te connais déjà beaucoup et par coeur, même si je ne t'ai encore jamais vue, did you understand my french words? you do not speak French in Medicine Hat of course, do you?, you are too far away in that Indian country, and what do you know about me?. there is much snow and lakes and we are not Americans, what is your dream? love love and love, but it is the general dream, all the people on the Planet are dreaming of love, where are the special peculiarities, do we have an attitude that is characteristic?, Nicolas has his own particular way of walking, talking, unusual uncommon exceptional ordinary person, and we receive each other privately, take each other aside parental authority etc., in our family we have the same name but we are not in any way related, where are you Phyllis in the universe, my sister?, it is a matter of urgency, this letter to you in the Queen's English, the wailing of newborn infant in wanderings, making regular journeys between A and B, roaming haphazardly, wavering in vacuity in canadian emptiness, freezing in the Pole ice from sea to sea, glorious and free, we stand on guard for thee beneath the shining skies, our home and native land, and the poor Indians, the lost Indian summer, o chère Phyllis, où es-tu, where are you, is your mother dating and going out and sleeping around a lot, what do you think about smoking pot, does it make you feel insecure and paranoid, and drugs like LSD, mushrooms, peyote and mescaline?, a lot of kids trip on acid, they think it is groovy, but they do not know the dangers, chère Phyllis, I have many questions to ask to you, my kindred soul, did you ever try suicide, slashing your wrists, did you have to see a therapist, are you going badly in school?

III

Like a stream that flows into the fleuve St-Laurent, I heave a sigh, I glance to you Phyllis in Medicine Hat, I jettison a letter, an interminable letter, to throw a bridge over a river, like ship driven ashore by the storm!, throw my letter out of the window, throw in the sponge, the die is cast, what is the score, the stakes are down, the truth is dawning on me, it is a day's journey, what is the date, what day of the week is it?, I saw him the other day, he didn't see me, day by day my every day clothes, wait till after the holidays, all the way from nowhere to nowhere, I stew in my own juice, Nicolas mon amour where is he, I swear we swore in twin beds when he came at home, now I am dying of natural cause, the cause of la maladie d'amour, it becomes apparent that I must die, it is my only escape from a world I cannot understand!, Nicolas, if you no longer love me and do not wish me to come back to you, will you not write and tell me so!, mister professeur d'anglais will not see my letter, because I do not want him to see my plagiary neither my thoughts, my spelling mistakes, my suicidal syntax, so Phyllis, the die is cast, the Labrador cannot be in the Rocky Mountains, what do my friends say to me?, nothing!, my friend Helen started smoking when she was in sixth grade, besides pot, she also smokes cigarettes, she is not like me, I am prudish compared to her, she began having heavy sex about a year and a half ago, just before her twelfth birthday, it was with a boy who she really likes, they had also intercourse, I could do that but I am afraid, I do not want to break my dream, my psyché, I psalmodize, I intone my love in my heart, I think personally that my friends who take acid and stuff like that and have heavy sex do not really have their heads together, I do not have friends, I am alone, just alone as the north Pole, are you alone Phyllis in Medicine Hat, what a wonderful name for a city, charming dream of a magician who let go out off his hat rabbits in the Prairies and also fantastic birds, and you are in that hat, that medicine hat, Phyllis?

IV

I am dying out like the Labrador duck, wild horses, giant bisons and the passenger pigeons who disappeared from the Earth, I will vanish, a girl like me cannot live, the destructive effects of civilization on life put me on the verge of extinction, we are critically endangered species, Phyllis, with our fragile, delicate health, and precarious happiness, are we on a threshold of a new awakening like professors say, our extraordinary propensity to isolate ourselves from love, anything that we do now or in the future becomes futile unless the growth of the non-lovers population can be stemmed!, in the permanent darkness of deep sea, we, brittle stars, insinuate ourselves into small crevices between rocks, we tend to be secretive, living on hard bottoms where light penetrates, o the light!, Phyllis, we feed on small particles of light, some courageous brittle stars extend arms into the water and catch suspended particles, but I am tired out, what medicine would act and would have an action to exhume me of the buried continent, Phyllis, do you have a remedy in your beautiful hat, for me wreathed with mist, a fountain of wisdom to save me from violence, discord and confusion, from pride and arrogancy, and from every evil way, a prayer to give me back my lover Nicolas, to defend our love and fashion us into one united person, Nicolas and me, brought hither out of many kindreds and tongues, to deliver us from evil, and grant us an entrance into the land of light and joy, in the fellowship of the saints, in the eternal and everlasting glory, oh I have a terrible headache, I will let my passport expire, I am losing the thread, the ship is in distress, the plane is crashing the ground, crippled with rheumatism, many questions will not be answered.

V

There is a baby growing inside my own body Phyllis, I do not believe it, maybe it is only a tumor or I am getting fat a little, I cannot realize that there is another human being inside of me, O Nicolas!, ce serait notre fils ou notre fille, notre enfant, our child!, if it is really a baby, I will keep him and raise him, I will drop out of school and stay home, I reject abortion, mother will help me, he will be my main reason for living, my mother does not want to speak to me, she acts sullen but the baby will be very cute and she will love her little grandson, if not I will move out of the potato family, the mustard family, but perhaps there is no baby, am I quite sure my developing fruit hasn't left yet?, I am a flower split open to show her fleshy receptacle, her interior ovary, her branches with leaves, her stamens and pistils, Phyllis, I am like lillies grown for ornamental purpose, but in the species of lillies who yield drugs and have poisonous properties, I have got three times as much as I need and I swim against the stream, the poison is against me, I absorb it to become asexual and sterile, I do not eat anymore, Phyllis, you are reading my testimony, I bequeath, I devise my petals, my dried tears, my ovules, my corolla, my wedding dress to you my kindred flower, I will be incorporated into organic world and be transferred to farm equipment, causing with dead leaves molecules and dung, ding dong the bells, I will move along chains of electron carriers to other lives, I will be a tomato plant or a pea, not a violated flower, I do not want to be nice and cute, my ice cube's heart is in winter blooming with health in thousands crystallized stars, you would think the marriageable daughter is asleep at the parting of the ways but she is crying something from the roof top of the Planet in the north wind.

VI

They experiment with the "distressed" look in makeup, they do not know what is distress in my class, they go discoing almost every night, burn incense in their bedroom, look older than they are, wash their face with soap and water twice a day, care, really care about their skin, how it looks, how it feels, they live like cattle, they give me a wry smile while, piece of wreckage, my stockings are wrinkled, they wring their hands in despair like wine that has lost its sparkle, their unfeeling heart, and they would consent to my execution on the charge of blasphemy and punish me by stoning, O Phyllis, the tortures and agony I endure are horrible enough, but the cruelest torment and my deepest anguish are not physical pains, my sufferings are moral, I am isolated, deserted, alone, no intimate companions, where are my friends, my brothers and my sisters?, O Phyllis do they reject me?, it seems hopeless, in the depth of my agony, I am tempted to despair, despite all outward appearances to the contrary maybe the marriageable daughter could enter into happiness, do you think she should commit suicide, choking with sobs in this self-supporting America that reeks of crime?, there are limitations to the conditions which various human beings can tolerate or survive, sex is nothing but fun, war is nothing but fun in the Earthly Paradise, the lights have fused, it is drizzling now, the cheese crawling with maggots, there has been a foul-up in the foundations of modern society, O Phyllis, excuse me, forgive me, send me a medicine from the magic hat.

VII

I am poorly adapted to the season because of flowering prematurely, I have been exposed to love and now, at 12, already in my menopause, feet close together, I live on continuous darkness, my internal and biological clock is broken, my leaves hang down, my friends are initiated in time to mature ovules (prior to frost or drought, unlike me), their dormant buds are made capable of withstanding unfavorable cold weather that lies ahead, thus the only season in which I would be capable to produce flowering again is hell, where I could find surely my polygamous father whom I poisoned with arsenic, in his soup, dead and gone, when the police inspector came, I put on my suitable expression, a poker-face, the funeral will be private, said my mother, she did not want to see all my late father's mistresses, decision taken by her majority, your father, said she, escapes uninjured and unhurt, one must choose the lesser of two evils, there is no harm in that, he has no cause to regret it, I will not speak ill of him, he packed his trunk as artful as a cartload of monkeys, saving us from all tormenting fear of condemnation in the day of Judgment, no more we loved him because he abandoned that care and concern for us, I was unlucky, a miserable five-cents piece in my purse, où irons-nous, Jeanne?, my mother asked me, (although I hate her I will help her) it is the worldweariness, I said to mother, just take a sick leave, but I have no more job, said she, I retorted: your job, it is me, mother, and very soon I shall go like father, oh my legs are giving way beneath me, Phyllis, it is the world war three, I am tilting at windmills like Don Quixote, I am a chatterbox and a bad windbag, do not listen to me, forgive me, O my darling in your fabulous hat, holy, holy, holy, Lord Hat Almighty, which was, and is, and is to come.

RIDING TO THE CORRIDA

BY PATRICIA ROBERTSON

Saturdays Darla and Micaela hitched downtown and stood in the video arcades, not playing but watching the slim-hipped boys bent over the machines. It was Darla's idea to watch, Darla who ran red lipstick over her mouth and stood with a hip thrust out in the gloom where the machines hummed. Micaela hung back, shook her bangs in her eyes, and stuffed her hands in the sleeves of her jean jacket. Later they wandered through the department stores, leaning into mirrors to hold earrings at their ears, turning their heads this way and that. Sometimes Darla slipped into a changing cubicle with a pair of lacy French-cut panties and came back with her own cast-off pair on the hanger. Micaela pretended to be looking at night-gowns.

At fifteen Darla's plump arms already left an afterglow when they moved through the air. Beside her Micaela was a dark elf. When they sat on concrete planters on the street mall Micaela hugged her knees to her chest and let Darla deflect the force of the men's stares with the bounce of her ponytail, Darla did not seem to notice; she applied blue eyeliner, freshly stolen. In between strokes she talked about the stepfather with his leather belt, the four younger sisters, the mother who sagged in the background, the boy she had slept with at twelve. Micaela listened. There were no echoes in her own house where her mother's mouth had swallowed her father's name. Her ears swelled with Darla's secrets. In gratitude Darla eased from the department stores the earrings and bracelets their limited money would not buy.

Patricia Robertso was born in Engla and grew up in northern British Columbia. She is a graduate of the Cr tive Writing Progr at Boston Universi and lived for sever years in Spain. He work has appeared in *The Malahat Rev* and *New: West Coa Fiction,* and her ra play *Marjorie's War* was broadcast last year on the CBC. S now lives in Van-couver, where she has recently comp ted a collection of short stories and a stage play. She is currently at work a first novel.

They stood on a downtown street, thumbs out. Darla counted makes of cars, the top lines: fifteen Cadillacs, five Porsches, three Jaguars, a Daimler. Micaela kept track of colours: maroon, taupe, metallic grey. This one will stop, I know it, Darla said, or: See that dark blue Rolls with the silver trim? That one for sure. As the cars glided past, sometimes carrying a man's smiling face or pink-tongued mouth, Darla wriggled her fingers after them. May your wheels fall off at the next stoplight, she said. May your radiator uncurl. May your engine block melt.

When the cream Cadillac stopped and the back door swung open, Darla jumped, Micaela crept in. The driver laid a pearl-cuffed arm on the back of his seat. Black hair, white teeth, about as old as a father. I am lost, he said. You can help? I look for *el parque*.

Sure, said Darla. You Spanish? My friend speaks Spanish.

Micaela pressed herself against the seat. Her palms were moist. Only a year of high school Spanish, she said.

My name is Juan Carlos, he said, nosing out into traffic. *Como el rey*.

Something about the king, whispered Micaela. Maybe he's related.

At the entrance to the park the fountain played, cherry blossoms scattered across the hood of the car. Beautiful, very beautiful, said Juan Carlos. He parked the car near the zoo. They walked in the sunshine from the seals to the orangutans. Juan Carlos bought a bag of popcorn and took a photograph of Darla kneeling on the ground feeding a squirrel out of her hand. *Ahora te toca a ti*, he said, motioning to Micaela. She squinted into the sun, shading her eyes. Maybe later, by the totem pole, she said. Darla jumped up, giggling, and threw her arm round Micaela's shoulders, her bare knees pocked with gravel. Ah, that is nice, said Juan Carlos, and bent down to take the picture.

They stood on the outdoor chessboard where the wooden figures were almost as large as Micaela. Darla was the white queen and Micaela was the black. Juan Carlos moved the pieces. *Los peones*, he said, have nothing. Like in life. *El caballero* stamps them in the dust. He replaced Micaela's pawn with Darla's knight. And *el obispo*, he is a man of God, yet he too eats them up. Another pawn fell. But *la reina*, she is the most powerful, she can do anything she wants. He pushed Micaela forward by the shoulders and rolled a white pawn from her path. She would have thrown coins and cakes from her castle balcony. In that sunlight gold coins spun and glittered towards the cobblestones below.

On the way back to the car he gave them each his card. Micaela traced the raised letters with her fingers. Juan Carlos Ramirez Solano, Comerciante y Representante. Calle Agustin Sanblas, 17, Barcelona. I am a businessman, he said. Import-export. Clothes, shoes, textiles. And oranges? said Micaela. Her mother had spoken of hitchhiking years ago along dusty roads past dark trees with golden fruit. Juan Carlos laughed. It is true, he said. Seville oranges. for *mermelada*. But no, I do not have.

Are you married? said Darla. Yes, he said, four children, the oldest is fourteen. María del Carmen. *Te parece a ti*, he said, touching Micaela on the arm. The hair is different, but the eyes are the same. He's a smoothie, said Darla in an undertone.

You have been most kind, he said. Can I invite you to take coffee with me? He still looked crisp and fresh in his grey suit with the small lace triangle over his heart. He held out his arms for them to take. Micaela's fingers touched the smooth grey cloth. Was this what a father did, walked arm in arm with his daughters to have coffee in a fancy restaurant? Her name was María del Carmen, and she looked up smiling at her father's handsome face.

He watched them in the rear-view as they drove out of the park, the blonde one, *la rubia*, bouncing up and down in her seat and the little dark one, *la morenita*, sitting back quietly against the red plush. *La rubia* might be sixteen or seventeen, it was hard to tell with her red mouth and blue-fringed eyes. The other one was probably the age of Mari-Carmen, looking lost and fragile in her oversize jean jacket. Where were the parents that they allowed their daughters to wander the streets and catch rides with strangers? He could take them to the distant mountains, or far south into Mexico, and who would ever find them? The world was vast and a child small and easily mislaid. And then no longer a child. He guided the car carefully into the main flow of traffic.

Tell me about yourselves, he said over the silver tea service on the marble-topped table. They sat under glass beside windows that almost spilled them into the harbour. A waiter in white gloves brought the pastry tray. Darla chose something that oozed chocolate and custard, but Micaela hesitated among the pastels of the petit fours. Juan Carlos took a slice of lemon with the little silver tongs.

Darla talked, licking her fingers at the end of sentences. Micaela listened. The man opposite her flew over blue oceans and wore pearl cufflinks and lifted silver tongs under a roof whose colour changed with the weather. How could she tell him about the cramped house on the east side, her mother in her red and white checkout-girl uniform, the father who was only a faded smile from a summer fifteen years ago? This man had beautiful daughters who wore crisp navy uniforms and white kneesocks like the girls who went to the Catholic high school. On Saturdays, he said, he took his family out for *la merienda*, coffee and pastries in one of the cafés on the Ramblas. While she and Darla stole.

I fly back tomorrow, he was saying to Darla. Just in time for the spring *feria* in Seville. Do you know it? It is very famous, people come from all over the world.

Darla wriggled forward, Micaela leaned her chin in her hands. Juan Carlos pulled up a razor-creased pants leg as he crossed one knee over the other. At the height of the sun, he said, the *caballeros* rode through the streets to the fairground in their short jackets and wide-brimmed hats, their ladies mounted behind them sidesaddle in flounced dresses and lace mantillas. From striped tents waiters rushed forward with glasses of pale gold *manzanilla* for the thirsty riders. Under the paper lanterns plump grandmothers and tiny girls danced *la sevillana*, their dresses frothing. The match- and water-sellers cried Fire! Water!, while the guitarists threw back their corded necks and sang. And punctually at five, every afternoon, the bullfight, *la corrida*, began.

Darla wrinkled her nose. Ugh, she said, I wouldn't go. Juan Carlos shrugged. There is a great respect for the bull, he said. It is difficult to explain. It is like a dance, a dance with no mercy, where every step must be exact. Where the *torero* wraps the bull around him like a dress.

But it's not fair, said Darla. My brother, said Juan Carlos, was training to be a *torero*. A bull caught him right here — he pressed his fingers to his groin — during a *farol*, a pass of the cape. They could not stop the bleeding. He was twenty.

In the silence the waiter appeared with fresh hot water. As the steam rose into the air the bull's flanks heaved, its neck with the gay *banderillas* glossy with blood. It pawed the ground in the turning sun. The *torero* drew his sword and sighted along it. The lady in the president's box stilled her fan. The *torero* ran forward, thrust the sword deep into the bull's hump, and leapt clear of the horns. The bull stood motionless, feet splayed, staggered and fell. Hats, scarves, flowers sailed into the air. The *torero* stood cap in hand with his cape over his arm and saluted the lady in the president's box.

If you were a lady riding horseback to the bullfight, Juan

Carlos said, looking at Micaela, the men would say *piropos* as you passed by. Compliments like *guapa, linda, hermosa*. I might say to you — and he swept an imaginary hat from his head to his heart — *que ojos más lindos!*

What? said Darla.

I am inviting you and the señorita with the pretty eyes to dinner, he said.

I better phone my mom, said Darla. Tell her I'm okay.

In the cream Cadillac they rode down a street where glass storefronts sparkled, people sipped coffee at white tables, men in flowing coats strode past women in high heels. Down to where the street almost dipped into the sea, then rounded the curve of the bay. People walked, biked, jogged with children, dogs, baby strollers. Juan Carlos and the girls walked under the chestnut trees. A red and yellow kite sailed over their heads. A man in a suit played a clarinet, the breeze ruffling the pages on his music stand.

We never rode in a cream Caddy before, said Darla. Black, the last one, and before that blue, and before that — do you remember, Micaela?

Micaela shook her head. You do so! said Darla. Micaela has this fantastic memory. That's why she gets good grades.

And you do not, señorita *caballito?* Juan Carlos tugged her ponytail gently. Darla squealed. I smack boys' hands when they do that, she said. Juan Carlos held his own out, palms up. Go ahead, he said. When Darla brought her hand down he caught and held it, laughing. Darla tugged and squealed. Micaela looked at the blue dissolving mountains.

You're mean, said Darla, standing up and brushing the seat of her skirt. She wandered down to a knot of girls and boys sitting on the seawall. Juan Carlos lay back on the grass and shut his eyes. Micaela sat cross-legged and severed a grass blade. A ladybug crawled along the upside-down blade and onto her thumb. Fire, whispered Micaela, water. The ladybug remained still. Juan Carlos sat up and pressed his fingers against his eyes. Four days of business, business, business, and I am tired. He laid a hand gently on her shoulder. Are you happy, *morenita?* Micaela coaxed the ladybug back onto the grass blade and laid it in the grass. I don't know, she said. Juan Carlos stood up and cupped his hands to his mouth. *Oye, niña!* he called. Down at the seawall Darla's blonde head turned as she shaded her eyes and looked up.

A swan of ice sailed down the buffet table, carrying slices of rose and pale-green fruit between its wings. Juan Carlos cut meat with his knife and fork and carried the fork to his mouth with his left hand. From time to time he dabbed at his lips with his napkin. Micaela watched his left wrist flex as he raised food to his mouth, then lifted her own. Darla stabbed potato with her right hand.

One glass of wine for each of you, said Juan Carlos, pouring. That is what my children have. The wine, a pale honey, tasted like acid on Micaela's tongue. She swallowed, ate some bread, took another sip. In Spain the children drank this wine, sitting solemnly at dinner with their parents. Juan Carlos lifted his glass. *Un brindis*, he said. To friendship. To our countries. To your queen and my king.

Micaela laid down her knife. Have you met him, your king? she said. At a reception once at a trade fair, said Juan Carlos. He shook my hand. I have a photograph at home.

Was he wearing a crown? asked Darla.

Oh no. He is a very modern king. He even has a pilot's licence.

Micaela looked at her plate. *The King of Spain's daughter, Came to visit me, And all because . . .* How did it go? Juan Carlos was talking. *I had a little nut tree, Nothing would it bear, But a silver nutmeg and a golden pear.* Yes, Juan Carlos was saying, the king often travels to other countries. *The King of Spain's daughter, Came to visit me, And all for the sake of my little nut tree.* But without silver nutmegs and golden pears, what hope was there? Still, the hand that had shaken the king's had rested on her own shoulder.

There was a little wine left in the bottle. Juan Carlos held it out. Darla placed her hand over her glass and the wine splashed onto her fingers. She flicked the drops at Juan Carlos, giggling. *Hui, que cara tienes!* cried Juan Carlos, and snapped his napkin like a *torero*. Micaela tried to remember the Spanish textbook. *Cara* — was that like *cariño*, darling? Darla's ponytail was bouncing, bouncing. Cheeky, very cheeky, said Juan Carlos. Micaela closed her eyes and swallowed her wine.

Juan Carlos was ordering something from the waiter, coffee and a glass of brandy. He drew a cigar out of his inside jacket pocket and tapped one end on the table. The waiter set dishes piled with cream in front of her and Darla. After this most charming evening, said Juan Carlos, I will drive you home.

Oh no, said Darla. We want to see your hotel first. Don't we, Micaela?

After three glasses of wine and two brandies he could not be drunk, but the lights in his room were too bright, the pattern on the carpet blurred. Overtiredness, no doubt. *La rubia* sat on the stool at the dressing table and spun round and round, making him dizzy. And *la morenita*? Ah yes, behind the drapes somewhere, staring out at the city lights. He could not remember why he had brought them here. *La morenita* was so small there was no bulge in the drapes to reveal where she stood. There was a knock at the door. *La rubia* answered it and came back with a bellboy who carried a tray of something. He managed to pull out some coins for a tip. Look what we ordered, said *la rubia*, and showed him a plate of something disgusting, some sort of sauce poured over chips. She held it out to him; he shook his head. Want some, Micaela? she called, chewing. The drapes parted and *la morenita* came into the room.

La rubia held his business card in her greasy fingers. We'll come and visit you, one day, she said. She hitched up her skirt on the side away from him and tucked the card in the top of her panties. In the dressing-table mirror he saw the line of round bare thigh scalloped with white lace. He beckoned *la morenita* over, took her wrist. *Dile a tu amiga*, he said, *que es bella*. She looked at him uncertainly. *Bella*, your friend, he said. *Guapa. Hermosa*. His tongue, thick with longing, would not form the English words. *Bella*, he repeated stupidly, which was not what he meant. Butter-soft flesh, melting between his fingers, but he could not explain that to *la morenita*. He traced her baby palm with his finger and kissed it, protectively. *La morenita* pulled away her wrist. Stood up and walked to the other side of the room and disappeared behind the drapes.

From the seventeenth floor all the lights of the city lay before her. Nets and arcs and columns of lights, red, gold, silver. All the lights in the world must be here, far from her own street where the street lamps were always out. Would the King of Spain's daughter be impressed when she came to visit? She would take her by the hand and show her the cherry trees, the wooden queen as big as herself, the roof that changed colours. After all, she probably had more silver nutmegs than she knew what to do with.

Behind her she heard Darla's voice, hushed, urgent. Micaela! She opened the drapes a crack, blinking in the bright light. Juan Carlos lay asleep on the bed, his tie crumpled, one shoe on the floor. Darla's hands dripped with lace, necklaces, cufflinks.

There's more in that suitcase, she said, filling Micaela's pockets. You got room down your front too, she said. Hurry up, she said.

In the doorway Micaela looked back at the man on the bed, his arm thrown sideways, mouth open.

CONFOUNDING THE DARK

A Symposium on Canadian Writing

We posed a number of key questions — for example, where has Canadian writing gone, where is it going? — to these thirteen panelists:

SAM SOLECKI:

Sam Solecki

Solecki, former editor of *The Canadian Forum*, is a member of the University of Toronto faculty, writes frequently on literary matters, and has recently edited important works on Michael Ondaatje and Josef Škvorecký.

GEORGE WOODCOCK:

Woodcock has authored and edited numerous influential works in a variety of fields, and is generally considered one of Canada's foremost men-of-letters.

LINDA HUTCHEON:

Linda Hutcheon

Hutcheon is Professor of English and Comparative Literature at the University of Toronto. Her titles include *The Canadian Postmodern, The Poetics of Postmodernism: Story, Theory and Fiction*, and *The Politics of Postmodern Representation*.

LARRY SCANLAN:

Larry Scanlan

Scanlan was Book Editor of the Kingston *Whig-Standard* until recently; he is now associated with CBC's *Morningside*, where, among other duties, he looks after book matters.

DONNA BENNETT:

Bennett's critical writings are extensive. She edited with Russell Brown the *Oxford Companion to Canadian Literature* and is an editor of *Descant* magazine.

Donna Bennett

IRENE MCGUIRE:

McGuire is a Toronto bookseller whose enterprise is the well-known Writers & Co., "the literary bookstore".

Irene McGuire

DORIS COWAN:

Cowan is editor of the revamped *Books in Canada* magazine.

Doris Cowan

ELEANOR WACHTEL:

Wachtel is a free-lance writer and broadcaster now frequently heard on CBC radio.

DOUGLAS FETHERLING:

Fetherling is a poet whose books include *Variorum: New Poems and Old, 1965-85* and *Rites of Alienation*. He is Literary Editor of *The Whig-Standard* in Kingston, Ontario.

Eleanor Wachtel

ALBERTO MANGUEL:

Manguel is free-lance broadcaster, writer, book and theatre critic, and translator. His best-known anthologies are *Black Water: The Anthology of Fantastic Literature, Dark Arrows: Chronicles of Revenge, Other Fires: Stories by Latin American Women,*and *The Dictionary of Imaginary Places*.

Douglas Fetherling

ANN MANDEL:

Mandel's commentaries on Canadian writing are widely published. She teaches in the field at Toronto's Glendon College campus of York University.

Alberto Manguel

DAVID COLBERT:

Colbert is a Toronto publisher.

ED CARSON:

Carson rejuvenated trade publishing at Stoddart and General Publishing Company and is now Vice-President, Publishing, at Random House of Canada

Ann Mandel

David Colbert

1. *What would you describe as the major changes in Canadian writing over recent years?*

DONNA BENNETT:

What impresses me is how Canadian writing has moved from being shaped by geographical regions to reflecting the changing ethnic makeup of Canadians. The patterns of immigration since the Second World War not only have changed Canadian writing but have altered the nature of regionalism itself. While region is still a factor, a writer's identity as immigrant (or child of immigrant, or member of an ethnically identifiable Canadian family) *and* his experience of Canada (what *he* has come to identify as Canadian) are likely today to influence both the "content" and the "form" of contemporary writing. I suppose one obvious example of the writing that has emerged is Joy Kogawa's novel *Obasan*. Or look at the short-story collection by a younger writer like Rohinton Mistry. Or the work of the writers who have begun to emerge from the Italian community in Canada, and the importance they attach to their sense of inheritance. And then there are those great writers in exile around — like the Hungarian poet George Faludy.

Because most people who come from "everywhere else" live in Canada's three largest cities, the old east-west, or prairies-Ontario, dichotomy has been recast. In its place there tends to be an urban-rural split. The more traditional British/Western European voice often comes from small population centres, regardless of geographical location, while the urban voice is becoming that of the new immigrant population.

ED CARSON:

The fictions we're telling ourselves and, increasingly, people from other countries are far more entertaining and challenging and interesting. We're turning a corner towards a quality of writing that is part of a new phase or generation of writers. Look for stronger, more inventive and intriguing story lines, with many more Canadian authors finding audiences in the U.S.A. and the U.K.

DORIS COWAN:

One big change has been in public awareness of Canadian writing. It's still not high, but it has increased significantly over the last twenty or thirty years. Whether the books are actually being read I can't guess, but the authors' names — sometimes even their faces — are now more often recognized.

ALBERTO MANGUEL:

If we can claim a greater maturity in our literature (by this I mean books that require no geographical or political excuses), it would be thanks not only to the books that have appeared but also to the books that have been read. Here, I believe, we have failed yet again as a civilized public. While certain important books received their dues (Atwood's *The Handmaid's Tale*, Munro's *The Progress of Love*), others were ostentatiously ignored: Gurr's *The Ringmaster*, Gail Scott's *Heroine*, and, in translation, practically all the stuff that comes from Quebec. Developing a literature is no doubt a slow process, and the goal is sometimes never achieved, but it can't be a one-sided business. Until we get some real critical sense into our papers and radio and television, the thing will not take off. I'm not saying that we'll ever be a country that takes its literature seriously, but at least we might be one that allows those who want to read to make a choice. Right now, the majority of readers don't even know what's out there. But all right, as far as changes are concerned, I think there have been fewer Sudbury-angst stories and more fiction concerned with giving a new sense to this tribe's done-to-death vocabulary.

DOUGLAS FETHERLING:

The poles change but the polarity is always the same. For every good there's a corresponding evil.

The good, it seems to me, is that women are at the centre of writing. It's not that there aren't some serious male writers, but that taken as a whole there's little audience for them. The realization of this has realigned energies and channelled abilities in ways that are quite exciting. This might be said to be the big shift, of which regional vitality could be seen as a part.

The evil is that in the contest between the Canadianizers and the Americanizers, the latter seem to have won. So in a way there *had* to be a reversal on gender grounds, since the males had made such a mess of matters when they had control, failing to convince the readers of the integral necessity of Canadian writing and letting the infrastructure decay to the point where it's now believed that the way to success in publishing is to publish books for people who don't read. This has led to an environment in which individuals have agents and take vows of celebrity.

DAVID COLBERT:

Read Canadian: A Book About Canadian Books, edited by Robert Fulford, David Godfrey, and Abraham Rotstein, is a collection of thirty essays on various facets of Canadian writing and publishing. It was published in 1972. Twenty-four of the essays were written by men; four were written by women. Don't bother asking about racial minorities, either as contributors or as authors of the books being discussed. Apparently there were no minorities in Canada in 1972. The list of "The Ten Best Canadian Books" is just as revealing:

Morley Callaghan's Stories, by Morley Callaghan
The Empire of the St. Lawrence, by Donald Creighton
Anatomy of Criticism, by Northrop Frye
Lament for a Nation, by George Grant
The Fur Trade in Canada, by Harold Innis
The Stone Angel, by Margaret Laurence
Sunshine Sketches of a Little Town, by Stephen Leacock
The Gutenberg Galaxy, by Marshall McLuhan
Collected Poems, by E. J. Pratt
St. Urbain's Horseman, by Mordecai Richler

Where are the rest of the women? Is every Canadian writer white? Why did the contributors to the book decide "Canadian books were defined as books by Canadian authors published originally in English only"?

Since that book was published we've moved towards a different perception of what constitutes Canadian literature. There's room for Rohinton Mistry, and Michael Ondaatje, and Neil Bissoondath, and Margaret Atwood, and Audrey Thomas, and Alice Munro, and others.

On the other hand, from the list of contributors I've seen, the book you're holding in your hands might not pass the test yet.

ELEANOR WACHTEL:

The most unequivocal change in the writing world — and a truism by now — is the prevalence of computer/word-processors. Speculations about the impact of this technology on literary production are rife, but why not risk a few? There is a trend or fashion for the prose poem — poetry that is indistinguishable from prose on the page, without line breaks — that some attribute to computer composition. It also seems that the machines have a disinhibiting effect on the creative "geist" that's resulted in more submissions to literary magazines.

Another significant change is the aging of the "renaissance" generation of Canadian writers — writers responsible for the growth of CanLit in the sixties and seventies. A couple of years ago, there was a promotion called "45 Below" to uncover "younger" writers. Meanwhile, in 1989, Margaret Atwood, Marie-Claire Blais, bill bissett, W. D. Valgardson, Patrick Lane, and so on, turn fifty.

Finally, there has been a gradual acknowledgement of ethnic diversity in Canadian writing. Joy Kogawa, Rohinton Mistry, Neil Bissoondath, Bharati Mukherjee, Marlene Norbese Philip, Di Brandt, and others come to mind.

IRENE MCGUIRE:

I see two major changes. The first, which has been the subject of much analysis, is the ascendancy of the short story.

The second change, and the most significant, is the increasing internationalization of Canadian literature. Canadian writers are using non-Canadian settings and/or cultural experiences to create a wide-ranging body of work that has altered our literary landscape. Recent examples include *Digging Up the Mountains* and *A Casual Brutality* by Bissoondath; *The Middleman and Other Stories* by Bharati Mukherjee; *Tales from Firozsha Baag* by Rohinton Mistry; *Running in the Family* by Michael Ondaatje; *Daughters of Captain Cook* by Linda Spalding; *Borderline* by Janette Turner Hospital; *Proud Empires* by Austin Clarke; *The Abbotsford Guide to India* by Frank Davey; *Coming to Jakarta* by Peter Dale Scott; and *Shoeless Joe* by W. P. Kinsella, which is one of the best baseball novels ever written.

ANN MANDEL:

Because the most visible and/or admired writers today — for example Atwood, Findley, Ondaatje, Kroetsch, L. Cohen, nichol, MacEwen — came out of the experimentalism and political activism of the sixties and early seventies, and continue to challenge the borders between genres, between art and history, invention and fact, younger writers can begin to write without having to pass exams on regionalism, realism, the lyric, the naturalistic play, the Canadian Identity. Young contemporary writers can confidently acknowledge the influences of, say, Phyllis Webb and Céline, Chris Dewdney and Marguerite Duras, Atwood and

Borges, with no sense of strangeness or embarrassment. They know there exists a body of Canadian writing worthy of being placed in an international context, however it might eventually "measure up".

Ironically, the process by which these visible writers have become so comfortably present has less to do with the inherent values and challenges of their work and more with the frightening rapidity with which art of all kinds is becoming commodified, co-opted by the marketplace — also part of that international context, at least within Western society. If Atwood and Findley use their visibility to speak about human rights and the ecology, if Ondaatje in his recent novel engages issues of class politics, the vitiating influence of the media and the market turns these ideological concerns into trends, fashions.

That there is more and better Canadian writing today than ever before is a legacy of a previous period when "literature" appeared to be rooted generally in vital cultural and social concerns, when "literary" and "community" seemed, indeed were, compatible terms. Today, the area of feminist writing is the one in which the activity of writing continues most clearly as part of larger social practices, though this is true also of other marginalized groups such as native peoples, gays, "ethnic" minorities. The strength and liveliness of feminist writing lies in the extent to which it refuses to limit its concerns to "the literary", indeed rejects the category. Feminist and other marginalized groups perhaps occupy the place of the experimentalists of twenty years ago, but do so with considerably more political canniness, much more urgency. Yet, unlike their earlier counterparts, who were helped along by an economic growth reflected in the rapid increase in literary presses, magazines, and Canada Council support, and by a widespread popular support for their work, young writers in the late eighties, from whatever background or ideology, must contend with an economic and social climate which marginalizes all artists and arts that can't "make it" in the marketplace.

So the young feminist writer can write within the sphere of feminist practice, contributing to the construction of a viable, necessary, but marginalized cultural alternative to the dominant power structure. But as the women's movement enlarges, as it does and will, is there any reason at present to believe it can successfully resist the commodifying forces of the age?

This question seems to me the most important one to ask

about Canadian writing, about the arts, today. Influential trends and fashions are likely to be just that.

LINDA HUTCHEON:

In both the literary and the critical communities recently I think we are witnessing an increased self-consciousness about those humanist "givens", those things we used to be able to take for granted: things like the universality and timelessness of the appeal of the canon of CanLit; the innocently curatorial function of our literary histories; the unquestioning authority of the author (as all-controlling yet inspired genius); the power of narrative to reflect (as opposed to construct) our world; the clear division of writing into separable literary and non-literary genres; and the list could go on. With the new challenges to all these things that once almost went without saying has come a fundamental reconsideration of what it is that we ought to be institutionalizing as "Canadian literature" in everything from our anthologies and reviews to the curricula of our schools and universities. This is also crucial because we have finally started to listen to the anti-centrist voices of women, gays, (non-Anglo or French) ethnic groups, native peoples, and other races and classes, and these now sound loudly in the ears of most of us. The once ignorable "margins" have become the productive "fringe" — and, of course, the fringe is the cultural space where exciting things have always happened. That canon can never be the same again, mostly because it cannot help being derived from social, cultural, and ideological contexts that are visibly changing, partly, no doubt, as a result of the politicized 1960s. Not only were these the years of rising nationalist sentiment for Canadians and increased support for the arts, but they also saw the rise of the civil rights and women's movements and of protest in the name of peace and ecological sanity. The writers "formed" intellectually and politically during these years are now offering us overtly political literature — yes — but also more implicitly committed art, art keenly aware of ideological issues such as gender, class, race, and sexual orientation. The sixties also saw the inscription into Canadian history of those belonging to these "fringe"groups which seem to be altering the direction of our literary values away from the eternal and universal and toward the particularities of our time and place: Canada in the late twentieth century. For some this will be seen as a loss; for others, as a liberation. What is unmasked is the hidden ideology behind those so-called universals like "human nature" and "Man":

that is to say, they turn out to be concepts in fact rooted in a particular place and time, a specific class and gender. A liberation, indeed.

LARRY SCANLAN:

What has changed since 1981 — when I began to earn a living from literary journalism — is the steady proliferation of Canadian titles each fall, with no apparent diminishing of British and American books. Toronto has become one of the busiest crossroads of publishing interests in the world.

The regrettable result? The fall is not seen, at least by those inside publishing, as a time to celebrate books. It's more a pre-Christmas lottery, winners take all. Small-press books and first novels are particularly apt to be neglected in the frenzy of book-peddling. If only publishers would hold some titles for spring publication. . . .

Perhaps readers enjoy this annual flooding of the shelves, but more is not better. Each fall I am shocked at how many good Canadian books there are, and appalled at how many bad Canadian books there are.

SAM SOLECKI:

If I had to point to a single important change, I would cite the "internationalizing" of Canadian writing in the past two or three decades. This seems to me to apply both to creative and to critical writing. Reading Canadian fiction, for example, I no longer have the impression — as I did in the sixties — that I am entering a time warp.

This is true as well of the critical writing in the country, which, even though in quality it lags badly behind its subject, nevertheless is more responsive — for better or worse — to foreign currents. If we do this survey in twenty years, perhaps the most pleasant surprise will be the appearance of a handful of home-grown academic critics whose work one will be able to recommend to readers with the same confidence we now recommend articles and books by Roland Barthes, Gerard Genette, Gerald Graff, Richard Poirier, Leslie Fiedler, and Irving Howe. When the criticism catches up to the writing, we may be in a position to launch a Canadian critical magazine worth reading.

The final and perhaps obvious point about the international dimension in our writing and criticism is the extent to which the past few years have witnessed the acceptance or mild popularity of some Canadian writers abroad. No doubt, some of this is the result of the scattering of External Affairs' monies all over the campuses of Western Europe. But we find what two decades ago we only dreamed of — CanLit being discussed within the international arena.

It will be interesting to see in the near future if these discussions will produce a consensus about whether or not there is or has been a Canadian writer of international stature. To those who claim that the whole idea of "the great writer" is *passé*, I can only answer that it sounds like nationalistic sour grapes. For better or for worse, the Western tradition — the lately much-maligned canon of classics, from Homer to Faulkner, Sartre, and Beckett — is a history of great writers and great books. Like it or not, *that's* where the action is, and we can't join that game by claiming to be producing masses of "good" writing or by advertising to anyone willing to listen that we're the best short-story writers in the world or by citing as evidence the testimony of second-rate European academics.

The dark side of this situation is that it is possible that the international influence on a colonial or neo-colonial culture like ours can ultimately be only harmful in so far as it ensures that that culture — especially in an era of mass culture, electronic media, and so-called free trade — will never achieve a sense of its own identity in and through its cultural products.

GEORGE WOODCOCK:

The most obvious and in some ways the most important change has been the quantitative one — Frye once called it an "explosion" — not only in the number of writers, but also in the breadth of opportunity for publication and the broader readership for Canadian books. Comparing the situation now with what existed when I started publishing *Canadian Literature* in 1959, I find astonishing changes in all these directions. Then there were few publishers; most of the important ones were branches of British or American firms, and the Canadian publishers were mostly jobbers who survived by distributing foreign books and published a few Canadian books on the profits of their agency sales. It was a good year then in which a dozen books of verse and ten novels by Canadians were published. Drama went virtually unpublished, since a live theatre hardly existed and most dramatists wrote for radio. Now one has only to look at the long lists of forthcoming Canadian books in every issue of *Quill & Quire* to realize how the situation has changed.

The quantitative expansion in Canadian publishing (and

hence in Canadian writing) has accompanied changes in the infra-structure of the Canadian literary world, without which it would hardly have been possible. There are far more medium and small Canadian-owned presses than there were in the past, and now that they have shed the naive nationalism that inspired many of them in the 1960s, they are increasingly publishing books for their intrinsic merits as pieces of writing rather than for their thematic intents.

Much as we may justifiably criticize the Canada Council — and I am constantly doing it — its role in fostering and protecting small publishers has been important. But patrons never create artists or movements in the arts, and the quantitative expansion in Canadian writing arose from deeper movements within the culture, which it would be simplistic to attribute to growing nationalism, but which are none the less related to the increasing maturity of our vision of ourselves as Canadians.

The quantitative eventually and inevitably merged into the qualitative. When there are few significant artists or writers in a country they tend to see their function as giving a voice in a rather direct and didactic way to its emergent self-consciousness, and so many Canadian writers, from Charles G. D. Roberts down to — say — Dave Godfrey, tended to be nationalistically inclined. But once there is a sense that the battle either has been won or has become irrelevant, that the distinctive character of the culture has been ensured, then the obsession with thematic considerations vanishes, writers are released to pursue their own imaginative goals, the aesthetics of form and language gain in importance, and as each writer increasingly pursues his own vision rather than some collective ideology, there emerges the restless variegation which is the sign of a mature literature.

2.   *What do you see as the most interesting areas of literary activity in Canada today?*

DAVID COLBERT:
The good stuff. Anything that reaches a level of excellence interests me greatly. We all know the off-beat structure of Brian Fawcett's *Cambodia* is as interesting as its content. But Michael Bliss's *Northern Enterprise*, a history of Canadian business, is just as iconoclastic if you look beyond the structure to the ideas within the text. It may not be as wild as *Cambodia*, but it is equally interesting and worth while.

In a more specific sense, I'll add that I'm especially pleased with the flourishing, and acceptance, of writing from minorities. For the most part, publishers employ few minorities. How many Black or Asian or Indian editors work for the large trade-publishing houses? None in Toronto. A few on the West Coast. Fortunately, we are past the days when a Ten-Best list selected primarily by white men could list only whites and still be deemed credible, or when publishers refused to use photos of their popular Black writers on book jackets. The contributions from minorities are too great to ignore. In this area, the schoolteachers, who are able to affect the tastes of so many new readers, seem to be ahead of the publishers. The continuing success of Joy Kogawa's *Obasan* in paperback is not difficult to understand: there's nothing similar out there for a teacher to assign. There will be more books, soon.

Some people are only interested in experimental fiction. I think it's as hard to master the old tricks as the new ones. There may be something admirably lonely about writing experimental fiction, but it's not necessarily a greater achievement than writing a moving story told by the old rules. Why do some folks think it is more difficult to write about writing than to write about people?

ELEANOR WACHTEL:

There are two areas that I've particularly enjoyed: (i) a variant of memoir, which could be called family history; and (ii) the short story. Writers always draw on their own lives, more or less, but Michael Ondaatje's *Running in the Family*, Michael Ignatieff's *The Russian Album*, and Bill Schermbrucker's *Mimosa* all uncover exotic family stories from before their own births.

As for the short story, it is curious that this perennial Canadian favourite is having something of a revival in the U.S. under the banner of "minimalism", but that we haven't been much affected by it. Here, writers like Audrey Thomas, Rohinton Mistry, and Edna Alford continue to create a diversity of careful, illuminating work.

DONNA BENNETT:

I'm struck by Canada's particular response to postmodernism. With the exception of the attempts of a few writers to play by some perceived set of rules, postmodern writing in Canada has been less flamboyant than that of its New World neighbours. Contemporary Canadian writers differ from American post-modern authors, in that they have never completely rejected the Canadian "realist" tradition, but rather have continued a transformation of forms that began with Modernism, a characteristic kind of transformation that typifies Canadian culture. I'm thinking especially of a writer like Alice Munro, who so often gets spoken about as if she were a realist — because at first glance her stories *do* seem as if they exist wholly in the realist tradition. As we're coming to realize, that is an inadequate response to Munro's extraordinary craft.

Except, perhaps, for a small group of writers (most of them associated with *Tish* and *Open Letter*), the overt marks of American postmodernism — disjuncture as structure, say, or the extensive disorientation of the reader — have not been important in Canada. Similarly — and even though there have been more moves in this direction — South American-style magic realism has never really been important in Canadian texts.

The influence of postmodernism has, however, recovered for Canadian writers techniques and perspectives that had been excluded both by the nineteenth-century realist tradition and by Modernists. So in this sense it has served to liberate contemporary Canadian writing. The perfect example of what can emerge from this new way of writing is Ondaatje's *In the Skin of a Lion*. Look at the freedom of narrative perspective in that book, and of even the way the parts of the story go together. And yet Ondaatje balances this kind of freedom — drawn from the resources postmodernism has given him — with an extraordinary evocation of the cityscape as a literal, lived-in place.

DORIS COWAN:

I find novels most interesting at the moment, because some of our best writers have turned their attention that way. It's often been said that the short story is the Canadian form, but in the last few years there has been a shift of interest away from the story to the longer form.

The interesting thing about these recent novels is that few of the writers seem to have accepted the narrow definition of the novel that earlier generations stuck to with dogged faith: that it must be a straightforward prose narrative involving a manageable group of characters and a realistic plot that reaches a clear conclusion. Now we have Ondaatje, Seán Virgo, and others writing novels whose narrative logic, structure, and language owe more to lyric or dramatic poetry than to traditional prose. Rick Salutin's novel incorporates extended arguments and meditations about history and culture in Canada, Germany, and Israel, which earlier writers would have said had no place in a novel, and the central character's ruminations continue after his death. Novels no longer have to be set in Canada. Some recent novels have been set in the Caribbean, the Solomon Islands, Hawaii, France, New Orleans, and Chicago. Toronto has also appeared in several recent books, unselfconsciously playing itself.

IRENE MCGUIRE:

I think that the increased recognition of Canadian writers internationally has generated a high level of expectation from the reading and book-buying public. That Margaret Atwood and Robertson Davies were short-listed for the Booker Prize, that Ondaatje's *In the Skin of a Lion* was short-listed for the Ritz-Hemingway Prize this year, that Canadian younger writers are being published in both the U.S. and England, and that Canadian books are reviewed in the *New York Times Book Review* has created a new sense of awareness of Canadian literature among the general public.

ED CARSON:

Without a doubt, the most interesting area is fiction, particularly that coming from the newer authors.

Fiction in Canada, as well as abroad, seems to be moving away from the rather narrow, self-centred works of the last few decades. Authors appear to be willing to risk more in subject matter, attempting larger and denser themes for their works. Social consciousness and an awareness of history are more and more appearing alongside strong characterization and a renewed interest in entertaining and interesting story lines. My guess is, as is my hope, that fiction authors are rediscovering or reviving the importance of first telling a good story — the well-told tale.

LARRY SCANLAN:

Here is what I've been noticing: a certain preoccupation, both here and abroad, with the redemptive qualities of nature and the wisdom of the aboriginal mind. These are, one must admit, familiar literary subjects. Pauline Johnson and Bliss Carman embraced them in this country at the turn of the century. What is new is that contemporary authors extolling these values are enjoying unprecedented popular success.

In an essay in *The Native in Literature* (ECW, 1988), Queen's University scholar Margery Fee argues that native people in Canadian literature are rarely depicted as individuals "because they must bear the burden of the other — of representing all that the modern person has lost." We need our literary Indians, she says:

"We are afraid that if we don't believe in Indians, we will have to become Americans." It's a good joke, and an apt one.

Rudy Wiebe, W. P. Kinsella, Robert Kroetsch, and Sandra Birdsell, each in a different way, have written about native people, and perhaps they paved the way for a shift in our thinking on ancestral values. M. T. Kelly's book *A Dream Like Mine* is a contemporary book about Indians, but with a difference. In this raw, searing novel, the dream referred to in the title is as much about Indian revenge for white transgressions (historical and current) as about native spiritualism. The panel that chose this book to receive the 1988 Governor General's Award for Fiction must have genuinely liked the novel (that it beat out Michael Ondaatje's *In the Skin of a Lion* caused some consternation), but perhaps at some level they felt that the time had come to recognize a novel that deals honestly with the land and its first peoples.

What I see, then, in Canadian and other writing, is some new evidence that the aboriginal mind is worth picking. That our pursuit of material goods is a hollow and dangerous pursuit. That sustenance can be found by reconnecting with the land and its creatures, as aboriginal people did before colonization changed everything.

Call it a fashion (back to The Land), but it certainly is catching on. I see it most powerfully in Canada in the poetry of Robert Bringhurst; in Kelly's poetry and prose; in *The Songlines* (about the complex mythology of Australian aborigines) by English author Bruce Chatwin; in American author Barry Lopez's *Arctic Dreams* and, more recently, his essay collection, *Crossing Open Ground*.

Writers have long admired nature, some have even admired peoples we long ago dismissed as "primitive". What is new about all of this, I would argue, is the sense of urgency. What I sense now is more and more writers pleading that our way is the wrong way. If the environment is to survive, if we are to survive, these writers are saying, then we must cease our estrangement from the land and see it with fresh eyes, with aboriginal eyes.

ALBERTO MANGUEL:

If we're going to use labels (how else do we go about describing "areas"?), then I'd say that in two "genres", historical fiction and science fiction, we have lately seen something of interest. Gurr, for instance, has come up with a superb collage to explore the pre-Nazi sensibility in Europe (Canadian antecedents are, perhaps, Godfrey's *The New Ancestors* and Findley's *Famous Last*

Words, and also Geoffrey Ursell's uneven *Perdue*). Mark Frutkin's *Atmospheres Apollinaire* is a quieter but equally successful example of the same use of history in fiction. In science fiction, William Gibson above all others has developed not only a new language (his "cyberpunk" is already a common noun), but also a new ethical and social code that stems from it.

DOUGLAS FETHERLING:
What I've found most interesting recently (if also least pleasant) is the international context in which Canadian writing resides so uneasily. I sometimes imagine that it must be only a question of time until CanLit begins to reflect the sense of despair one is starting to feel about the important global changes taking place in politics now. With *perestroika* and *glasnost* in the USSR, the rate at which Japan is accumulating wealth, the pace of political improvements in Latin America, even such signs as the riots in Korea, there's a growing perception that the action is everywhere but here — Canada, Britain, and America. That might still leave some faint hope of interesting Commonwealth culture but for the fact that Thatcher has practically dismantled the Commonwealth concept, partly because she despises it on racist grounds. Canada's too much in the American sphere, clinging ever more tightly to the dying giant, to have taken part anyway. The sense that things are opening up everywhere else but closing down here, this must erupt in the writing one day, I'm sure, just as fear of the Bomb once did. Writing is written while waiting for the other shoe to drop. Curiously, the much-trumpeted multicultural aspect of Canadian writing shows no signs of playing an especially significant part in this. But then our multicultural art always has had an artificial feel to it, hasn't it? More a political convenience, to be acknowledged by a few well-chosen examples, than a vital force.

SAM SOLECKI:
The single most interesting and challenging area both here and abroad — and for better or worse — is all the work in various genres and disciplines associated with feminism. In a manner of speaking, feminism is to the seventies and eighties what Marxism was to the thirties. It's a very good time — perhaps the best of times — to be a woman writing creatively or critically.

The down-side of this is that a mountain of drivel is appearing under the feminist banner as publishers and granting bodies rush to join the march of progress. Delacroix's Liberty led all of the people; the feminist muse — critical and creative — allows only one sex, one gender, to follow behind. How many male critics have you seen lately included in anthologies of feminist criticism?

It's a good time to be a woman writer.

GEORGE WOODCOCK:

Personally, I think there are interesting developments in every genre. Everywhere the image of the writer as prophet is tending to diminish, and we no longer have larger-than-life figures in our minds that dominate and represent a whole decade, as Hugh MacLennan tended to dominate the 1950s and Margaret Laurence to dominate the 1960s in fiction, or as surrogate mother and father figures like Frank Scott and Earle Birney and Dorothy Livesay tended to dominate the same period in poetry.

With the myth of the Great Canadian Novel, we have happily lost the myth of the Great Canadian Writer; we have even, one hopes, abandoned the whole pernicious concept of greatness. Delusions of grandeur having passed, forms like the short story and the novella have come amazingly into their own. At the same time the grips of realism and nationalist ideology on the novel have weakened, and novelists are able to benefit from the experimentalism of other fiction writers.

Drama has gained immensely from the decay of the CBC as a cultural agent and from the rise of live theatre. Radio always imposed limitations on the playwright, so that few plays for the air stood up to reproduction in print, and television never took off in Canada as a dramatic medium. These circumstances released playwrights for the stage just at the time when theatre was achieving a success in Canada it has never enjoyed before. The result has been a good many plays that are as interesting and memorable on the page as on the stage.

Finally, criticism, which has an essential mediatory role in any mature literature, has developed extraordinarily in both skill and insight. When I founded *Canadian Literature*, the academic panjandra of the time told me (a) that I would never find enough Canadian writers worth discussing and (b) that I would never find enough critics to discuss them. But it was a time when the flow of new writers that characterized the 1960s was already beginning, and the vitality of the situation called up new critics, who emerged in response, many of the best of them being practising poets and not all of them, praise the Muses, academic critics. The Northrop Fryes have had their uses, but the time has come for a kind of criticism related to creation and not to category.

3. Can you identify any influential movements/trends/fashions (domestic and/or international) in contemporary Canadian writing? What effect has postmodernism had, for instance? Where stands regionalism? Has realism lost its hold? Is there a definable mainstream?

DORIS COWAN:

I don't know of anything I'd call a movement. I think that can really only be identified after the fact. There are always fashions and they are usually damaging to writers who follow them. And of course there are, as always, schools or sets that band together for courage and confidence. If there is a "mainstream", I don't know what it is.

ALBERTO MANGUEL:

No, I don't think there's a definable mainstream. And if there were, would it be worth mentioning? From a distance, we blur things — we speak of the Victorian novel, the tenth-century sagas, or the short-story writers of the turn of the century. Those "general lines" tell us less about the subject than about ourselves. I'd rather concentrate on the individual authors, or rather, on the individual books. I don't much care to guess how history will see them; right now the books I like have an intimate importance, and that alone justifies their existence.

DONNA BENNETT:

I'm uncomfortable with the word "trend", which tends to mean something not only exploited by "those in the know", but probably created by them as well.

If by "movement" you mean something that depends on the consciously acknowledged associations of and consciously interdependent patterns of influence, then I think that I see few, if any, new movements. The strongest associations of newer writers are undoubtedly those formed around an interest in feminism. A woman writing in Canada today is likely to be in close contact with other women writers. This feminism *is* shaping new Canadian writing, because emerging women writers are learning that the forms, styles, and subjects that they are currently employing have their own tradition.

LINDA HUTCHEON:

The realist novel is not dead in Canada. In fact, what I would call the particularly Canadian variant of "postmodernism" is based precisely on the premise that realism is alive and well — and can therefore be challenged. The postmodern challenges in Canadian literature always seem to operate subversively from within the conventions of realism, milking their residual power even as they contest it. The postmodern always underlines and undermines prevailing conventions, and the Canadian version is, I think, no exception.

DOUGLAS FETHERLING:

The proof of a genre's value, other than as social history, is that some people should be doing valid work in it long afterward. One day magic realism must inevitably be about as fashionable as social realism is now, but there still will be people working within its conventions. There's a kind of writer who's always susceptible to allegiances, the way others are to bronchitis, and another type who's interested in pursuing to the end whatever view he or she came to at the start of his or her career. When such people continue into extreme old age, the effects are often heightened. Earle Birney is an example of the one. He changed his style any number of times out of genuine curiosity and love of poetry and a desire to prolong vigour. Morley Callaghan, who's only one year older than Birney in age, is an example of the other. He hasn't deviated very far from the diction he came to in the 1920s and 1930s and has kept his generation alive by writing that way and refusing to be swayed. Which is better? Who's to say?

ELEANOR WACHTEL:

Ah, fashions. Well, there's postcard fiction — a do-it-yourself phenomenon popularized here by Kent Thompson in his anthology *Open Windows*. Some of these clever pictures — especially by Thompson himself in *Leaping Up Sliding Away* — are evocative and imaginative. There is some blurring of borders here between the prose poem, the very short story (e.g., Atwood's *Murder in the Dark* or Shields's *Various Miracles*), and the postcard. All, to some extent, cater to the ostensibly short attention span of the modern, TV-saturated, reader.

Trends: journalists writing novels. For example, Heather Robertson, Gary Ross, Carol Corbeil. The appeal of novels hasn't diminished, despite a "thin" season in fall '87.

The most exciting work I've seen in the last year is Robert Lepage's "Dragon Trilogy", a theatrical mix of performance, dance, theatre, in which words — in three languages — are perhaps the least important component. But this drifts into theatre and performance, where boundaries are even more elusive than in writing.

As for "a definable mainstream", it would remain the naturalistic or realistic, often autobiographical, novel. There's also been a marked increase in genre writing — science fiction, thrillers, and, above all, mysteries. The latter has been furthered by the creation of a Canadian crime writers' association with its own (Arthur Ellis) awards.

DAVID COLBERT:

A mainstream? Sure there is a mainstream: it's television. These days, all of us in the book world are fringe.

More important than any domestic or international fashion that has become a trend in Canadian writing is a Canadian fashion that has become something of an international trend. The world has finally discovered story collections, and many Canadian writers have benefited by this departure from the old rule of publishing collections only after great success with novels. Isabel Huggan, Ann Copeland, Rohinton Mistry, Brian Fawcett, Linda Svendsen, and Guy Vanderhaeghe are just some of the writers whose first books in America or Great Britain were, or will be in a few months, collections. Ten years ago these writers might not have been published abroad until they wrote novels. Jonathan Galassi of Farrar, Straus & Giroux in New York was one of the first to notice this trend in the United States, and he has said it arose out of the acceleration of everyday life. People worry that they won't have time to read the latest 600-page novel. But stories seem like short, attainable goals. Walter Bode of Grove Press, also in New York, has noted another possible cause. Word-processors have eased the task of producing a manuscript, he says, so more people are producing them, and more people consider themselves writers. These new authors are buying collections and first novels to keep up on the work of "colleagues".

ED CARSON:

Because I believe we are at a turning-point in contemporary Canadian writing, it's very difficult to isolate any discernible "trends" or "movements". The Atwood generation of writers will continue to sell, but won't chart the coming new directions. I suspect there will not be a "mainstream" of writers, but rather a whole series of strongly defined and substantial tributaries. At the heart of these tributaries will be the new writings and experiences of Canada's new and expanding cultural minorities. If there is any one group that will prove to be most influential in the coming years — influential in the sense of charting new themes, new perspectives — I suspect it will be the rich and varied experiences of these minorities. Coming from all over the world, they will both bring that world to Canada, and take Canada out into the world.

GEORGE WOODCOCK:

Literary movements are for the most part fictional inventions. They are imagined by literary historians after the event in an attempt to arrange the fertile chaos of what hundreds or thousands of individuals write and publish. Or they are created by academic critics intent on enhancing their own self-importance by trying to give literature the shape of their theories.

I find most of the labels bandied about by critics these days, and sometimes foolishly assumed by writers, as insubstantial and evanescent as yesterday's farts. We are all — with the possible exception of Louis Dudek — postmodernists by definition since the death of Pound; even the classic modernists, Joyce and Eliot, Pound and Lewis, turned out in the end to be pursuing very different goals. Much that passes for postmodernism arouses a strong sense of *déjà vu*. Fiction writers have been playing around with meta-fictional devices since *Don Quixote* and *Tristram Shandy*; parody and palimpsest and pastiche are ancient tricks. No reason not to use them. But to claim they are revolutionary? Experimental? More stale hot air. As for destructionism, it's a fading fad. Derrida, who was he? Another presumptuous academic trying to tell writers what they are doing. Some writers pay him lip service, but often their work, as in the case of Robert Kroetsch, has turned out much more interesting than the theories to which they bowed.

SAM SOLECKI:

The question of a "mainstream" can be approached on the basis of which writers are seen as dominant and most *influential* in the country. In other words, whose "voice" do you hear when you read the young and younger writers? There's little doubt in my mind that among women poets between twenty and forty,

Atwood has been the central influence — not the only one, but the most obvious. In prose, I'm less certain, but would be surprised if Atwood, Munro, and Laurence weren't among the most important Canadian influences on both style and content on the novelists and short-story writers of the seventies and eighties. Among male writers, I don't see any line of dominance or influence. Harold Bloom may be right in suggesting that male writers practise a kind of patricide on their predecessors. Women seem to have a different, healthier, less cannibalistic sense of the writing family.

It's possible, however, that to look at the idea of a "mainstream" from a predominantly national point of view is wrongheaded. In other words, the real mainstream today is international. The best work from other nations is translated so quickly into English that we may want to start thinking of a free-floating international literature in English to which any idea of a mainstream or trend will have to be referred. Josef Škvorecký and Milan Kundera, for example, are as much French or English as Czech writers. And where shall we "place" Rushdie or Naipaul?

It may also be true that you can't have a national mainstream without a dominant central figure whose voice casts a shadow (yes, yes, I know that's a mixed metaphor) on his or her near successors: they wrestle with it during their formative years and either imitate it or transcend it (by using it in a unique way or rejecting it completely). I suspect that many women poets have faced this problem in their reading of Adrienne Rich and Atwood.

4. *Is there a discernible change in the audience for Canadian books?*

IRENE MCGUIRE:
Yes. The average reader is definitely reading more Canadian books now than he or she was five and ten years ago.

ELEANOR WACHTEL:
Yes, it's grown.

There's a steadier, more loyal audience, who will buy fiction by certain Canadian writers no matter what the subject or the reaction of reviewers.

The "market" has been responsible for an explosion in non-fiction books. These are often "instant" books, political biographies or memoirs, written or ghosted by journalists. The saleability of these books has resulted in substantial advances to writers, an increase in the number of literary agents, and greater competitiveness amongst publishers for a seasonal "blockbuster".

DORIS COWAN:

Besides the slight increase in the Canadian public's awareness of its writers, there is a *much* larger audience for Canadian writers outside Canada.

GEORGE WOODCOCK:

Undoubtedly, by conscription and proselytization, the readership for Canadian writing has grown considerably. The conscript readership consists of the schoolchildren into whose course material Canadian books are more or less forcibly injected, and while this may be a moderately effective form of nationalist propaganda, and may help writers' royalties somewhat, I am doubtful about its permanent effect in turning children into readers of Canadian books. The chances are that the availability of Canadian books will draw them towards Canadian writers. But, as one knows from the number of school-created Shakespeare-haters among the educated English, patriotic force-feeding is not a particularly good way to help a literature survive. Broad availability of books in school and public libraries is much more effective.

Canadian literature courses in universities and colleges are somewhat different, since an element of election enters in. But whether students who do not follow academic careers or themselves become writers continue to be interested in Canadian books is a question I have never seen addressed, and perhaps it should be.

One certainty is that more Canadian titles and more copies of Canadian books are being sold. Perhaps books of verse still sell mostly about 500 copies each, but many more titles do reach print and somehow find a public even if most bookstores don't stock them. The problem of how to increase further the voluntary readership comes back to the need for adequate exposure for literature in print and the other media, and this involves getting the newspapers to change their reviewing policy and trying to make the CBC go back to giving adequate treatment to literature and the arts.

LARRY SCANLAN:

Keath Fraser once told me that his audience would fit in the back seat of a Honda. He wasn't just being humble.

This is conjecture — I don't have figures to support my

belief — but I suspect that the typical reader of Canadian litera-ture is a voracious type, who dips broadly into our literature and others.

Picture it then: a small but devoted readership. Writers who typically specialize in short-fiction collections, which don't usually sell as well as novels. Small wonder that the Writers' Union of Canada has made such an issue out of payment for public use and copyright in libraries. Writers need every penny to survive.

Matt Cohen and Brian Moore no longer write novels that one might define as literary and regional. No more Salem novels for Cohen. No more Ginger Coffey in Montreal for Moore. The locales of their more recent novels have become international, like their audiences. Perhaps this is where their writing took them; perhaps they grew weary of their small but devoted audi-ences, their small royalty cheques.

DOUGLAS FETHERLING:
I think the general middle-of-the-road audience, descended how-ever distantly from the liberal humanist tradition, the audience for which Ryerson and the old Macmillan used to publish books, has withered owing to television and other American influences. But what remains has grown far more cosmopolitan the past ten years or so. Lester & Orpen Dennys's list is merely one of the indica-tions of this. Maybe it's even more discriminating too, if not quite so wide-ranging. At other times, however, I'm less sanguine.

ED CARSON:
Several years of "CanLit" education, not to mention hard work by authors, publishers, and booksellers, have made Canadians more aware of this country's claim to a substantial and world-class group of writers. My hope is that writing in Canada no longer needs or requires the CanLit label. Years ago, this kind of thing was perhaps necessary, if for no other reason than to make people familiar with what was available. But not now.

It's clear that we are at the beginning of a major interna-tionalization of writing by Canadian authors.

LINDA HUTCHEON:
From a teacher's point of view there has certainly been a change in the classroom audience. When I began teaching CanLit ten years ago (with no formal instruction ever offered me in my English training before that), I had a very real sense that teaching Canadian was a subversive activity, not to say a political act. Part

of the reason was the fact that many of my colleagues were either English or American and that the English curriculum was predominantly British-oriented, but part was also the realization of how little my students knew about their own culture. Today, however, I teach classes of students who have already studied much of the canon of CanLit before they even reach university.

Another change in audience is the increasingly large European readership, particularly within the academy. Many countries have Associations of Canadian Studies which hold annual conferences, host Canadian writers and critics, and publish their own journals. However, I can still recall my embarrassment when a room full of Italian professors of Canadian literature expressed utter disbelief that Canadian literature did *not* have the same status in Canadian English Departments as Italian literature did in Italy. I believe I muttered something about colonialization.

Some things still need changing.

SAM SOLECKI:

My impression is that there is a larger audience out there because Canadian writing has been publicized, written about in the daily papers, and taught in the schools. Whatever the drawbacks of the intensely nationalistic attitude that we took towards literature in the sixties and seventies — and I would argue contra-Metcalf that the attitude was and is, for the most part, justified — one of the results is a readership that will continue to grow because every year more and more people are reading Canadian writing in the schools. For those dubious whether these people continue reading (or reading Canadian) after graduation, I can point to various groups all over Toronto that I have talked to about Michael Ondaatje, Josef Škvorecký, and others.

The only thing that isn't clear yet is whether this audience will *pay* for its entertainment. In other words, what would happen if we charged admission to readings?

I also have a hunch, by the way, that the audience is more sophisticated than it was — at least to the extent that the people I see and talk to at readings are interested in Canadian writing in the context of contemporary writing in general. Some of my better students talk about Ondaatje in relation to Salman Rushdie and Milan Kundera, and of Margaret Atwood side by side with Margaret Drabble and Marge Piercy. It's as if they take it for granted — in a way that we didn't in the more nationalistic and therefore more anxious sixties — that there is a solid body of Canadian writing and that it can be seriously discussed side by side with the work of other nations. It's an attitude, a confidence, that was simply unthinkable before we had the work of Mavis Gallant, Mordecai Richler, Alice Munro, Margaret Laurence, Robertson Davies, Al Purdy, Atwood, and Ondaatje. Next to this, the majority of the poetry and fiction published before 1960 is simply not worth reading. Yes, yes, it's part of the "tradition" and we should know about our "heritage", but as for actually reading all that stuff, let the professors read Frederick Philip Grove and Morley Callaghan for us.

Which brings me to the last, though by no means least important, part of the new audience — the university professors, high-school teachers, etc. For better or worse, we now have a large group with a vested interest in our literature. Tenure decisions, promotions, publications, grants, and leaves are now part of the fallout of the rise of CanLit. The professors, as much as the publishers, profit from this body of work. Nobody is going to "stand on guard for thee" ("thee" = CanLit) more than the professoriat, especially that branch of it with a graduate degree in "Canadian" and no expertise outside the quotation marks. By their footnotes shall ye know them.

DONNA BENNETT:

This is a subject about which I am most pessimistic, although I hope that I am wrong. Two things make me fear that readers of anything longer and more complex than a piece of tabloid journalism may be a dying breed. First, in this century, literary writing has moved away from the needs of a general readership in direct proportion to the increase in the availability of mass media. Perhaps writers realized, at least on some intuitive level, that they could not compete with the reductiveness of popular culture for the "undemanding" reader. In many countries this branching of audiences into two rather separate streams, one for high culture and one for mass culture, has not been such a serious problem. However, in a country with as small a population as Canada, especially with its tradition of only a limited group of individuals going on to post-secondary education or into the arts, such a fractioning of the audience has resulted in economic catastrophe for the artist. Not enough readers exist to justify commercial literary publication for most of our writers, even some of the very best. This problem is, of course, greatly exacerbated by the competition offered by — and the educated Canadian's frequent preference for — British or American writing.

A second influence on contemporary readership is one

that is a function of the changing social structure. Traditionally (from the eighteenth century into the twentieth) a great number of literary readers have been middle- and upper-class women, because they had enough unstructured time that they were able to read both fiction and poetry. However, the recent changes in the place and the nature of women's work (and women's leisure), the move from the home and its flexible demands to the market-place and its rigid structure, have effectively cut many women off from literary reading. To make matters worse, professional men and professional women once belonged to a class that considered a passing knowledge of serious contemporary literature a neces-sity for a cultured person; now both find themselves a part of a work ethic that no longer separates home and job, and that increasingly requires after-hours social involvement — as well as after-hours attention to the flood of information necessary to stay abreast of one's field.

DAVID COLBERT:

The readership has grown considerably. The most important fac-tor is the number of Canadian books being published abroad. A rise of a few percentage points in the domestic readership is to be celebrated; but publication in France or Sweden or the U.K. or the U.S. can quickly double or triple the audience.

Traditionally, English-language Canadian publishers, for lack of either interest or expertise, have been almost entirely ineffec-tive in securing foreign publishers for their authors. When literary agents began to operate in Canada about twelve or thirteen years ago, they started opening new countries for Canadian authors.

In six years of doing this myself, I've found that no publisher is interested in a book for its Canadian origins or content; often the opposite is true. But if a book is *good*, they will publish it. Some of the government efforts to help this process of agents selling rights actually hurt it, by promoting the national origin of Canadian writers instead of the quality of their writing, as if a Maple Leaf brand name can sell literature abroad the way it sells sausage here. On the other hand, writers like Alberto Manguel and arts promoters like Greg Gatenby help immeasurably. Both of these generous men, who proselytize the cause of excellent Canadian writers, are respected abroad, and do more good work than a corps of flag-waving cultural attachés. Alberto will often return from a trip and let the agents know which foreign publish-ers are interested in which writers, so the agents can follow up and secure foreign publication.

As publishers improve their foreign-rights sales staffs, and as the number of internationally respected agents operating in Canada grows, this increase in the foreign audience for Canadian writers will continue.

L'ENVOI

George Woodcock
and
Sam Solecki

GEORGE WOODCOCK:

I had embarked on a long tirade, but decided that for the moment it was better to be brief, or briefish, and utter what seem to me a few sensible suggestions for rules of conduct. Distrust Department of Communications bureaucrats and anyone else who talks about "cultural industries"; they are only interested, ultimately, in what makes a profit, not in sustaining literature or the other arts *per se*. In dealing with the Canada Council, always be prepared to bite the hand that feeds, for that agency has the same tendency towards bureaucratic ossification as any other, but it still responds to strong enough criticism. Agitate for more representatives of writing and the other arts on the Council itself, which tends to get clogged with party-lining dilettantes. As for the CBC, most people forget how good the corporation once was in its fostering of literature, and how vital it was regionally as well as nationally, until — say — the middle 1960s. They still go on praising it without really listening and remembering. In reality the CBC gets steadily more useless as a source of real support for literature or any other of the arts, and the organization has become so completely ossified that it cannot be changed. Too many efforts to do so have proved fruitless. I say this as a supporter of public broadcasting, but not bureaucratically straitjacketed public broadcasting, which has lowered the CBC in quality to the level of the private networks with which it cannot hope to compete in its chosen task of trivialization. The public broadcasting I would like to see is a kind linked to the sources of Canadian culture, which are regional. It should consist of a network of centres operated co-operatively by artists, producers, and technicians, with the bureaucrats in minor roles as employees, not as dictators. Would it work? Only trying can tell. But it couldn't possibly work less well than the CBC today. Well, I suppose that *is* at least a mini-tirade. But I get exasperated with Pierre Berton and other pompous literary figures who claim to be "Friends of Public Broadcasting", and accept and defend the CBC when it is no longer in any true sense "public", but merely the fief of the clique of Philistines who are its bureaucratic controllers.

SAM SOLECKI:

A parting thought. I wonder if I'm the only person in the country who thinks that the only change or development in Canadian writing that will decisively alter the way we think about our literature and ourselves will be the appearance of an undoubtedly major figure, someone we can discuss in the same breath as . . . (here each reader can fill in the blank with his or her own non-Canadian nominees; my own would include Solzhenitsyn, Grass, Pynchon, and Rushdie). The flip side of this is our lack of a post-Frye critic of international stature. The appearance of either figure would work wonders for the quality of our literary discussions. If nothing else it would help us to separate the major from the minor figures, the first-rate from the second-rate, and it would make reviewers and university wits more wary of crowning each new writer they like as the king of the castle. The appearance of X would also do wonders for all discussions about the canon. Like Stevens's jar in Tennessee, all Canadian writing would be reread in relation to X. At a time when the very idea of a canon is under fire from all those committed for theoretical or political reasons to questioning it (even though they couldn't question it if (1) they didn't know what a canon is, and if (2) they weren't trying to supplant one canon with another), the canon would be inevitably resurrected by the appearance of a major figure if for no other reason than that he or she would force us, however reluctantly, to read Canadian literature teleologically.

Is it possible that we won't produce a major critic — whose home base is Canadian literature — until we produce a major writer? Is it even possible to write a first-rate book of criticism about a good second-rank literature? If the answer to the second question is no, then a first-rate man of letters like George Woodcock may have been wasted on us.

"We will now discuss in a little more detail the struggle for existence."
— **Darwin**

POSITION PAPERS

Over the summer of 1988, and on into fall, over eighty poets, novelists, short-story writers, and dramatists were invited to contribute what I shamelessly insisted on calling Position Papers: brief documents that would lay out the writers' literary aesthetic, define major operating principles, encapsulate aims and objectives, describe the philosophical lodestone that steered the individual writer's work — and in the bargain consider, generally, the way of literature in the world. Is the humanist tradition, I asked these writers, ragged and crippled and largely defunct in these postmodernist times, or can literature still shoot, as Cynthia Ozick and others insist it must, "for a corona, subtle or otherwise, of moral grandeur"? Can it prop up humanity's flagging spirit, somehow make easier the sleep of the innocent, vanquished dead? May it still speak for those who have not the means to speak for themselves? Or are these outdated notions in these besieged and harassed times when drama, fiction, and poetry reportedly can't compete with the news?

What does postmodernism mean?

My letter of invitation noted, too (or at least the first forty did), the overwhelming influence of French linguistic theory on current *critical* writing in North America, and observed that an increasing number of Canadian poets and novelists appeared to be "embracing, or investigating, or being affected by" this phenomenon (even as French writers and critics rush to disavow it). I had an interest, then, in measuring, by teacup poll, the impact of that movement.

Statements on their craft by 37 Writers

Order of Appearance

1. John Newlove
2. Louis Dudek
3. Clark Blaise
4. Rudy Wiebe
5. P. K. Page
6. Jane Urquhart
7. Elizabeth Spencer
8. Doug Jones
9. Don McKay
10. Carol Shields
11. Raymond Souster
12. Phyllis Webb
13. Robert Bringhurst
14. Dorothy Livesay
15. Susan Musgrave
16. Susan Swan
17. Diane Keating
18. T. L. Duff
19. Ray Smith
20. Josef Škvorecký
21. Don Coles
22. Keath Fraser
23. Linda Spalding
24. Norman Levine
25. Trevor Ferguson
26. Rachel Wyatt
27. Stephen Scobie
28. Janette Turner Hospital
29. W. P. Kinsella
30. Kent Thompson
31. H. R. Percy
32. Robert Harlow
33. Timothy Findley
34. Paulette Jiles
35. Aritha van Herk
36. Seán Virgo
37. Ron Smith

Why do you write? That was finally the question got down to.

Some of the people one would like to have heard from are not to be found here. A good many I simply never got around to inviting, and some many of those receiving the summons were engaged in other activities. Margaret Atwood was deep into a novel, as were Graeme Gibson, Matt Cohen, L. R. Wright, Joy Kogawa, and any number of others. Alice Munro continued to maintain the pose whereby she insists that the left hand knows not what the right hand is doing, or why, and Michael Ondaatje, working a similar route, hooked his eyes upon the floor in such manner as to give one to understand that such probings invited the black cat to cross one's path.

Mavis Gallant wrote back amiably that she preferred to let such investigations rest with Sartre, who said, "Literature is an end in itself." Spider Robinson wanted — reasonable enough in an ideal world — an up-front fee and royalty terms favourable to his children's old age. Robertson Davies responded civilly that European duties, and attendant mercies, were likely to be consuming his time.

A good handful said they would contribute, but didn't, while a smaller group said they wouldn't but did. Numerous others conceded that the questions raised were the very ones they had been pondering as the invitation arrived, but they preferred to let the pot simmer a while longer. Robert Kroetsch laughed and said, "What? Do it again?" Audrey Thomas, speaking to the issue quite clearly and profoundly in a private letter that ended up alleging how she couldn't, couldn't, couldn't, was one of several who found and followed that model.

A good many spoke of "plates too full". By the same token, several said they were in their beachwear or otherwise in prolonged analysis of summer's torpor; still others were "up a tree, generally" or just generally ("Don't ask me why") unavailable. Several mentioned that they were feeling particularly destitute of meaning and purpose at the moment, and could not fathom taking finger to paper. Others stressed the inarticulateness to which they had succumbed, and stated their intention to give up, not only writing, but *speech* into the bargain.

A few professed to zilch interest. Playwrights, notably, were not heard from at all (itself suggesting a line of inquiry defensibly worth academic pursuance). A cadre of good citizens felt kinship with the project, and gratitude for the opportunity, but refused out of firm disagreement with John Metcalf for his variety of stands on assorted issues related to art and society.

Be the above as it may, for my money what you will find in these following statements is often stunning, and not infrequently beautiful; in the diversity of its reach, and under the full orbit of your close attention, is wealth vital to the heart's journey. Good medicine for the long march. You have here the odd dollop of impurities, but you also will find a good share of the nation's soul-runners. From my position, I'd say the corona is evident.
LR

JOHN NEWLOVE

Did You Run All the Way Home?

This is a hard thing to say, but you cannot know until you know. And then you may be wrong. I write to entertain myself, for I can never console myself.

To be able to think about the technique of anything at times makes the technologist so self-conscious that he is liable to lose sight of the thing itself. Thus, "concrete poetry", "sound poetry". We are a species of mammal, for God's sake, that has to be taught even to walk. Why talk about technique in poetry, unless there is a desire to run?

People ask, meaning to be kind by showing an interest, why did you write? who influenced you? and if you name a name, being kind and interested yourself, they will say, Well, that was the influence. He started writing because of Wallace Stevens. But in everything human there is both instinct and desire, and they are as unseparable as content and form or soul and body. No one influences anyone to write. The existence of other writers merely makes the idea of writing available. That existence suggests the possibility of my existence. Otherwise, we are all first causes. Everything begins with our selves.

Who was the first writer?

In each case, the answer is: Me.

What an odd word it is.

We do not live in the world, we live in time.

Working for the civil service of the soul has made me wordy, but reluctant to say anything.

I worry about line lengths, syllables, about the foolishness of ending a line of verse with "and" when "and" runs all the way home to the start of the next line. I remember Mallarmé saying that poems are not made with ideas but with words.

Technique is the intrigue of things, it is a kind of giving away. It is a method of making your soul a part of the living machine as opposed to making a machine that can only print our big display cards saying: THIS IS MY SOUL, and which when turned on only spits out little driblets — and they are interchangeable — of venom and love.

It is much harder to think about the Why than about the How. I can tell you, to a degree, How. A friend once told me he could teach anyone to draw. The only difficulty is that if you learn How from me rather than from yourself, you will become Me, diluted.

That is not important, unless you want to write poems. There's no shame in not. Most people you know are just careering along in any case. Everyone will forgive them except themselves; most of us lose our way when the time comes, and to tell the truth it's very hard to say what this life is about, or even why it is.

It's like saying, I can't tell what that woman's up to. Of course you can't. Neither can she. And as for you, you fool, what are *you* up to?

But did it move you, did you cry? Did you run all the way home? To my arms? Please? Even bitterness must have its beauty.

August 15, 1988
Ottawa

LOUIS DUDEK

Authenticity

I think the difference between the literary situation today and that of about fifty years ago, when I started writing, is that literature as such, literary art, was very important then, and it is not very important now. Great writers — Eliot, Joyce, Mann, Proust — dominated the contemporary scene; and the English literary tradition, from Beowulf to Hardy, was the required foundation for all literary study from high school to graduate school.

The prestige of literature and art in general was simply taken for granted, although dire prophecies of decline ran rampant, and the philistine society in general often ignored or disparaged the serious arts in the popular media and entertainments. Even Hollywood, tinsel paradise itself, honoured the real thing, through Stokowski, Deanna Durbin, Grace Moore, Jan Kiepura, and the numerous "classical" themes in their repertoire and story lines. The great thing was genuine art and literature, to which all aspired, even though most preferred the simple satisfaction of junk.

The situation has completely changed since then. The culture of the popular media has now established itself everywhere, even in the universities, as the measure of life and art. The very idea of "literature" has been tainted with a suggestion of pretentiousness or élitism. The junk has simply floated to the top and covered the whole surface.

Now, by "art" I do not mean some kind of inhuman, bloodless imitation of past monuments and artifacts. Nothing of the sort. I mean a living, authentic record of contemporary human experience. In poetry, it is language and rhythm in the most vital, condensed form, expressing our sense of life, our enduring passions, at this historical moment.

In other words, art is the highest entertainment. It is not dead or boring. It is not a mere echo of past masterpieces. It is a new masterpiece, which probably will shock you, and make you think that artists are incontinent, tasteless, beastly brutes, who ought to be locked up for their own good and the benefit of society. Reality is like that.

But the artist doesn't set out to shock. He sets out to tell the truth, as he sees it — and unfortunately that sort of thing is liable to shock.

The word is authenticity. God's truth, if you like. What the world needs most.

We live in a world where there is little of it. Where the news is packaged day by day in deadly professional sets of capsules, to be taken after breakfast, after supper, and before bedtime. Where the entertainment is highly moral, but violent, or farcical, or sentimental, and is interspersed with nauseating attempts to "fake sincerity" in the rhetoric of selling goods, called advertising. Where everything you buy, touch, taste, or smell has been doctored with the counterfeit of commercial glitz, the inauthentic glitter and shine of money-bait.

So *authentic* is a profound and far-reaching concept. There is something in nature, in man, in the very creation, that demands authenticity, that wants a true report and expression of itself. Every new movement in art, like the turning away from the sentimentalities of the nineteenth century to the clarity and forthrightness of the Modern, has been a search for this truth, this authenticity. (Postmodernism is nothing but a hysterical variant of it.) This was the meaning of Eliot's early poems, of D. H. Lawrence, of Ezra Pound at his best (*Ching Ming* — "precise definition" — "straight as the Greek"), of Auden in the thirties, of Spender. Yes, and of Allen Ginsberg, and all the Beats. Also of our own poets, Alden Nowlan and Raymond Souster, and lately of Ken Norris and others, as well as of Ralph Gustafson.

In short, if modern literature, modern poetry, was intended primarily as a corrective to the inauthenticity of modern culture — a corrective, from the *Cantos* and *The Waste Land* to *Howl* — then the worst thing we can say of our time is that this literature has been worsted and defeated. The age has become progressively more dishonest and mercenary, and the arts have grown progressively more hysterical and demoralized as a consequence. They seem to have lost their way. They are helpless before the power of commercialized exploitation, the wilful violation of the human spirit.

But, of course, defeat in these things is never absolute or complete. As long as one conscious artist remains, as long as one individual exists who deeply hungers after truth, the game is not lost. And somehow nature has designed it that this individual is there, that he will always be there, until the end of time, to nurse the little flame that may yet light the world. May his fate not be too painful and bleak; may he find companions to forward him on the long trek toward that far-off land which is never reached, whose reflection shines in the illusions of art, and in the architectures of literature.

June 10, 1988
Montreal

CLARK BLAISE

Casting from the Shore

I cast from the shore, I don't troll. I throw out a line or two, and sit. They're out there — I see them jumping. All the boats are out, hired by great hulking brute-writers, out at sunrise with their states-of-the-art. They come back at twilight with empty cans and sandwich wrappings, bearing *tales*, stringers full of iridescent trophy-stories.

We all love to fish, but I never bought the serious equipment. Just as well — I get seasick and blistered. Perhaps I never wanted fish — I only wanted *to* fish. Or worse, perhaps I *am* a fish, trying to communicate with the man on shore.

The mosquitoes are bad. I'm being chewed to death.

To catch a story, I use worms, doughballs, squashed grasshoppers, roaches, and leeches. My true bait is patience. I am the fish, the weeds, the turtles and snakes. I am everything below the surface, everything that bites, sucks, cuts, and nibbles, everything unseen from shore.

I am an archaeologist of the self. My stories were all laid down generations ago. One day in the mid-1950s, in the basement of my parents' furniture store in Pittsburgh, following an *eloi* of my fancy, I stumbled across the adit. I removed the boards, the cobwebs, kicked aside the rats'-nests, and followed the trail of cold, stale air. Every day, I went a little deeper. Lights gave out. Old butts, bottles, matches, papers, disappeared. I was alone.

For twenty-five years, I've been poking through layers. The store is gone, the parents, Pittsburgh, but the cave stays put. If I can wedge myself through a few more crannies, I think I'll enter an enormous room with petroglyphs and bones and evidence of rituals no one has ever described. Of course there are bats and blind fish and probably blind, albino versions of everything known in the outer world. In these cinders are trace elements of vanished worlds. Neutrinos from novae at the dawn of time have passed through the world's crust and lodged down here. Its pure darkness is rather handsome, like a cloud-chamber, where silent collisions go unseen but for their radioactive decay.

So, I'm down here in the cave, or standing on the shore, every day. I have come to believe that the world has scratched a rather complete record of itself on the walls of a pitch-black cavern whose exact location, and whose language, are known only to me.

June 6, 1988
New York City

RUDY WIEBE

Without Goodness, Beauty Is Unknown

At various times in the past twenty years I have tried to say something about writing; when some of these public statements are isolated from their surrounding texts, their perplexing and indeed contradictory nature — even within themselves — becomes apparent. Here are four:

a) " . . . to touch this land [the prairie] with words requires an architectural structure; to break into the space of the reader's mind with the space of this western landscape and the people in it you must build a structure of fiction like an engineer builds a bridge or a skyscraper over and into space. . . . You must lay great black steel lines of fiction, break up that space with huge design . . . build giant artifact."
— 1971

b) " . . . writing a story is much like rappelling up a mountain whose top may not exist because it can never be known by anyone but yourself. For me, the climbing — that is, the writing itself — rarely takes as long as deciding that this is the particular mountain on which I want to spend my energy."
— 1972

c) "Let me say that writing is like taking a long journey. You must travel every day, and every day you decide roughly where you would like to go, what you would hope to see, but you never know if you will actually get there. You do not really know where you will eat that day, or what, or where you will be able to rest, if at all, and you may not even have a place to sleep when night catches you. The only certainty is that you are travelling, and that travelling with you is another person. This is a person you love; you are together in everything you encounter, whatever you eat, wherever you rest or sleep; whatever the circumstances there you two are together. And that is enough. Together you are enough for anything, anything in the world."
— 1984

d) "Story is always a living closeness; there's an endless fascination in making them. Anyway I don't even think I write stories; I find them. I'm more archaeologist than inventor. You never know when, or where, but you're always looking and suddenly you unearth a marvellous archaeological site and then, if you're smart, you dig very carefully indeed."
— 1984

It is obvious that these images of what (fiction) writing is carry not only affirmations but also logical negations ("rappel", for example, means descending, not ascending, a mountain on a doubled rope; is "writing" the journey, or the lover, or both together?). They also imply worth. All these actions are good for something, for someone. Perhaps when I consider doing something as important to me as writing (after all, I have been doing that or trying to do it all of my adult life), whatever image I discover is always rooted in a certain moral necessity of goodness.

At the same time, I am aware of the contemporary disdain of connecting "goodness" with "art". Last year William Gass published an essay in *Harper's Magazine* entitled "Goodness Knows Nothing of Beauty" in which he argued that art can and does give to any human meanness "a glorious godlike shape", and that beauty and morality hold nothing in common with each other. To me the cool, glance-down-the-nose intellectualism of such thinking is not absurd; it is merely ludicrous. Goodness is as hard to come by (and as essential) as beauty; when you find one (or find it within your capacity to make one), you cannot but find (make) the other as well.

Flannery O'Connor wrote truer than Gass: "It is in the nature of fiction [art] not to be good for much unless it is good in itself." I would hold that for something to be art, that is, to be beautiful, it will be good in every possible ramification of that word. If it isn't one, it can't be the other.

June 1988
Edmonton

P. K. PAGE

Why I Write

because my right lobe creates images my left lobe must
   transcribe
because a drum in my head demands words of me
because in this dream I laugh and I weep
because the man in the moon hides his face from me
because I must hear and because I must see
out of fear that my ancestors excommunicate me
because I taste silver because I taste gold
because of the six-winged seraphim
because of the ocean because of the sky
because the unknown is writing me

July 1988
Victoria, B.C.

JANE URQUHART

When I was a very small child, about six or seven, my
family moved from a location that my father always
referred to as "the bush" — a tiny mining settlement two
hundred miles north of Lake Superior — into the boxed
regularity of North Toronto. It was my introduction to the
dailiness that I've been trying to escape from ever since.
Where once I'd been able to watch my father's friend
"Fearless Fawcett" settle his rattling, ill-repaired bush
planes down on the surface of a frozen lake, now I gazed
through the windows of my house at a row of post-war
brick houses, all terrifyingly similar, at concrete sidewalks,
and at rectangular patches of green. At this point, since
very little of the external urban world interested me, I was
forced to invent and miniaturize landscapes in order to
make them accessible to my whims. Two spots, beauti-

fully suited to this activity, were within my grasp — one terrestrial, one architectural — and I delighted not only in the smallness of these areas but in my ability to control everything that happened there. And believe me, plenty happened there.

I built a county, perhaps a province, within the terrestrial perimeter of my backyard sandbox and peopled it with a collection of very small, brightly coloured plastic busses, trucks, and automobiles. First I made several mountain ranges, all equipped with perilous roads where tragedies were bound to occur. I spent, I remember, one full afternoon attempting to fabricate a lake (where more tragedies were bound to occur), but its waters obstinately disappeared, despite the fact that the garden hose was able, with no difficulty whatsoever, to melt the mountains. I began to understand and appreciate the idea of natural disaster, and as events concerning busses and trucks began to unfold, the giant green flood snake lurked just beyond the sandbox border ready at any time to throw chaos into the narrative.

One great big yellow bus, I seem to recall, fell inappropriately in love with a little blue car who was engaged (by her parents and against her will) to a rather dull but possessive and tyrannical brown truck. The bus and the truck took part in a lot of dangerous driving, playing chicken, etc., on the twisting, tortuous roads, and eventually, inevitably, the truck lost control and plunged to his death. The bus then had to rescue the hysterical blue car from the piece of track on which my brother's toy train (borrowed from his room) waited, near the non-existent lake, to play its part. Would the bus get there in time? I rather thought not, but miraculously he did. The lovers embraced as best they could, their bodies being rigid plastic. I built a little chapel and planted a score of trees around it to make a picturesque setting for wedding photos. And then, although it broke my heart, the snake struck, the floods came, the mountains dissolved and all the trees were swept away. The lovers died in each other's arms.

This was, of course, seasonal employment. In winter the little architectural world of the doll-house dominated. Here lived four small dolls: Mother, Father, Bobby, Susie — all suffering from some form of wonderful derangement. Bobby hid most of the time under beds, behind the sofa, sometimes on the roof. Eventually he drowned in my mom's laundry-tub. There was a terrific funeral in November, in the sandbox, during which Mother doll had to be restrained from throwing herself into the grave. She was sedated and put to bed for several weeks, and, as time rolled by, Father and Susie found themselves having the best days of their lives — staying up until two or three in the morning, eating nothing but desserts, going to neither work nor school, lounging around the house on various pieces of tiny furniture. Bliss does not, however, last forever, and when Mother awakened, weeks and weeks later, she felt well enough, and angry enough, to sell Susie to an orphanage and to run away to New York with the large amount of money that she had been able to get for her.

Father doll was a broken man. He wandered around the house singing, "I've grown accustomed to her face, / She almost makes the day begin. . . ." (I'd just been to New York myself and had seen *My Fair Lady*.) He was singing about Susie, not Mother, and finally the little girl escaped the orphanage, appearing, stage left, just before her father was to drink the draught of poison he had been busily preparing.

The conduct of my own parents, I should add at this point, was exemplary. Nothing resembling dramas of this dimension took place in our house. But that was just the point. I wanted, when I was playing, an alternative to the safe predictability of my outer life, an alternative to sidewalk squares and tidy rectangular lawns. I wanted Sir Walter Scott and Lord Byron. I wanted secret trouble and moments of profound awakening. (When Father doll, for instance, discovers that it is Susie, not Mother or even the poor drowned Bobby, who really matters, or when the doomed truck and car realize in their last moments that doomed lovers must remain doomed lovers.)

Having only just learned how to read fluently about this time, I was beginning to develop enough distance from words to see them for the extraordinary magical things that they are. They were being transposed from the ordinary rituals of shared bedtime stories into something I could savour in secret, apart from adult rules. The sound of them began to appeal to me. "Wynken, Blynken, and Nod one night / Sailed off in a wooden shoe — / Sailed on a river of crystal light, / Into a sea of dew." I said these lines over and over to myself in the dark, loving the lilt of the syllables. I began to write a poem or two on nursery themes:

> Hi and goodbye
> I wish I could fly
> I'm on my way to market
> To buy a pig
> Who can dance the jig
> And drive the car
> And park it.

I discovered that I enjoyed doing this almost as much as drowning Bobby or banishing Susie or playing with the doomed lovers. Finally, of course, I found that I could have it all, despite what my mother said about having your cake and eating it. And that's why, and that's when, I began to write.

Exactly the same thing is true today, except that I have neither sandbox nor doll-house in which to work out plots. Perhaps I should resurrect them and thereby strengthen my narrative line. But the point is, the reason I write now is the reason I played (and wrote) then: to live for a while an intense inner life that I cannot seem to do without, to provide myself and the few others who miraculously understand with an alternative world which nevertheless mirrors, on some levels, our own, and to play with, to control as best I can, the music and the meaning of words.

June 19, 1988
Wellesley, Ont.

ELIZABETH SPENCER

Why do I write? Well, it was an urge, like nail-biting, etc., that started when I was too young to know what it was. I tried to paint it out but had no talent, had no ear for music, and jumping up and down and calling it dancing didn't work either. So writing down made-up stories did, and that's how it started. I also loved hearing stories, read or told. Then we get more serious. What's it all about.

I write to straighten things out that seem kinked-up in my experience, or society, in the small or large sense, and I do think there are many dimensions that get involved — the moral "corona" as you put it, maybe; the metaphysical perhaps; the comical most certainly. As much as you can bring to bear. Some of it may miss most readers. Some, private to yourself, is forever secret, but gives the heart-beat.

I write because I believe in the reality of my own perceptions.

September 1, 1988
Chapel Hill, N.C.

DOUG JONES

Poets? Some of the bright ones are now in advertising, using sophisticated technology to reinforce contemporary conventions. Horace, I presume, would approve. Others still fish by obstinate isle.

At the moment, I would have to explain why I am not writing — not why I write. My mind of late has been filled with academic crises, taxes, lumber, and a septic tank.

One influence which did lead me to write was "Lycidas".

> Yet once more, O ye laurels, and once more
> Ye myrtles brown, with ivy never sere,
> I come to pluck your berries harsh and crude,
> And with forced fingers rude,
> Shatter your leaves before the mellowing year.

This is an old story, but also Bloomian, and, one might argue, post-Modern. It begins with repetition and proceeds, almost immediately, to violent appropriation, a kind of rape.

Milton inherits the language of father and mother, the ancestors, exfoliated, layered, thick as autumn leaves, the daemons wall-to-wall in the underworld. He strictly mediates the thankless Muse, her sibylline utterances, her sweet nothings, her hero, consort, king's commandments, epigrams, pastorals. He comprehends their composted authority, their *frissons*, their power and their glory — which the *infans* could not utter or command. Then he imitates; he expropriates; he storms the master's castle and the mistress's bower. Confronting the fate of the upstart son, Orpheus/Christ, he rolls the disconsolate nymphs, the Muse herself, in the monstrous deep, among the monstrous dead. He, however, asserts his still-living breath. He is master of the word now. He gives ratings to the dead heroes, assigns them their astral stations, allows them to live on in his reiteration of the names. And he ends with his *oeuvre ouverte*.

> At last he rose, and twitched his mantle blue:
> Tomorrow to fresh woods and pastures new.

The poem, says Wallace Stevens, satisfies belief in an immaculate beginning. Once more, and yet once more . . .

A contemporary and feminine variation on this theme is Anne Hébert's "Le Tombeau des rois" and "Mystère de la parole".

Poetry is a specialized area in which this ambiguous intercourse between convention and experience, ancestral codes and the barbaric yawp, repetition and belief in an immaculate beginning, may be worked out to produce, as Stevens says again, a satisfaction.

These statements, confessions, apologies, credos, fiats, obiter dicta, or manifestos tend to be either melodramatic (poets are the unacknowledged legislators of the world) or examples of meiosis (poetry is a superior form of amusement). One doubts that any poet, at least since Homer, has had the influence of Karl Marx. And the power of poetry, in any immediate sense, pales before rocket-launchers and atom bombs, acid rain or the green-house effect. The power of poetry works through individuals (even if they work with the communal symbolic code) and requires very little high-priced technology. And it is, distinctively, playful, experimental, heuristic — an instrument of what Northrop Frye, among others, calls an open mythology. I sometimes suspect that half the population, at least in adolescence, writes poetry. Good.

I would like to say that a neighbour's daughter who two days ago threw herself off a ten-storey building would not have done so if she had written poetry. But this, too, is probably baloney. She may have written poetry. And some of the best poets throw themselves off bridges.

I like Leonard Cohen's "My lady can sleep/ On a handkerchief/ Or if it be fall/ On a fallen leaf". (I've wondered if this owes something to a Chinese sketch of a lady sleeping on a banana leaf, I think in a museum in Boston. If it doesn't, it should.) George Bowering writes of a leaf that falls on its shadow. We all do. Once more and yet once more . . . with variations. Robyn Sarah notes, and takes the trouble to articulate, the growth of dust, how it gathers the household effects, marbles, pencils, paper clips, into an amorphous whole. Whether one can allegorize this into an example of what language might do without poetry or not, I like the attention to fact and to language. I once noted, myself, the necessity of dusting off the old typewriter. Make it new as Pound, following some Chinese emperor or other in his bathtub, said — once more and yet once more.

July 1988
Quebec

DON McKAY

Some Remarks on Poetry
and Poetic Attention

Things occur to me, in the midst of writing, following my nose into whatever, and I'll pass some of these along.

There's an affable iffiness to these in the original sniffing and browsing, which I will allow to diminish in the interests of shape. Also, I don't want them getting pushed around by the big-bullying theories of the schoolyard.

— I suspect that the quality of attention surrounding a poem is more important to me than poetry. A species of longing that somehow evades the usual desire to possess. Or, I should add, to use.

— Art comes across; it occurs as tools attempt to metamorphose into animals. Language, for example, opens its ear to the other. Once you have tools plus longing, you have poetic attention.

— Probably these notions incubate during bird-watching, which in my experience involves a mental set nearly identical to writing: a kind of suspended expectancy, tools at the ready, full awareness that the creatures cannot be compelled to appear. (Bad writing: a trip to the zoo.)

— Poetic attention registers with me as a different form of knowing from the commodity sold in schools. When Martin Heidegger speaks of "tarrying alongside" whatever it is we're "knowing", he shifts the relationship away from knowledge as ownership, and catches reverberations with both visiting and distance. And, underlying this, a sense of shared mortality you don't get when you're Knowing with a capital K. You swim awhile with a fellow creature of time.

— But language, you might say, has a life of our own, and a writer can start there instead, with the energies of the prison-house, or house of being, or mother tongue, body speech, animal music, or word-as-such. All these various linguistics interest me, but less and less the closer you get to solipsism, which comes about from spending too much time indoors. I need a linguistics I can talk with. The meetings of experience and language — negotiation, abrasion, dominion, cross-pollination, intercourse, infection; the "wondrously tedious monotony and variety of the world" (Francis Ponge); wildness invading language as music, which occurs as soon as syntax is seen as energy rather than enthroned as order: this boundary is not a line but a planet rich with ecosystems. I'm not wild about the taste of paper or the narcissism of the "signifier", however free or ideologically correct the play may seem in those salons of the spirit where it is pursued. I don't believe that "reference" is a consequence of imperialism, late capitalism, or the patriarchy. Freeing words from the necessity to refer is equivalent to freeing Tundra swans from the necessity to migrate, or, getting down to it, freeing any creature from its longing for another.

— I suspect, too, that poetry brings us back to that longing, back to poetic attention.

— In one version of our evolution as a species, we become outfitted with a capacity for poetry (all the arts, maybe) as a natural check on our genius for technology: for making things, for control and reduction, for converting the world to human categories. Poetry, that wonderful useless musical machine, performs the actions of technology but undoes the consequences. In this version, Auden gets modified; poetry makes nothing *happen*.

September 1988
Ilderton, Ont.

CAROL SHIELDS

Everywhere it seems there is an impatience with the conventions of literary realism, and with good reason, for the "real world" is too often shown as fragmentary, a sort of secondary lesion of the senses, trailing off in *diminuendo*, interrogated on every side by technology, unwilling to stand still long enough to be captured by definition. Language itself, our prized system of signs and references, frequently appears emptied out or else suspiciously charged.

Post-modernism — it's sometimes forgotten that post-modernism is a theory, not a mode of writing or a methodology — seemed for a time to offer a new perspective. Writers were relieved of the responsibility to create a believable world and to invest that world with meaning, to tell a story that derived its tensions from the springs of cause and effect, from psychological motivation or moral consequence. Writers could lean in their inarticulateness on the absurdity of the endeavour, and their *texts*, that curious but useful word, could be crisped and refreshed by the knowledge that this was, after all, a game.

But how anxious theory is, and how arbitrary. This "beautiful nonsense", as it has been called, proved all too tendentious, too labyrinthine, too much a hypothesis deduced from materials that were themselves unproven. How disappointing it was to find that even a theory that illuminated and delighted the intellect could fail to convince. There was also, and from the beginning, a disparity between theory and practice that signalled a certain effort of accommodation and an easy forgiveness of imprecise expression or ironic aloofness — some would say élitism. Language, which might have been liberated, instead shrivelled; we have seen how writers, overdosed on theory, became incomprehensible. (The poet Don Coles has written about a tragic Portuguese child who was kept by her parents in a chicken coop and who, when finally rescued by neighbours, was found to "talk" like a chicken.)

But if post-modernism has proven a synthetic discourse, unanimated by personal concerns, it has at least given writers a breath of that precious oxygen of permission and, more important, time to see in what way the old realism failed us.

It was, perhaps, not real enough. It focused too compulsively on those phantom inventions, comedy and tragedy. It trafficked too freely in moments of crisis, imposed artificial structures, searched too diligently for large themes and too preciously for graceful epiphanies (*mea culpa*). It banished certain parts of our language to certain emotional parts of the house. The people who appeared in "realistic" fiction were almost never allowed the full exercise of their reality, their daydreams, their sneezes, their offended appetites, their birthday parties, their tooth-aches, their alternating fits of grotesque wickedness and godly virtue. Their meditative life was neglected. Realistic fiction passed too quickly through the territory of the quotidian, and it dismissed, as though they didn't exist, those currents of sensation that leak around the boundaries of vocabulary. The realistic tradition stressed

— why? because it was more "dramatic"? — the divisiveness of human society and shrugged at that rich, potent, endlessly mysterious cement that binds us together.

These are interesting times for a writer. The crisis of meaning, and we nearly died of it, has brought us a new set of options. The strands of reality that enter the newest of our fictions are looser, more random and discursive. More altogether seems possible. The visual media, television and the cinema, have appropriated the old linear set-ups, leaving fiction, by default, the more interesting territory of the reflective consciousness, the inside of the head where nine-tenths of our lives are lived. And writers seem more happily aware of their intimate connection with readers and with other writing. (I love the work of Audrey Thomas because she understands that the books we read form part of the tissue of experience.)

In the books I read — and I find it hard to separate my life as a reader from that as a writer — I look first for language that possesses an accuracy that cannot really exist without leaving its trace of deliberation. I want, too, the risky articulation of what I recognize but haven't yet articulated myself. And, finally, I hope for some fresh news from another country which satisfies by its modesty, a microscopic enlargement of my vision of the world. I wouldn't dream of asking for more.

July 26, 1988
Paris, France

RAYMOND SOUSTER

To rediscover and redefine the heroic — this would certainly appear to be the task of poetry, world-wide and especially Canadian, as we rapidly approach the end of another decade.

It seems to me that writers are presently bogged down in an obsessive examination of self which has all but outlived its usefulness. I don't know if this is more true of poetry than of prose, but I wouldn't be too surprised if it were.

There's no doubt the heroic exists all around us even in this present world, awaiting the artist who is prepared to grapple with it. I look forward to the work of a new generation which will approach the status of a Joyce or a Malraux, a Jeffers or a Char.

July 27, 1988
Toronto, Ont.

PHYLLIS WEBB

"There Are *the Poems"*

An editor asks me to put it all down: the reasons I write. And I thought "it" was a gift. *Homo ludens* at play among the killing-fields of dry grasses. Playful woman making a space to breathe. "There *are* the poems," Sharon says, she means, between the critical flash. There *are* the poems, like fists wearing birthstones and bracelets, her "roses and bliss". Or they're like legs running, bounding into the fields of force, momentum, for a quick roll in Darwin's tangled bank.

And there are the poets doing what? And why, the editor asks. What does he want? Contributions to knowledge? Civilization and its discontents? Chaos among the order — or, oh yes, French doors opening onto a deck and a small pool where we can watch our weird reflections shimmering and insubstantial?

The proper response to a poem is another poem. We burrow into the paper to court in secret the life of plants, the shifty moon's space-walks, the bliss, the roses, the glamorous national debt. Someone to talk to, for God's sake, something to love that will never hit back.

September 1988
Salt Spring Island, B.C.

ROBERT BRINGHURST

Reflections on the Stone Age

Very little is being written, or has ever been written, in Canada except in the two official languages, both of which are recent imports. But a rich oral literature existed in the older tongues, and traces of it still exist in some of them. At the end of the nineteenth century, some of that oral literature was transcribed by the German anthropologist Franz Boas and a group of linguists working under his direction. Those transcriptions constitute nearly everything that remains of the real, ancestral Canadian literature, but they are very rarely taught as such in the schools. If I could send a generation of young Canadian writers off now on a grand tour, it would not be a tour of European capitals; it would be a journey through time, mind, and landscape involving the serious study of these ancestral North American languages and literatures. This may sound like a romantic project, but I mean it as a very classical one indeed. I would expect results as valuable as those produced in Europe five centuries ago by Erasmus and his colleagues, through the secular study of Latin and Greek.

The essential features of literature seem to me, if not beyond the reach of time, at least beyond the reach of history. Indeed, one might define literary history as the study of literary inessentials. (It is a fascinating subject, of course, but that is usual with inessentials.) The ancient stories collected in northern Europe by Jakob and Wilhelm Grimm, Peter Asbjørnsen, and Jørgen Moe, for example, though they had passed through many filters, and were pressed again through a fine mesh of nineteenth-century patriarchal sensibility when these gentlemen wrote them down, often seem immune to human time, impervious to history. One may say the same for the *Metamorphoses* of Ovid, the *Eventyr* of Hans Andersen, or the stories of Lewis Carroll.

When we look at the literary canon, however, it seems that the earliest European literature we possess belongs to the late bronze age, and most of it exhibits what Northrop Frye once called, in another context, a garrison mentality. That is to say, quite simply, it is obsessed with military life. Aboriginal Canadian literature is not without its references to warfare, but it is free of any references to the military profession, and to military and political institutions, including warfare, on any major scale. It speaks from a deeper layer in the phylogeny of human culture, and from a more intimate and habitual confrontation with the world beyond the limits of human technology, craft, and control.

The remnants of paleolithic oral literature that have been salvaged in Canada are an artistic and spiritual link with that earlier world — one whose value and relevance to us has not expired, and in my opinion *cannot* expire. It is even a world to which, in a practical sense, we may soon return. When our profiteering culture has finally eaten itself out of house and home, when its ever-increasing mortgages on the future finally fall due, when the last river is dammed and the forests and fossil fuels are exhausted, and when the idea of perpetual growth has become once again an innocent joke, like the idea of perpetual youth or perpetual motion, then whatever creatures remain on the earth may have to learn to walk again, and to do their flying in their dreams. The stories and songs of the paleolithic will make fresh and vivid sense to them.

I have no reason to think anyone in that world will learn to read books, still less to think that anyone then will memorize my unharmonious verses. I have no reason, in fact, to suppose that the inhabitants of that future will be other than prokaryotes, dinoflagellates, and rhizopods, or cockroaches and feral laboratory rats. Yet it pleases me sometimes to ask whether our paleolithic descendants could make sense of some of my own poems if they heard them. That seems to me a test of poetry more to be trusted than the judgments of current reviewers. But the test I value most depends not at all on the prospect of human survivors. I like merely to ask whether a poem dishonours or honours the world. I like to ask whether it is fit to be thought about next to a glacier-scarred stone or the limb of a mountain larch or a grass blade, or fit to be listened to with kingfishers and finches. It is not that I confuse, or wish to confuse, culture and nature. They are as different one from another as herbs from herbivores — and as intimately linked. But the works of art that matter most to me are bridges between us and the world we live in: a means of making that difficult crossing. The hardest journey of all, and one we can never make too often, is the journey to where we are.

April 1988
Bowen Island, B.C.

DOROTHY LIVESAY

Memory as Myth-making

In writing memoirs, as I am doing myself, the conflict arises when one seems obliged to choose between using recorded material from the past — diaries, letters, essays, and stories — or relying upon memories. Malcolm Muggeridge believes that memoir evokes those important impressions, emotions, and events which have truly influenced our lives. Whereas the daily journal, so significant when first written, is found to be irrelevant years later.

To the writer, the differences between diaries and memoirs are fascinating to explore. My mother's diaries tell me what she did every day for a period of six years, at a time when she was working in a newspaper office and being courted by two different men. In her diary she called them "Mr. Box and Mr. Cox". Nowhere does she record her dreams, never does she complain about being "put down". There is a yearning, however, to be "just pals" with men. This is as much as she permits herself to record. My memory of her is quite different. I relate her problems to the Old Testament myth of Adam and Eve. Eve is not a person in her own right, she sees her origins as a creature created out of Adam's rib. So then, after I have spent some time musing upon this, I have a dream — actually three dreams. These dreams take the myth and turn it inside out; or, if you like, upside down. With this thought in mind, I begin writing the images down. In the first dream, the myth is reversed. It is not the snake, but the man, who is treacherous, who leads Eve into temptation. In Dream 2, we see the pair banished into the modern world. In this dream Eve is helpless. Unable to cope. She cries to Adam for help. Dream 3 sets the pair down in a motel. There is no way out for Eve, if she accepts the myth of being an appendage. Such is the Judeo-Christian patriarchal pattern. Other civilizations, other religions, however, take from their environment entirely different views.

Recently I saw a TV documentary about Java. The thing that struck me most was, first, that gods and goddesses are within the reach of all of us; and secondly, that there exists a mountain where a human being, a man, awaits the coming of the goddess. Once a year she comes to be his bride and once a year there is great festivity amongst the people down below. Here then we see that this goddess bestows divinity and creativity upon Adam. The documentary points up the fact that environment determines the myth. In western countries the sun is beneficial; in hot countries the sun is treacherous and destroys crops. In a poem on this theme I reverse the western idea of a benevolent sun. It is the moon who brings us creativity and water. Here is a section from a longer poem entitled "Disasters of the Sun":

> Keep out
> keep out of the way of
> this most killing
> northern sun
> grower   destroyer
>
> Sun, you are no goodfather
> but tyrannical king:
> I have lived sixty years
> under your fiery blades
> all I want now
> is to grope for those blunt
> moon scissors

Fact or fiction? The event, or the myth about it? What does it matter? What we are trying to record is the experience of being human. None of our ancestors, be they dinosaurs or monkeys, have evolved to a point where they can record their lives. It is because we *have* evolved to the point of recording, not only our own lives, but the surmised lives of many creatures on this earth, from whales to snakes to eagles, that we are doing a great service to the history of human existence. Diaries, novels, poems, oral histories, have something valid to say on behalf of humanity. To my way of thinking, it does not matter if their words refer to personal reminiscences, or physical reconstruction, or historical research. All these approaches are vital, valid. All must be recorded. Hence you will see that I object, first, to those critics who make frantic efforts to sift the actual from the imagined; and secondly, to readers who desire to know all about an artist's personal life, be she or he a musician, a painter, or a writer. What matters is the message we can receive from this carefully sifted experience. Above all, do not take it as "*the* truth". Take it rather as a signpost, a guide to finding the truth about human existence here and now.

Lastly, it is my belief that what the woman writer today is doing is reversing the man-made myths, bringing female confidence and consciousness to the forefront. We must make women realize that they represent half of the population of this earth. They have the power to save our planet from self-destruction.

June 1988
Victoria, B.C.

SUSAN MUSGRAVE

Speculating on the Sex Lives of
People in Elevators
or
How I Don't Work as a Writer

When Knut Hamsun said, "I write to kill time," he couldn't have had a six-year-old daughter. When the poet John Berryman, however, wrote, "Life, friends, is boring," he'd probably spent the morning making ogre-noses out of modelling-clay instead of working on his *Dream Songs*.

My daughter is bored. I tell her, "To be bored means you have no inner resources," and take her to the library, where she chooses, among others, the encyclopedic *Book of Games and Pastimes*. Together we come up with a list of "Things to Make". I suggest she begin with the wormery, and send her to the garden to dig for worms.

This could take time. While she's occupied I take out my old nib pen and a sheet of blank paper and try to begin a poem on the theme of immortal love. I haven't got past the immortal-longing stage before she's back inside. She's decided she'd rather make invisible ink.

I relinquish my pen and the sheet of paper, which is still blank. Together we squeeze a lemon into a jar and I show her how to dip the nib into the juice and write her message. Back in my office I decide to forsake the poem and instead do some fine-tuning on my latest novel.

"Mum," I hear after a short interval. "How do you

spell 'summer holidays'?" I close my file marked CHAPTER ONE, DRAFT TEN. I'm already past my deadline, anyway.

When her message is dried, we hold the paper near the flame of a candle. "I love summer holidays because I get to stay home with my Mum and we do lots of fun things together" appears as light-brown writing. "It is magical, isn't it?" I say, genuinely touched. "No, Mum," she replies. "It's because lemon juice has a lower combustion point than paper, that's all." My daughter already believes in reason over passion.

But even passion has limits. I don't want to create an Underwater Volcano out of milk bottles and poster paints this morning any more than I want to play Old Maid, do crossword puzzles, or watch *Fred Penner*. My hatred of all board games is on a par with that of bingo and bowling, an admission that caused my therapist to conclude my "problem" is I'm indifferent to the usual values of life. Living, he said, is mostly boring formalities. He charges thirty-six dollars an hour for revelations like that.

Graham Greene, in an autobiographical essay, tells how he used to play Russian roulette after a course of therapy left him "correctly oriented" but totally bored with life. "I think boredom went far deeper than love. It had always been a feature of childhood. For years . . . I could take no aesthetic interest in any visual thing at all; staring at a sight that others assured me was beautiful, I would feel nothing. I was fixed in my boredom." Greene took his brother's revolver, loaded one chamber, pointed it at his head, and pulled the trigger. When the hammer clicked on an empty chamber, he experienced a sense of release from the tension.

When my daughter announces she is bored with *Games and Pastimes*, I experience a sense of tension that goes far deeper than either love or boredom. "Come on," I say to her, "I'll race you to the beach." I'm determined she's going to have a normal childhood and not develop pastimes like Graham Greene's.

As she washes out to sea on her inflatable alligator, I put on my dark glasses and indulge in some light summer reading. "How contrive not to waste one's time?" queries the protagonist in Camus's *The Plague*. "Answer: by being fully aware of it all the time. Ways in which this can be done: By spending one's day on an uneasy chair in a dentist's waiting-room; by listening to lectures in a language one doesn't know; by travelling by the longest and least-convenient train routes, and of course standing all the way; by queueing at the box office of theatres and then not booking a seat. And so forth."

By the time my daughter has washed in again I've gained a whole new perspective. When I suggest we go home and play Monopoly, she looks at me as if I've had too much sun. Testing me further, she says why don't we do the 5000-piece jigsaw puzzle I've been saving for "the right occasion".

While she's turning the pieces right side up, I make a mental list of more things I can do so as to be fully aware of time. I can take the slow route to town. I can spend the afternoon sitting in my therapist's waiting-room because I haven't made an appointment, and when he fits me in, finally, I can fire him because I have solved my own problem. On my way out — if I still need reminding that time is passing — I can speculate on the sex lives of people in the elevator.

I concentrate on the jigsaw puzzle. Getting an edge on it should use up most of the afternoon; later we can catch a political debate on the French-language station. After watching me for a long time, my daughter, with a concerned look, brings me another of her library books, *Having a Baby*. She presses it upon me, saying gently, "Here, Mum. This is how it's done. I think you need something to keep your mind occupied."

I help her put the puzzle back in the box, and suggest we play Tiddly-Wink Golf instead. That would be *too* boring, she says. We settle on Ropeless Tug-of-War.

August 3, 1988
Sidney, B.C.

SUSAN SWAN

On the window-blind of my first office, I once painted the words: to astound, to delight, to inform, to shock, and to provide hope. A few years later I crossed out "to shock" and replaced it with the phrase "to startle". I was getting older and starting to realize that writing to shock didn't require all that much courage. In fact, shocking people was much easier than I'd ever dreamt. But I still believed fiction must startle the reader on some level with the depth of its vision if it is to work.

These phrases are the closest I've come to defining why I write. Later I found out that, phrase by phrase, my credo was almost identical to the motto of the BBC. That discovery ended my public motto-making. No more blinds were painted with words that could be confused with the mandate of a bureaucracy. Besides, saying why I write is almost impossible. The need comes from an inner compulsion which feels biological, like sex. It's an urge to put language into form, and if I ignore it, I feel as if I am on an errand for somebody else's life and not living my own.

It's easier to say what I am trying to do when I write rather than why I do it. First of all, I begin with an odd, almost sensory awareness of IT (the book) as a thing in my mind waiting to be expressed. I am pregnant with something that distracts my mental processes, teases, and suggests haunting scenes and bits of conversation. I feel IT growing in me slowly and languidly no matter what I do. Then I sense a few hazy instructions that go with THE THING. Again, these instructions persist in being the vaguest of notions which just the same exert a relentless pressure on me to obey. These instructions are important. When I recollect them later (after the work is done), they amount to a description of what I am attempting to do. Or in other words what literature as I make it means to me.

In the two novels I have written so far (and a third just started), I seem to be interested in depicting a consciousness that threatens to eclipse my own unless I can express it. Sometimes this consciousness seems directly related to me — as if I am writing about a former self, her ideology and her motivations after I have outgrown her and become somebody else. This happened with my second novel (*The Last Golden Blonde of Summer*). I was aware while working on it that I wasn't creating a new character into which I could put some of my old conflicts but identifying and dramatizing an old self. When this happens, I have the uncomfortable feeling that I may not live as others live, but instead experience a series of fictions that I will later reshape and regurgitate. In other words, that I am just a series of selves I live through and discard and later reanimate in fiction. I also experience a second *blob-like* haunting during creation. I find myself wanting to express a consciousness that is like me in some indescribable way but was never mine. I'm not then dramatizing an old self but I feel the compulsion to give this invented self all the complexities of me.

From this, I deduce that I am most interested in exploring the complexity of the individual in fiction. The way a man or woman can survive through an interior life that intersects with the external world but is not ultimately defined by it is what most deeply fascinates me. I believe Hugh MacLennan was right when he said that creative non-fiction has taken over the traditional story-telling forms and left the novel to go underground "into the subliminal regions where are found the well-springs of human motives" ("The Changed Functions of Fiction and Non-Fiction", in *The Other Side of Hugh MacLennan*, Toronto: Macmillan of Canada, 1978).

I am also more interested in depicting a consciousness than in telling a story, although I rely on a narrative to do this. A narrative to me implies a progression into a more deeply felt understanding of the patterns and thoughts behind human lives, whereas a story seems to demand a plot and is therefore similar to a fable with a moral at the end like a cherry at the bottom of a Coke swizzle. A story seems clumsy and obvious — a man-made object that requires effort to suspend disbelief — while a portrait, if it evokes consciousness deeply, is like a terrifying flight into the beauties and wonders of the inner self.

A narrative must be aesthetically pleasing. It must have an intuitive logic that feels right, but it must not have a manufactured quality. And the narrative must let the characters talk as if their voices sprang to life without the intervention of the author. As if the vitality or wisdom in the idiosyncratic nature of each one was only waiting for the author's nod before they burst out and became themselves. I don't want to play God the author; I'd rather be Moses touching the rock of Horeb on God's advice to make a spring of water pour forth for the thirsty Israelites.

I'd feel happy if my novels were like an interesting head the reader could put on to deepen his perspective on human experience. Like a bionic mind tool with a spiritual resonance perhaps. Of course, what I am trying to do when I write is a personal matter. The philosophical reason for writing fiction is an intellectual subject. I am always eager to see how others define what writers are doing, and I read criticism as a way of reaffirming the act of writing itself. In the 1970s I worked a great deal in performance and was struck by the way this format uses language as an element (like image or sounds), rather than as a textual underpinning as theatre does. I also noticed that ready-made units of language (such as conversations about the weather) seemed to pop up and proclaim themselves for use in performance. These units by themselves wouldn't work as naturally in fiction unless they were filtered through a character or a narrative voice, but they stood on their own in performance as recognizably human. It wasn't until I read the Russian critic Bakhtin that I realized I had been exploring speech genres, the units of communication whose content and even ending can generally be predicted from the first words at the start of the speech.

The fact that I was using intuitively what he had already described analytically delighted me. I love analysis and theory and use it whenever I can to extend the permission I sometimes withhold from myself in a country like Canada which tends to favour a traditional view of literature as social realism. In short, I take it on faith that theory extends the possibilities for appreciation of literature but in itself has little to do with the act of creation. Which isn't to say that it can't be the subject of creation, as it is in many of Italo Calvino's narratives. And I even know a case where a theorist friend is borrowing performance techniques to give an academic paper.

Do I think literature has an obligation to uphold moral values? No. I think literature's first job is to express the vision of the creator. I believe the fiction writer is a lone spokesman for individual consciousness in a tribal culture. We live in an electric society dominated by the mass media, whose art forms like most television and Hollywood films tend to institutionalize the imagination. The fiction writer may well be an advocate of thought in a world of sensation and for that reason as necessary as ever.

September 16, 1988
Toronto

DIANE KEATING

Writing is life or death for me. Nothing else really matters. I approach it each time with a dry mouth and a pounding heart. It's the only thing I ever want to do, but I'm always afraid I'm not going to be able to do it. Even as a thirteen-year-old, when I was supposedly asleep, I wrote dismal odes to God by the light from the street falling across the bottom of my bed.

The force impelling me to write feels like a kind of existential loneliness that began with the gates clanging shut on my quasi-paradisiacal estate of childhood. The older I become, the greater the compulsion to return and peer through the bars of those locked gates.

One recollection that produces "an awful warmth about the heart" is the artesian well in the small prairie town of Birtle, Manitoba, where my grandparents lived. It was located in a grove of willows at the end of a flat, dusty road that led from their house to the river, and I never saw anyone there except batty old Beatrice. She was over eighty and hobbled along on legs so bowed that the townsfolk said a pregnant sheep had once jumped through them. Whenever I passed, she would shake her cane at me and cry out, "Water is the food of life, not honeydew."

On long, boring summer days when the sun beat into my skin like nails and the cicadas shrilled so loudly they seemed inside my skull, I would make the excuse of fetching water in order to go to the grove. Entering this cool, quiet place which had the numinous quality of a sanctuary, I would heave aside the rough wood cover of the well, lie on my belly on the mossy stones, and, with my chin in my hands, lean over the clear water.

First, I would stare at the shimmery reflection of my face, the overhanging bushes, the tree-tops, the brilliant snatches of sky, and, in that last summer of my childhood, the vapour trail of the Strategic Air Command bomber. Next, I would stare down through the water, dancing webs of light slowly dissolving into gloom, and then into darkness. Darkness that had no bottom. Finally, I would amuse myself by trying to look at the surface and the depth simultaneously. But this always made me feel queasy.

Before leaving the willow grove, almost as a rite I would cast a pebble into the centre of the well and watch the ripples fanning out, obliterating the reflection. On the way home, as the water from the tin pail splashed down my legs, I would think of where it came from — the sea in the still, black centre of the earth.

If I compare the Birtle artesian well to the role of literature in society generally, the grove is the creative process and the well is life. The pebble cast into the water becomes the influence of a literary work. Just as the pebble sinks through the surface reflection into darkness, so does the literary work sink below the personality into the unconscious or common imagination that we all share. Writers, by expressing their private feelings and ideas, reflect the feelings of everyone.

E. M. Forster said it in two words, "Only connect." But here at the gates of the post-modern twenty-first century our lives are becoming darker, more dusty journeys. (I don't have to go on about nuclear weapons or ecological disasters.) The wells of being are drying up. There is less and less feeling for the spirit or the essence of things. What will become of writers, particularly poets, when their words no longer have the power to touch others? Perhaps they will be village idiots like batty old Beatrice. Tolerated but ignored, they will hang around shopping malls and talk to everyone who passes — mimicking a society of which they have no part.

October 1988
Toronto

T. L. DUFF

Wanted

This is what I want from my own writing and the writing of others: writings of conscience. Literature that is *useful* to the human condition. Literature that is marked by a reinvestment in the humanist values. Writing that acknowledges a moral responsibility or at least moves towards that spectrum as it faces away from the idea of literature as play, as game. As *head*game, rather than *heart*game. Writing that has *meaning*. Writers who can without shame confess to a notion that literature *can* change lives. That it *can* bring the news. *All* the news. And writers who know that literature can achieve this without resorting to the didactic. Who know that it is there in the web.

What I want are more writers who have some conception of the literary tradition that has brought us to this doorstep. We have an entire generation of authors who have somehow escaped into the writing life largely without this knowledge. Writers, for instance, who would be dumbfounded if one pointed out to them the straight line that may be said to run from a writer as ancient as Ovid to one as current as Richard Ford, with stops along the way for Chekhov, Virginia Woolf, Camus, J. M. Coetzee, and ten thousand others — all of whom would insist that literature is meant to serve humanity. That it is meant — even if your novel is a first-person narrative about the most heinous creature who ever lived — it is meant to prop up the flagging spirit. Through language, through tone, through some solace there in the print's texture. The heart's words, the heart's papers.

When we speak of a book as having resonance, it is this, by and large, that is resonating: the inquiry, that solace, those fictional lives that have application to our own place in the world.

The absence of this is killing good prose at about the same rate as so much poetry is killing itself: yet another poem about poetry, yet another poem about another poet

— with the world excluded. Yet another novel where the writer is the hero of his or her own text.

Yeah, and this, too. We're out of the crib and need to stop going at it with crossed fingers.

What we need is writing that pours out the wrath and mercy of good people in deep, deep trouble.

October 1988
Marysville, Ont.

RAY SMITH

Werner Who?

Should literature ever come to be understood and defined by someone with proper philosophical training, it will be seen to be fuzzy.

Critical labels for movements — realism, post-modernism, metafiction — name bulges, tendencies; they serve fashion, not truth; they are crutches for those who need help reading, judging; crutches for editors, agents, journalists, and other such literary middlemen.

A successful critical theory must be analogue and multidimensional; it must be able to deal in unknowns and indeterminates. But most critical theories are digital and two- or three-dimensional, puny constructs one can walk around in an hour or two.

Any paradigm of the social role of the artist and his work must allow for Jane Austen as well as Solzhenitsyn; for Rembrandt's self-portraits and Vermeer's interiors as well as *Guernica* and *Los Desastres de la Guerra*; for *Der Rosenkavalier* as well as *Fidelio*. The arts and politics are arts of the possible; but the possibles are different. The great political artist finds his soul in the great world, the great private artist finds the great world in his soul; the little political practitioner is a hack, the little private practitioner pares the nails on his effetes. (Clearly I mean that the artists and works that begin this paragraph are great; anyone who thinks I mean they are equally great cannot read.)

Art is a just rendering of the world. The better the work, the more just the rendering. By "just", "rendering", and "world" I mean things beyond the complexity I can get at in this paper (or anywhere). I mean this not in the (properly) limited sense of the endeavours of the statistician, the lawyer, or the historian: *Tristram Shandy*, *Wuthering Heights*, and *Finnegan's Wake* render the world with a justice of a quality with *Emma*, *War and Peace*, or *Madame Bovary*; all sing in their different fullnesses. Let some critic take it from here; let us have some useful and generous delineations, distinctions, definitions; let us have a vocabulary of fiction. My own attempt at such a vocabulary is described in a letter to John Metcalf and published in his *Carry On Bumping*; the same letter includes my readings of modern critical theory.

While I was writer-in-residence at the University of Alberta, I wrote a piece for aspiring writers entitled "Three Propositions on the Art of Writing". They are:

I. Writing is an activity. (It is the doing of it that matters to a writer.)

II. A writer is someone engaged in the activity of writing. (Not in research, thinking, planning, drinking, talk-showing, award-receiving.)

III. All writer's questions about a piece of writing can only be resolved through the activity of writing. (A writer needs practical answers to such questions as "Will it work?", "Does it fit?", or "Can I manage it?" Theoretical answers here are meangingless.)

The most important aesthetic perception a writer has is that the dichotomy between style and content is false, does not exist for a working artist. It should also be false for a reader reading or a critic cricketing; but you can't undo two millennia of western thought based upon the dichotomy.

I have read lots of interesting critical theory (along with lots of trashy theory), but the only stuff of any use to me in my writing was done by other writers or painters or musicians.

I am constantly amazed at the certainty of critics: the only large certainties in the arts must embrace uncertainties. Critics are never uncertain; writers always are; I am a writer.

Who Heisenberg?

July 11, 1988
Westmount, Quebec

JOSEF ŠKVORECKÝ

Any meaningful pronouncements on literature depend on definitions. As for myself, I mean fiction when I speak about literature, which does not mean that I exclude poetry or drama but merely that I feel a certain qualification to speak only about fiction. Fiction for me is entertainment, but, of course, you can entertain people on many levels. The only level on which you cannot entertain anybody but yourself is the purely egocentric level of writers totally immersed in their miserable selves, although nothing really bad ever happened to them. That's as far as I am prepared to go to define this kind of writer.

The others may entertain on a very high level of significance; their sensitive and intelligent readers may rejoice at the way they have been able to express the *situation humaine*: how it feels to be a human being anywhere in the world, including Canada. Or they may entertain on the humble level of fiction written for what is usually meant by "entertainment": on the level of crime stories, westerns, adventures, science-fiction, horror, etc. But, as Chandler believed, what makes people read such stuff is not merely the suspense, the enigma, etc., but "emotion created through dialogue and description". In other words: the "literary", i.e. the aesthetic, qualities of the text. Only such works of low entertainment are reread. I don't think anybody ever rereads a Ludlum. Ludlum is simply not literature in the sense of an art constituted uniquely by language and vision.

Between these two extremes — top entertainment through expressing human situation, and low entertainment through creating emotion by means of dialogue and description — lies the vast country of fiction. For me there has never been any doubt that this fiction is a humanizing factor; sometimes its effects are barely perceptible, and perhaps only those already humane enough are moved by them; at other times its effects are almost immediate and very visible: remember all the various *Uncle Tom's Cabins* and *Huckleberry Finns*, *Grapes of Wraths* and *Intruders in the Dusts*, not to speak about the many works of writers from totalitarian countries, which are never perceived as merely experiments in form or explorations of the moribund state of the novel. Literature *is* very definitely for humanity. It does not compete with the news because it is about the soul, not about gun-shots. It is concerned not with moral grandeur but with truth. The truth about human beings, among whom some are better than others because — whether by exercising freedom of the will, or by the grace of God — they resist evil better than others. These better human beings are always compassionate. Thus literature is about the eternal values of good and evil, and about compassion. It is never relativistic, because literature is never fashion.

June 1988
Toronto

DON COLES

Philip Larkin writes somewhere of the sort of person who "will forever be surprising/ A hunger in himself to be more serious." I think there are many such persons; and I find this hunger (so often suppressed or unacknowledged by oneself, or mocked by others) very moving, as moving as anything I can think of. I believe also that for me at any rate this "hunger to be serious" fulfils itself with great difficulty, and seldom or not at all in the daily circs of life (one is either too rushed, or, as some unprogrammed encounter with seriousness looms, too inhibited, too embarrassed); but I know that writing allows me to draw close to it, even to live for long periods of time within it. For this I am grateful to writing, grateful that forms and traditions (for example, lyric poetry) exist within which I can stalk seriousness without needing to justify what I am doing.

It follows that a real role for literature in our society is to enable readers to know that this seriousness-hunger which they have privately felt is not, after all, isolating, but is widely (if, again, and almost invariably, quietly) shared. And referring now to this symposium's opening query, the one that asks me to reflect on the principles affecting my approach to my own work, I can say that the same emphasis shows up here: if access to my own deeper seriousness is what my work allows me, is in fact what my work more or less continuously and reliably incites me towards, and if I value this movement and its accompanying partial-understandings, those intermittent slow-flaring lights in the dark, then it's natural that I should want my work to evoke (in addition to whatever else it may evoke) similar feelings in anyone who reads it.

Much follows from this, in terms of craft, in terms of theme, in terms of the audience I think I write for. Some of this relates to clarity, the need for, some to subtlety, the need for. "Write as though for a generation infinitely more subtle than your own," advised Stendhal. Good advice, up to a point, and I think of it often, for instance when I am deciding which way to take a given line or metaphor: towards a kind of transparency or towards some shadow-ier place, more demanding of a reader's involvement. In fact I suppose I really feel that there's no either-or here at all, that it is in the nature of good art to be subtle, just as it is an absolute of art to communicate, that is, to have some relationship to clarity. But there is a spurious form of subtlety abroad in the land which is damaging on all counts and is too seldom challenged on it, and which matters a very great deal, not because of the writers, the poets, perpetrating it — they should be laid aside and never thought on more — but because of the decent folk their witless works turn away every year by the thousand from the real experience of art. I'm speaking now of the alienation that an over-private vocabulary or an intimidating syntax/formal structure can cause, whether in the work of the latest, freshest-faced recruit out of an Olsenite open-field creative-writing workshop, or of some multi-published-and-awarded but equally hapless senior coterie-poet. I have no interest in poets who fail to take note of this danger (or who, if they do note it, are either so inept or so insecure that they persevere in their convoluted indirections, their narcissism; it's very often the case, anyhow, that having pitiably little to say they're simply trusting in the opacity of their page to keep this barrenness from discovery). They harm us all: writers, readers; they keep us apart; they prevent our serious speakings and our serious listenings from coming together.

Enough of that. My point: clarity matters, subtlety matters, it *is* possible to be both demanding (of one's reader) *and* accessible, it *is* possible to speak suggestively and elusively *and* at the same time in a recognizably human voice. Not just possible, *necessary*. Or so I think.

Much more to be said about all this, of course. This seems to be what is closest to my mind at the moment.

July 1988
Cambridge, England

KEATH FRASER

When Is Style Moral?

If a writer's style pleases us there is usually something deceptive about its spontaneity. What we know of style suggests that unlike personality, say, it is an act of deliberation, second thought, correction — and not really spontaneous at all. In this way style, I think, is closer to character than to personality: to the shaping of character (the writer's own) but also, in the case of fiction writers, their own imaginary characters. Character is moral in a way personality isn't. You can say that personality is pleasing, for example, but you cannot call it moral the way you do character. Character is the quiet blooming of imagination and not the corsage at a ball. Personality is social and occasional; character private and persistent. The one is necessary, the other inevitable. Character accepts revision endlessly without feeling threatened. In this sense it is masochistic but not tortured, working toward the day of its release. Getting knocked about appears to cheer it up, perversely, and instead of losing spontaneity it bit by bit acquires it. This is the paradox of style, the essence of its deception: the surprising lack of bruises. (You can detect writing of personality because there is something specious about its desire to be tough in the company of straw men. It curries acceptance for congenial outspokenness and shuns self-imposed scruple.) Personality is constantly at risk from entropy; but character works against disorder, uniformity, collapse. Something unnatural in character wants to dissent from natural law. It chooses over and over not to fizzle out. Refuses to give in to time, a deadline, above all death. Art is long, we know, and around art as around character the decisions for melioration are endless. Style is moral, you conclude, when it has made of choice a world.

August 3, 1988
Vancouver

LINDA SPALDING

Scraps

A warm day, full of moist air and the urgent call of crows and I am back in my grandmother's steady house. The sound of crows will always resurrect her for me because, like smells, sounds are recreators of lost places, places that live in the bloodstream and in the deep, unconscious part of the brain. Crows and hand-pushed lawn-mowers and streetcars — their rockety clanging — and the uphill hum of a treadle-fed sewing machine; those sounds live in the same pool where swims, like a giant, overlooked creature, my grandmother's method of letting me be.

She was a tall woman, her hair perfect white and her skin like fine cloth. None of us — daughter, granddaughter, great-granddaughters — has inherited this texture. But I have her shape and her great-granddaughters have it too. I don't remember her as cheerful or sombre. She was simply steady, methodical, and canny. Having no sense of herself as a creative being, she was miraculously able to dream up the way to make a thing or fix it. She invented pockets in the hemline of my floor-length flannel night-gowns so that I could keep my feet warm as I curled against myself in bed. Never inflexible, she changed her recipes with every baking. She made garments for the clerics of her church and for my dolls and they were equally gorgeous. "Why, I'm no needlewoman!" she'd remark, when we praised her, thinking, no doubt, of her sister's exquisite and justly famous clerical embroideries. But she'd make wild tapestries of the left-over church silks and velvets, mixing them with the secular strains of neck-ties and bedspreads and knotting all of this together with a medley of invented stitches. When I look at food or handiwork I still compare it to that odd mixture of grace and invention she brought to everything she meddled with.

She had a bird-bath in her yard. I believe there were more birds in those days in Kansas City than there have been anywhere since and that they sang and screamed and cawed louder than they do now. My grandmother, who everyone called Katie, fed a family of local white-bellied squirrels out of her hand. She lived in a small stone house where my mother and her brother, who later died in an airplane crash, grew up. Because there was no sign of my mother in that house, I never believed she had really lived there, any more than I did on my yearly visits. Both of us were ghosts, dreamers who took our books up to the sleeping-porch, a room surrounded on three sides by windows, just beyond which were the long, thick arms of some huge tree, probably an elm. It was a solid, unpretentious house, exactly like the houses in my Greek neighbourhood in Toronto; set well back from the sidewalk these houses are, with deep front porches and bay windows on the dining-room side. Katie's dining-room windows had a long window-seat, where sat at one end the cookie jar shaped like a rocking horse, and at the other her telephone. She always spoke on the telephone very formally, sitting erect in her deep Morris chair, and there at her side would be the clean windows and the polished oak of the window-seat with its drawers full of carefully folded linens for the dining-table she almost never used. There was a smell in that house of things made and saved, especially in the attic, which had long planks down the middle and thick stuffing on the sides into which, if I fell, I was told I would plummet into the living-room and ruin a perfectly good ceiling and my reputation and my back. I pictured this as sure and ignoble death — descending through the clouds of stuffing and the thin plaster into Katie's neat and unused "front room". It was confused in my mind with my uncle's death and with all airplane travel ever since. How could two weeks a year have so much impact?

Although my mother read to me nightly for years and always read stories from *The New Yorker* to my father as we drove any place, I don't think Katie ever read at all. My mother can't remember a time when there weren't books in the house and when she wasn't taken to the library to bring home more, but none of us saw Katie read. As a child she'd been moved from one railroad town to another. Her mother, as far as we can tell, was the one who demanded an unheard-of, scandalous divorce, after which Katie was packed off to an Episcopalian convent school where she was taught, among a few other things, to walk by stepping first on the toes and then rocking back on the heel. No wonder she escaped school as we all did, to elope, although she did it younger, at the age of sixteen.

My mother and I were allowed to dream in Katie's practical house while she put up preserves, mowed the grass, sewed things for women who occasionally rented her skill and for the church, which borrowed it, grew spider plants, baked cookies, fried chicken, and poured boiling water over the dishes she washed in the same tin tub she'd washed my infant mother and her baby brother in. The house was quiet in a way no house could be today. There was no music, no TV. In the summer evenings, we listened to a radio program and then turned the radio off, hearing the sounds of the hot night. Windows were open. There was an electric fan moved from room to room and gyrating slowly. There was a woman in a yellow dress, her hair swept up, her shoulders bare, in a beautiful brass frame on the wall. When I asked who she was, Katie looked surprised. She was the woman who had come in the frame. Alien to us, I imagined her life.

I read the books my mother read. *The Water Babies. Beautiful Joe.* And all the Oz books, which had been purchased for her by Katie when they were banned from midwestern libraries because of their populist convictions. I set up an office in my grandmother's front bedroom and furnished it with my grandfather's legal stationery, and I was left alone at the old schoolwork desk for hours. Nothing about my visits was surprising but our solitude. My grandmother lived alone. Her dead husband and dead son were photographs, her daughter lived in another state. I must have been what she cherished most or most looked forward to, but she mended her broken steps and shutters and furnace and left me alone. She had no social life except for a few small words after church, no novels or soap operas. There was the radio for company, and her work. Hers was the only life I knew that was sufficient unto itself, and her work, therefore, her creations, were made for reasons other than the ones I was familiar with at home. Katie did what she did without an audience. Her cookies sat uneaten in the rocking horse. Her watermelon pickles and her candied ginger and orange peel sat in boiled jars on paper-covered shelves. Why was there so much whimsy in her craft? Why did she make those crazy quilts at all? Why in her solitude did she leave me to mine on those long summer days when our only excursion was an annual one to Swope Park on the streetcar with a picnic basket full of food? Other days I rummaged through boxes in the attic or sat at the schoolwork desk or lay, on those furious, hot afternoons, in the claw-footed bathtub talking to myself for hours, inventing houses, peopling them with characters who had habits and wardrobes and possessions and delicate conversations. Perhaps my grandmother, in the hot kitchen, did the same, moving her lips silently around things she imagined or remembered as she silently mouthed the hymns at church. At any rate, without a word, she taught me to survive divorce, run my own house, raise my two daughters, and make my own crazy quilts without succumbing to the terror that was always underfoot. She taught me to enjoy my solitude and use it, keeping paper handy to record the things that I imagined or remembered when there wasn't anybody there to tell. Maybe, I think now, maybe I chose that solitude that has become essential to me. Inside it, I am sure of where I am. Maybe for the same reason I chose this house with its old brick walls and the huge tree that shadows my bedroom window and the grandmother across the street who wears black shoes and stockings, a black dress, and a black kerchief on her head. When she carries her large grandson in his bright jacket she looks like a crow with a large blue bead in its beak. How wasteful not to make up that last piece of purple Easter cloth, that piece of velvet from the doll's cape, and the taffeta that is a remnant from a dress, the lining of the cape, and who knows what else. How wasteful to let all those scraps and pieces go unused. All those bright things we bring with us from one place to another — why not stitch them together and transform them? Why not transform them, make them into a new pattern? Even if it's put up in a jar and saved for nothing, even if it's a woman you never knew and only imagined, it's as close to immortality as you come.

October 1988
Toronto

NORMAN LEVINE

When I read your invitation, all I could think of was a sentence in a book that I reread two weeks ago for the first time in twenty-three years. It is the *Letters of Ford Madox Ford*, published in 1965.

I got the book in Fredericton, New Brunswick. I was there that year. And I must have read it closely and enjoyed it, for I reviewed it. But there was nothing in it that remained with me.

Now, twenty-three years later, a sentence in one of his letters sums up, very well, the way I feel about things:

> Life is a commonplace affair and it is only by piling one damn commonplace complication on another that you arrive at the tragic-comedy or comic-tragedy that life is.

I'm tempted to leave out "tragic-comedy", as I'm more inclined towards the comic-tragedy.

July 18, 1985
St. Ives, Cornwall

TREVOR FERGUSON

Silence as its own voice . . .

Thematic considerations are vital to me, although how I use them shifts from the norm. A book's theme becomes the novel's fuel, not its point of view. None of my novels would have achieved conclusion had I not been egged on by thematic impetus. And yet, by design, the themes are invisible.

Which is to say that I do not welcome anything interfering with the book's quest to find its own nature. If characters, occurrences, language are bent to serve any ulterior purpose, the work is being twisted out of its natural shape. That shape, cadence, appearance will be organized by the book itself, both by its organic growth, and by the pruning through (many) subsequent rewrites; that is, the book must discover a logic beyond the author's precognition.

No book deserves to be freighted with the baggage of its author. No reader deserves to be oppressed by an author's point of view. Any statement that can be entertained in another form — slogan, treatise, speech — has no business cluttering my novels. Step one, if you will, in proceeding to embark on a new book, is to identify the mind's bias, as well as the emotional gripes and joys of any particular season, in order to keep these out of circulation.

To start clean does not mean starting blank; it's a matter of inhaling an atmosphere not previously breathed.

Step two is rhythm. Feel the beat. Catch nuance like a scent. Live with it awhile, wait to see what images pop to mind. How much is being floated to the surface by the subconscious, how much is mere intellectual posturing? A time to make choices. If the scent, rhythm, nuance capture its author, we're on our way, mated for a spell, words our issue.

Other approaches. I work primarily in long form for a reason. I do not delineate: I explore. My pet peeve is authors who pit themselves above their characters, who assume that knowledge of that character's being is their privileged domain. Bullshit. Fictional characters must be as slippery as any living being: what is unknown is far in excess of what can ever be known, or supposed. In this regard, I'm suggesting that I believe in author humility. And I work novels rather than short stories because my preference is one of exploration rather than delineation, discovery as opposed to discourse. Epical.

Yet length demands its own discipline. I consider my work to be compact. Accused of exaggeration, I protest. What is occurring is a deliberate compression of the world into a narrower time frame, and geography, than is common, so that the world can be viewed without the illusion of the mundane, without the illusion of boredom, without the illusion of alienation from itself: without illusion. I fudge time, and distances, but don't seriously mess with reality.

The reason is twofold. Condensing the world, pressing it within a limited geography and time, allows the reader to act as the book's release valve. What tends to come across as energy is, in effect, this liberation of combustible gases, the blowing out of what has been compressed. *Whoosh*! Which is really a compression of time; things *do* happen at once, rather than sequentially, as things do happen all over the earth at once. As well, it allows the writer to inhabit the whole world and all its ages simultaneously without that being a silly, or unworkable, endeavour.

The nation is the writer's perspective; but the planet's his map. An age his utterance; but timelessness can convey continuity.

Other conventions and assumptions. Despite the fact that writing is partly a matter of extending antennae, ultimately authors write from the core of their beings. (I think most writers would like to avoid that.) Yet it is the core, and the ability to get to it, that count. The cracks in the psyche that permit access belong to the realm of psychology, accident, and experience, and familiarity with that inner being permits navigation of the zone. Fiction is the vehicle into that underground, to assay and carve the rock. Many writers like to shirk (catching the note of anger here?) this *expectation* of writing, because this is the treacherous land, and its excavation cannot be faked, manufactured, or modified.

Some books support the interior sojourn better than others.

But this is the territory that I wish to inhabit, and the thing that keeps me writing when all manner of common sense would have me shove it. One side of a war zone. Political, psychological, societal formats are freely protested from any quarter, but the inner life is a spent flame in our society. And whoever takes the trouble has to return not with a jumble of dreams, or, worse, an analysis of experience reduced to jargon, but with the connecting links and motifs which detail the inner life as it informs the outer world.

And then comes craft, so that the whole thing is seamless and unobserved. And language, so that the whole thing has resonance, impact, and, when it is appropriate, beauty.

The best words are those distilled by silence.

Finally. Imagination is vital in its own right. On a fractured planet, wholeness is witnessed only through the imagination's 3-D viewfinder. Narrative is under attack where vision is diminished. Writing owes its roots to the story-teller in the tribal circle, cave and campfire voices, songs in the tepee. The writer's job remains what it has always been, not to point out persecution hither and yon (we have been relieved of that temptation anyway by the camera's eye, and the journalist's access), because people bleed without a novelist's description, but to reshape the evidence and outcry and lament, forge identity always with the human heart, and whisper again that every solitary human transgression is individual long before it is corporate, bestial long before it is bland. The human gut and heart (dare I mention soul, that quiet rider?), musty, debased, passionate, resolute — whatever: without these there is only blither.

And never deny that a life is damned mysterious.

Silence can be known through its opposite twin, dissonance. The words come out from, and precede, the silence. They herald the silence. So that the silence will not be unheard on a noisy planet. And, when heard, will not be noise.

June 1988
Montreal

RACHEL WYATT

Where I Live

There is a vivid soundscape on my street, children playing, neighbours chatting, cars going by, trains in the background. These voices and sounds as well as others I have heard in places as different and as far apart as Banff and Baffin Island are the stuff of radio drama. Radio is a near-perfect medium for a writer. All those phrases and places and characters which juggle for space in our heads can be brought together to convey the state of fear and muddle and hope in which most of us exist.

I came only lately to writing for the stage. I try to set out those scenes in our lives when we go about our daily business often deeply involved in the trivial, heedless of sixteen-ton weights which hang Monty Python-like over most of our heads. The dangerous comedy of manners.

When I began to write, my children were very small. For years I wrote very short pieces. I never touched the typewriter on weekends, during school holidays, or at times of family crisis. (Some years this led to very little writing.) And when people asked me then why I wrote, I would shrug my shoulders and say, "Because they wouldn't employ me in Loblaw's as a check-out person," or some other flippant thing.

We talk about this from time to time, my friends who are writers and I. Why *do* we write? None of us is rich, so it is not for the money. None of us has had to bear the burden of great fame, so it is not for that. But there is a moment in this ritual conversation when we smile at each other in a secretive way and shut up. We have reached the point of almost admitting that we are, in a discontented way, content with what we do. That for us there can be nothing else.

I live on a very short street, forty-two houses. The people in the houses are various. There are men and women from Eastern Europe, Western Europe, and the United Kingdom, as well as people who were born here. Some have families and are trying to create a future; others lead quietly desperate lives; one has withdrawn into her own language and speaks to no one.

Some of the immigrants on my street deal in broken language and broken images. An immigrant myself, I write often about people who are out of place. But on this street, as on any other, it's not only the immigrants who are displaced. The deracinated are a large tribe. A person does not have to be from thousands of miles away to perceive himself as the stranger in town.

Born in Yorkshire, I began my life by thinking that I came of a superior race. Not only was I aware that Yorkshire people are larger (except for those few descended from the pre-Roman Brigantes, who were short and dark and square), but I knew we were better and cleverer than most others. As I grew into my teens it became clear to me that the rest of Britain did not share this opinion. To most

Southerners I was one of a tribe of oafs. Large, yes, but primitive, my brain most likely numbed from walking about wildly on the moors in the rain. And when I spoke, my accent confirmed their beliefs.

New in Canada, a young mother from the one-time Mother Country, kindly welcomed by many, I discovered that for a few the word Briton was a pejorative term. My accent was wrong again! Moving around, living in Niagara Falls, in Oakville, in Montreal, in Fenwick, though returning always home to Toronto, I met many aliens, and not all of them were from far away.

In my novels I attempt to describe all kinds of dislocation, not only the effect of the new place on the newcomer but the immigrant's effect on the place of choice. All immigrants try not only to adjust to the landscape but also to make it fit their specifications like some Procrustean bed. And in this alteration of the landscape, this putting back together, nearly always wrongly, of broken pieces, I find the comic and sad and sometimes surreal backdrop for my fiction.

Since, generally, it was better for me to keep my accent to myself, I began to speak through the voices of others.

August 11, 1988
Toronto

STEPHEN SCOBIE

Your survey contains a question about literary theory, and how we as writers, or as academics, respond to the remarkable rise of interest in theory over the past few years. For me personally it has been the most exciting and stimulating thing to have happened in years (even if one of its effects has been to make me very suspicious of phrases such as "for me personally"). It has transformed the criticism and teaching of literature in dramatic ways; perhaps less obviously, but no less critically, it has informed my own writing and the ways in which I read my contemporaries.

I am aware, of course, that theory has met with a lot of resistance, both from academics who are suspicious of its claims to override or modify traditional methods of teaching and scholarship, and from writers who are wary of *any* abstraction or intellectualizing of what they see as an imaginative and instinctive activity. Objections to theory have followed many lines of argument: we used to be told that it was a passing fad which would never amount to anything, and then suddenly we were told that theory was now passé, and had "had its day". (That day must have been somewhere around August 17, 1986.) And we are told, ad nauseam, that anything that theory says has been "said before", by anyone from Plato to Sartre. Frankly, most objections to theory bore me: they are so dull, timid, unimaginative, ignorant, and tedious. But there are two lines of argument that are serious enough to require some response.

One is the repeated assertion that "theory" — that amorphous body of various and often conflicting approaches which all seem to begin in "post-" and end in "-ism", with something French in between — produces a technical vocabulary, a jargon, that excludes all but a privileged inner circle of readers. I make no apologies for literary criticism's having a specialized and complex vocabulary: if language is the most complex of human activities, and if literature is the most complex mode of language, then it would be absurd *not* to expect that a serious and sophisticated discourse on literature would need a very complex vocabulary. It seems to me very naive for readers to suppose that an advanced discussion of a literary text would be any less difficult than an advanced discussion in nuclear physics or dentistry.

That is not to say that a specialized vocabulary cannot be misused: of course it can. Within the field of literary theory, as within *any* field, there is good and bad writing; and some of the bad writing undoubtedly takes the form of displaying "jargon" for its own sake, as obfuscation. But the fault does not lie with the theory itself, only with the way it is used. The correct response is not to say, "All theory is simply jargon and obfuscation," but rather to learn to read theory well, to read it with as much care, imagination, and critical attention as one would bring to a conventionally "literary" text. Again, this requires a great effort on the part of the reader. Theory *is not easy* — and I see no reason why it should be.

When I say that theory should be read with as much care and imagination as one would bring to a literary text, I am approaching the second great objection to theory: namely, that it constitutes an attack on the prerogatives and privileged status of "the author". At its most extreme, this is summed up in Roland Barthes's polemical phrase "the death of the author". Again, I see nothing wrong with treating critical writing on a par with so-called "creative" writing. These genre distinctions just will not hold. From the "theory fiction" of Québec feminists to the astonishing poetic meditations of Jacques Derrida, the barriers between these categories are collapsing: I would say that they are being "deconstructed" (properly understood, that would be the most accurate word), but doubtless someone would accuse me of using jargon.

What dies in the death of the author is not (obviously — but some critics are very literal-minded) the author herself, or even the use of biographical information in the process of criticism. What dies is the *authority* of the author: the idea that the main end and purpose of criticism is simply to recover or represent the author's "intention" or "original meaning". Deconstruction would argue, in great detail, that all such terms as "intention" and "original meaning" are highly problematic, and have to be rethought in much more subtle ways. In one sense, all that is being said here is that no author is completely in control of everything that goes on in a text: a point of view that has been recognized for centuries in the figure of the Muse. (Aha! you say, it's all been said before. Well, no, not quite: for "the Muse" would also have to be deconstructed.)

Some authors feel very threatened by theory, or indeed by any form of intellectual abstraction about their work. Fair enough: if that's what works for them, if that's the way they can write best, more strength to them. My own feeling is that the more one knows about what one does, the better one is likely to do it — but then, that's what works for me. My own poetry is not as openly theoretical or experimental as my criticism is, but the theory certainly does inform it. I invite any reader of my poem *The Ballad of Isabel Gunn* to consider it within the context of everything that Derrida has said about "signature". (But that of course is my "intention", so, while it is present in the text, it is not a limiting or determinant factor in any given reading.) Theory has enabled me to think about writing and language in new ways; it has opened far more possibilities than it has closed off. It is now a part of our experience of literature; to ignore it is not only stupid but impossible.

August 1988
Victoria, B.C.

JANETTE TURNER HOSPITAL

1) What is my literary aesthetic?
Here's a credo of sorts:

I believe in the slippery, dangerous, shimmering, salty power of language to confound the simplistic and to go on pulling fresh questions out of the hat.

I believe that somewhere behind such volatile and sliding signifiers as *truth, dream, reality, justice* and *injustice, victim, oppressor, loss, sorrow, redemption, love,* down at the end of the corridor of mirrors, beyond the inflections of history and gender, deep in the Platonic cave, there are numinous shifting essences of which those words are the fuzzy reflection.

I believe that the writer sets out on a non-stop and hazardous journey in search of those essences, driven by the same sort of obsessive excitement and fear with which Leichhardt set out to cross the dead hot heart of Australia and with which Franklin set out to cross Canadian arctic ice, and with roughly the same chance of success.

2) What are my literary ambitions?
I endorse Picasso's statement, made to André Malraux in a 1945 interview:
"I paint against the canvases that are important to me, but I paint in accord with everything that's still missing. . . .
"You've got to make what doesn't exist, what has never been made before.
"A painter should never do what people expect of him."

3) Do I see myself as a post-modern writer?
Yes.

4) What does post-modernism mean?
It is what happens when Diogenes the Writer, equipped only with lantern and pen, sets out on the journey mentioned in (1) above and trips over the lip of a Black Hole labelled: The Present (post-Einsteinian) Time. In the free fall down the rabbit-hole of literary history, Diogenes (her first name is Alice) finds out that time curves; that pockets of space are void of space; that a clock on a shuttle in orbit round the moon runs slower than a clock on the ground in Toronto; that sub-atomic particles (which are only particles when they are not waves) cannot be said to be at rest, nor can they be said to be in motion, but they do have *tendencies to exist* in certain places; that the Mad Hatter on a space-shuttle joyride returns younger than his twin, the March Hare, who stayed at the picnic table; that every few minutes one human being on this planet tortures and kills another, and that much of this can be watched on television, in the privacy of Alice Diogenes' living-room, in between a commercial for Labatt's Blue and another for high-fibre cereal.

When Alice Diogenes opens her mouth to describe this state of affairs, the same half-dozen Protean myths that she and her forebears have been recycling since the curved surface of time began come stumbling and lisping from her lypths.

She takes a quantum leap. She pours the same six stories into new, more adequate moulds. She pours them into Einstein–Bohr thought boxes; she draws off new hi-tech hi-clarity uncertainties; she twists them into totally new, totally unrecognizable shapes.

And Proteus (with Schroedinger's cat in his arms) rises up from the new moulds and says:

"Once or twice upon a circle of time, when Diogenes the Writer, equipped only with lantern and pen, as I may have said before said before said before . . ."

August 16, 1988
Kingston, Ont.

W. P. KINSELLA

I am an entertainer in the oral tradition. All my work is meant to be read aloud. A fiction writer's first duty is to entertain, in fact a fiction writer's *only* duty is to entertain. If a writer can slip in something profound or symbolic, so much the better, but fiction-writing evolved from the days of the caveman, when, at the end of the day, Ugh would stand up and say, "Listen to me. I want to tell you a story." If the story wasn't interesting, the audience would quickly disappear. It is the same today. The navel-gazers, and those who mistakenly think their own lives are interesting and should be thinly disguised as fiction, have a few dozen readers, while the true story-tellers have the large audiences. That's it. Except that the average book-buyer does not give a flying fuck about the overwhelming influence of French theory on current critical writing, nor should he. I'd be surprised if there are twelve people in North America who know what French theory is, and probably only a dozen more who would care if they were told. Books should have an audience before they are published; the pretentious few can exchange pretentious correspondence.

June 1988
White Rock, B.C.

KENT THOMPSON

No-Win Situation

My impulse is always to demonstrate — not analyse, or explain — what I mean by fiction, or the function of fiction in our culture, or its value to the great wide world. But then, if I felt otherwise, I wouldn't be a fiction writer, would I?

But that impulse is due, too, to an increasing suspicion about the value of abstract discussion, and that, in turn, is probably because I make my living turning fiction into abstract discussion — and I'm not at all sure that that's a good thing.

Look at it this way: every work of art that we consider — a play, a poem, a painting — is translated into abstractions the moment we begin to talk about it or write about it. We read a play, for example, and talk about it in terms of its cultural background and contribution, its place in literary or theatre history, its interpretation according to one of several popular systems of analysis: philosophical, psychological, Marxist, Freudian, Feminist, or Anthropological Linguistical. In all of these exercises we have translated art into something other than it is so we can talk about it in other terms. Then the other terms become valuable, and it is the other terms that we judge, not the work of art.

This is very dangerous business, because abstract discussions are frequently a means of avoiding experience. In my opinion, however, the value of art is in the participating experience that it demands.

An anecdote that might illustrate the point: The other day I was involved in a theatre exercise in which I and another performer were given the task of improvising on a scenario. I was a widower; she was my almost-middle-aged daughter. I wanted her to come home and look after me. She wanted to borrow some money from me so she could maintain her own apartment.

We went at the exercise more savagely than our audience of young actors expected. I as the widower had prepared a meal for her, my daughter, as a gesture of goodwill toward her (one point for me) — but had done it badly to demonstrate my need for her. She reacted by throwing the mess in the garbage. (One point for her for refusing to be intimidated or manipulated.) She then offered a perfectly reasonable compromise: she would come to my apartment once a week to clean and cook for me — meals could be put in the freezer, and I could take them out as needed. This was so reasonable that I could only respond by being unreasonable — and gamble on her love for her father. I said no, that I wanted all or nothing. Then I pushed my advantage: I gave her the money (one point for her), and threw her out. Big point for me. She could only slam the door as she left. (Half a point for her.)

What we were demonstrating, or embodying, was the old conflict which trades on love: I was demanding always more, saying that what she offered was not enough. It was nasty. It was our version (as we realized later) of *King Lear*. (The young people who were our audience were aghast at the savagery; they thought we must be immigrants. Honest.)

What we were demonstrating was a no-win situation — which I have come to see lies at the heart of all serious drama or fiction, because it demonstrates what abstract thought cannot: that human beings are damned to be individuals, and as such are tyrannized by their separate feelings and individual characteristics. *Of course* a reasonable person would have accepted the compromise offered by the daughter to her father. A psychologist would advise acceptance; Ann Landers would agree. But the father was not reasonable; neither was Lear. The individual need for love was too great.

But it was the experience of this scenario that was valuable — to actor, audience, writer, or reader — the experience, not the translation into abstraction. In Henrik Ibsen's *Ghosts*, Pastor Manders asks Mrs. Alving what she gains from reading challenging, unconventional books. She replies, not with an abstract model of understanding, but with the simple statement that they give her confidence.

Yes. That's worth seeking.

July 1988
Fredericton, N.B.

H. R. PERCY

The Lure of Language

I was captivated when very young by the magic of words, and knew I would be a writer. My voracious and haphazard reading was motivated not so much by a thirst for knowledge or a desire for vicarious adventure as by an intuitive response to the power and beauty of language. The reason I still write is rooted somewhere in that early fascination. Other motives emerged, of course, over the years: the story-telling urge — the desire to observe and record, to catch life on the wing; the need to air opinions; occasionally the didactic impulse. But these have always been alloyed, in some way, with that early perception of language as something more than the stuff of everyday communication: as a medium of art.

This duality imposes on literature an obligation to have meaning in a way that music and painting in their purest forms do not, but I sensed then, although I did not formulate the thought, that *how* something was said was at least as important as what was said. Stories by Robert Louis Stevenson were much more fun, though far less sensational, than those in the boys' magazines my parents called "twopenny bloods".

Because of this early obsession, I found myself possessed of a "way with words" long before I had anything significant to say. It took me a long time to discover that the grist for my literary mill was all about me; that nothing in creation was too trivial to be written about, because the "something to say" becomes significant only in the saying. By the wizardry of words, the humblest of human beings become more commanding than kings; without it, epic events shrivel down to inanity and towering passions fizzle in the mire of the paperback romance.

The process of writing, for me at least, is organic. In the growth of a story, events, moods, characters and the scenes among which they move, shape one another continually, and all are influenced by the language used to evoke them and to orchestrate their interaction. It begins with some thought or image tossed into the murky waters of my life's assimilated experience — of which language is part — and from that subconscious deep there rise, refined and often transformed by their long immersion, half-forgotten impressions and observations germane to the job at hand. Futile, therefore, to formulate "plots" or to prefabricate characters. Inhibiting also. With every sentence new alternatives present themselves, new doors open, new choices must be made which, if one's instincts are true, incline the work towards its ideal and seemingly inevitable conclusion. Any preconception serves only to slam all these doors in the face of creativity.

Art is a purely selfish activity. It cannot be otherwise. Any attempt to saddle it with a purpose beyond the fulfilment of its own potential is to submit to prostitution, which doubtless we all do in some degree: the furtherance of a cause, the dissemination of a message, the expression of an opinion. None of these are valid unless they are intrinsic to the work itself, spontaneous products of its organic growth.

But if the creative act does not have an audience in mind and does not seek to please it, if it does not anticipate the barbs of criticism, how can it benefit society? Perhaps because one's only window upon the universal lies within. The only reader I truly know is the reader whose tastes I have been refining through years of study and experiment. No critic could be more exacting.

It is futile and probably harmful to approach any art with a view to defining its function. It is a flowering of spirit that does not have to be justified, to be proved useful, any more than does the flowering of nature. It is there, and we each take from it what we will for our own enrichment. A work of art has certain properties, to which we as individuals bring our own perceptions according to our bent. It would be as ludicrous to say that the function of literature is to inform, to record, to instruct, or whatever, as to suggest that the function of a tree is to produce lumber. Literature will never be superseded by the advances(?) of technology any more than trees will become obsolete if we ever stop using wood.

August 16, 1988
Granville Ferry, N.S.

ROBERT HARLOW

I came to adult consciousness after I returned still young from the Second World War. One of my first discoveries was that I wanted to be a writer. Shortly thereafter I found that nothing I wrote would be published here because there were no Canada-oriented publishers, just publishers who mostly processed books accepted and edited elsewhere. There appeared no peaceful means of change, and I wasn't a revolutionary. I became the first in a lengthy line of Canadians who went to Iowa to find out how to write and to join America's dominant culture. Everyone who went from here to there may have learned a good deal about themselves and about writing, but I don't suppose many of us joined the culture. My own best experience was that I came back knowing for the first time that I had a country, that I belonged to it, and that, not altogether onerously, it belonged to me.

But finding myself a shy and untried nationalist was a bad fate in a country that had given up its film industry by signing a cultural trade agreement in 1923 that made Canada part of Hollywood's domestic market; gave away its book and magazine literature to the cultural consciousness of Britain, the U.S.A., and their branch plants; and relinquished the promise of its radio and TV to cultural accountants below the border. With no Canadian audience available, the choices appeared to be to quit, to disguise oneself as a foreigner, or to continue to write as the best kind of amateur one could be. I think my generation might have had for a while that sense of freedom that comes, as the song says, with having nothing left to lose.

But, whether I liked it or not, I was indigenous, worked then for the CBC, and was in touch with the best (perhaps only) sense of how to tell our story that we had at the time: the documentary, which, if you've got no culture, is the sanest place to begin. In short, the fifteen years from the war to 1960 was only a time of preparation. Then came — on the lyric and documentary side — Margaret Laurence, and shortly thereafter, going in another direction, the important young *Tish* group, who established both a seminal mimeographed magazine and an apparent conscious policy of importing literary theory and applying it to Canadian content.

Both these energies are still with us, and over the past twenty-five years we've created a literature that at the same time ignores and uses both. Again, in short, we have created a normal national literature that acts pretty much like every other national literature — partly documentary and partly energized by current theory, which at the moment appears to emanate from France. Frankly, I think it is only interesting that the French are back dynamiting the foundations of literary theory. It's been a habit of theirs since Flaubert and Baudelaire, through Breton to Robbe-Grillet and beyond. And if there's a lesson to be learned from this it is that each fashion achieves the status of the prick of noon and then soon loses its potency. Notwithstanding, these exercises are necessary and important. They signal formal exhaustion and are meant to reinvigorate western literature.

But our writing has so far grown mostly outside this sophisticated tradition because its function, the interior aim of the whole spectrum of our literature, has been to help Canada's colonized people become conscious of themselves as a nation, and I believe this has happened in both Anglophone and Francophone Canada.

A strong sense of this successful struggle over the past half-century has now let us see that we have established our consciousness of ourselves as exportable in its own terms. This, in turn, has allowed us to begin to join as equal partners in world literature.

My personal odyssey has run parallel to the one I've just described. I began as a disciple of Flaubert, Forster, and Faulkner, each of them a contributor to a mature literature in their own countries. They were authors wonderfully aware of their craft and appeared to me to be able to indulge in the art of the novel for its own sake, while I was only aware of the need to begin saying that it was okay to write about a place no one (who counted, that is) had heard of. So *why* I, and others I knew, wrote was clear, if at first hardly recognized in the beginning either in or out of the country. But *how*, and under the aegis of what aesthetic, were harder questions.

For myself, I've never given up believing in the approach of my mentors. To me, each of their novels had an aesthetic of its own, forged according to its purposes and needs. When we say "Faulknerian" we're talking content, not craft. His novels, from *Soldier's Pay* to *The Reivers*, use any techniques, borrowed or manufactured by him from whatever literary theory, that best allow his novels to get themselves told. *The Sound and the Fury* is still successfully avant-garde. *The Old Man* and *Wild Palms*, first published as alternate chapters in one book, are, when separated, two of the best-made American novellas (a form still little understood outside of Europe). And *Sartoris* is a straightforward family novel in structure if not in tone. All of the techniques and theories since his favourite King James Version were available and used by him.

My sense of my own work is similar. If my craft is secure and working truly, then that makes me free of any one theory and allows me to go about my business of becoming more conscious (an artist, by my definition, tries always to be the best consciousness of his/her time and place) and perhaps more useful to the society I'm happily doomed to try to help nurture.

August 1988
Vancouver

TIMOTHY FINDLEY

Who Do They Think You Are?
(with apologies to Alice Munro)

When the photographer arrived, I was not quite ready for him and had to call down from an upper window: "I'll be with you in a minute."

The cause of my delay was trivial and, soon enough, I had joined him on the driveway, where he was supervising the unloading of his van. His assistant had already piled a number of shiny metal boxes and coils of black extension cord on the grass and he was currently struggling with something. I could not quite see but certainly it was something white, with slats and a railing, and I thought: *how curious — he's brought a fence. . . .*

It turned out, however, not to be a fence but a child's white crib with high, slatted sides, a dirty mattress, and a bunch of old bedclothes.

I wondered aloud what the purpose of this crib might be — given that we had assembled for a portrait session.

"It's for you," the photographer told me.

"Thank you," I said, somewhat flabbergasted. "But why?"

The photographer laughed. "It's not for you to keep," he said. "It's for you to be photographed in."

"I beg your pardon."

The alarm I felt in that moment can barely be described. Visions of the notorious photographs of Carroll Baker, when she was playing Tennessee Williams' *Baby Doll*, rose up before me. These were the pictures in which Ms. Baker, wearing nothing but a pair of baby-doll pyjamas, had been posed as Williams' thumb-sucking, semi-retarded, sexually provocative heroine in a white metal crib exactly like the one now sitting on my lawn, waiting for me to climb inside while the camera clicked.

But what had Baby Doll Carroll Baker's crib to do with me and the purpose of our photo session?

"It wasn't my idea," the photographer protested when I had put this question. "The editor thought . . ."

Aha!

The editor thought was all the clue I needed.

I smiled. "I see," I said. "Well — I'm sorry your assistant has gone to all the trouble of setting it up, but you can tell him to take it apart."

The crib was duly dismantled and I never saw it again.

Later, over lunch, the photographer explained that the crib had been intended to represent my supposedly unhappy childhood. I was to have been posed in such a way — perhaps standing upright in the crib with my arms extended to the sky — that a caption might describe the scene as *Author rises triumphant from the trauma of his child-hood!*

"What might I have been wearing if such a photo-graph had been taken?" I asked. I could not get rid of the image of Carroll Baker in her pyjamas. But I need not have worried.

"I was told to ask for naked," said the photographer. Now why didn't I think of that?

The article for which the photographer had been commis-sioned to take what turned out to be an excellent sequence of pictures had been written by one of Canada's leading academic biographers. The thesis upon which this article flourished had to do with the assumption that all writers of fiction are merely working out their psychological prob-lems while creating their stories and novels. In my case, so the theory went, the darkness in most of my work stemmed from the darkness hidden in my childhood.

True, I should have been forewarned. All through the sequence of interviews during the course of this aca-demic's search for the real Timothy Findley, there had been an inordinate number of questions about my child-hood. Not what I would call a great deal of interest had been shown in the rest of my life. The fact is, yes — there had been trauma in my childhood; specifically, around the age of two or three. One thing that happened then involved a baby brother who had died in a moment when I was also deathly ill. It seems to me, however, this trauma might have affected my parents more than me.

It did affect me in one way, however. Indirectly, the death of my brother may have saved my life. My mother, it seems, was determined not to lose two children in the same venue — and when the doctors said they could no longer help me and that I was going to die, my mother said: "Die, maybe — but not here." And she took me home. Almost at once I began to recover.

Perhaps the interviewer had been just a bit too delighted to have stumbled upon this story. It provided the perfect basis for the theory that the travails experi-enced by some of my characters arose out of my own early difficulties. The only trouble was that one day the inter-viewer arrived and said, with some alarm: "The most terrible thing has happened."

"Yes?" I said. "What?"

"I went to the hospital records, just to be sure we had the dates right, and I discovered that . . ." Here there was a dramatic pause. And then, "you never had a brother who died."

"I beg your pardon?" I was laughing.

"I'm afraid it's true. *You never had a brother who died.* Besides which, *you were never ill*. What," the interviewer asked, "am I going to tell your mother?"

I heard myself saying: "I'm not sure I understand what you mean by 'What am I going to tell your mother?'"

"About the fact that she never had a baby who died! About the fact that you were never ill! About the fact that for over fifty years your mother has lied to you!"

Goodness.

What had started out being funny was now patently crazy. Here was this person who barely knew me telling me that one of the basic truths of my parents' lives was, in fact, a lie. "The hospital has no record of it!" I was told.

"Go back," I said, "and try your exercise in research again."

"But the hospital . . ."

"Go back," I said. "And try again."

The next day I received a telephone call. "I apologize," the interviewer said. "Of course there was a child who died — and your illness did occur."

"Thank you," I said.

"I'm so relieved. I cannot tell you how relieved I am."

"Why?" I said.

"Well, now I don't have to explain all this to your mother. How she lied and everything. . . ."

Somehow, I hadn't thought such an explanation would ever need to be forthcoming.

On the other hand, a certain image persisted. Perhaps the editor had the wrong person in mind when he saw me rising triumphant from the crib. I mean, the trauma of my childhood. Such a photograph might have been more appropriate if the subject had been my would-be biographer. Perhaps in baby-doll pyjamas . . .

June 29, 1988
Cannington, Ont.

PAULETTE JILES

Fast Fish

I write because I always heard people speaking well and talking really good talk and then it disappeared into thin air and was never heard from again and I thought I would like to seize onto it. And also because I had so many adventures in my head and these are easier to work with if you get them on paper.

And then thirdly there are beautiful language expressions and cross-correspondences that arrive like fish up out of places you can *hardly imagine*. You have to be fast to get these.

October 11, 1988
Malta, Montana

ARITHA VAN HERK

A Re/position on Death

Writers ought never to forget that the ultimate position is beneath, below. We stand beneath the stars, the sun, beneath our own pasts and implacable futures. Underground, even. Beneath the surface of the skin, be that skin earth or sky, flesh or the imagination, our torrid progenitor. For even abhorring it, the best position is beneath, the proper or appropriate place under, whether that be baseball and the ball or the movement of the trombone's slide and the fingers. These dispositions or arrangements of the body, these positional variants, linguistic and otherwise, whatever brings them about, life or sex or death, or even that most blamable of all blames, civilization and what we have done to it — used always as metaphor or excuse, when in fact we are all under the sky of the world and we are all making love to our imaginations, whatever our accidents of birth — become the crucibles of our words.

I write underground, a mole or more appropriately a gopher, tunnelling quietly through the earth of being and language, although I know so little philosophy I am ashamed, just as I am ashamed of the poverty of my expression, that I have not the tongue to celebrate properly the incandescence of this beneathedness. It is beneath that looks us up, points our chins toward the stars or the beclouded sky — looking toward heaven, light, the possibility of angels (ah, Handke knows that angels are sad, sad, gloriously sad, that they sorrow with us, that they long for the taste of coffee, however bitter and black it scalds). And the absolute certainty of death.

All too much has been said about death and writing. Too glibly, too easily it slips into our alliances, when we ought to take care, step softly, take care.

— "we wish to command and resurrect (pay homage to) the dead." (Butor)
— "the figures of fiction, both fat and starving, stand in awe of the brooding face of death." (Fraser)

Oh yes, we die. Oh yes, we do, we will, we die by inches every day, our skin sloughing itself, our brain quietly losing information, our lungs gasping from the uphill climb, and even that old mother of invention failing us. We fail. And yes, "in every parting scene there is an image of death" (Eliot), and yes, "there is not room for death" (Brontë). But, but, but. We romance that dying, rush it into our writing, make a virtue out of death and titter our way through its palpitations, thinking, oh, what a lovely effect. And fail to die at all, having made that most private of acts a public speculation. But why not? If fiction is one of our minor triumphs over death, why not put death into fiction? And how can we progress a fiction with death in our eyes? Enscribement seems the only solution.

And oh, although the flesh dies, flesh never dies, and being flesh must die, and dying must be part of flesh and so part of the fictions of the flesh. How then to *restez calme* in that eye of the flesh's hurricane, dying and waiting for death to come. And so, all our feverish embodiments to create on the page an othered life, longer-lasting than our own. This too has been said too much — that writing is an act of need, to make a mark, to say, "I was here." The human person's ego paramount and rising. And feeding too the insatiable and prurient curiosity of the reader, the repeated wish to drag away the clothes the author puts on words. That reader's search for the author beneath the stones of words, the author, if ever him or herself daring to renege on authordom, as I often wish to deny my maimed and abortive children who tumble clumsily upon themselves in their need to recount a story. In their surge toward death. For which we all need consolation, reassurance, even assistance, a good push in the right direction. So death has become our high priest, our confessor, our great mystery, our apologist. Everything is dying, we lament, and bend our knee. And there is good reason, isn't there? As John Fowles has his playwright/scriptwriter ponder in *Daniel Martin:*

> It had become offensive, in an intellectually privileged caste, to suggest that anything might turn out well in this world. Even when things — largely because of the privilege — did in private actuality turn out well, one dared not say so artistically. It was like some new version of the Midas touch, with despair taking the place of gold.

Can there be a substitute for despair? And are not knowledge and despair the same?

I almost inevitably wish that I could be declared legally dead until a good five years after one of my books is published, in order to escape the consequences of words, both prizes and punishments. That is, of course, a coward's sentiment, but the inevitable follows: I am a coward. The exaggerations of fiction are the purview of good cowards, a way to insist on their own safe otherness from the extant world. At the same time, they offer an almost impervious watchtower from which to snipe at the world, that ungrateful and relentless domain of non-fiction. Which might be why we dwell on death so pleasurably.

But let me speak the voice of doom. Death is a theory, the most dangerous of all, and the most tempting. And there is scant label that can accommodate its reach.

So call on death to justify the fiction, to fence the real, to compilate the myriad bad-breathedness of characters who *will* annihilate themselves, come hell or high water, no matter how we insist on them jumping into the one available lifeboat, clinging to the drifting spar (? — wrong kind of wreckage) from the *Titanic*. Death underwrites us all, and gives the nod to realism with a relish that I can only find suspicious. The fact is, death is a fiction, and however we enlist it to our cause, use it to shore up our puny aspirations for immortality, blame our pedantic realism on its presence, death is extremest fiction, the world we do not know, a world we have not entered. Using it as justification for the vagaries of fiction is as great a meta-fiction as the most common of all possibly common postmodernist ploys citing their own mirrored fictionalizing within the text they make. And in the fictions of death, we mongers of its potential, we miners, we scavengers on its hopeful bonepile, are as fictional fictioneers as the most insistent of narcissistic poseurs. Death *is* a happy ending, goddamn it, the one ending we know but cannot know, the loveliest of endings because it is utterly imaginary.

And however much the moral police of fiction may use it as their backstop (dear god, I hate baseball), its fictional justification is as vindicatory as the theory that would make us see all language double, make us duplicate all language into the pinpoint of perspective. We are talking usage here, employment. How close do vindications and propagandas come? And oh, we usurers, we fictional fictioneers, how dare we claim death's territory as our own when it be as theoretical as the breath of language? Except that we know it happens, and it will happen to us, it will, it will, and perhaps to our words too.

1988
Calgary

SEÁN VIRGO

fiction

We are all, endlessly, quoting. Sorting through grave dust for new configurations which Time finds anyway were always predicted. The more we are genuinely original and distinctive, the more we are linked to our roots.

Grave dust. Auden said writing is "to break bread with the dead". I quote a dead man quoting a dead man who quotes a dead man: Berryman, Kierkegaard, Hamann. Two voices: "Write." "For whom?" "For the dead whom you loved." "Will they read me?" "Yes, for they return as posterity."

They watch at your shoulder. The only audience. Telling you if at least you are working in good faith.

Each of us has their beloved dead. Some we delight in, some we honour. Even those who excited us once, whom we've now grown out of. For we *have* grown out of them.

The enemy is a sense of the *other* audience, across the desk. The reader is to be created by our work, not stroked, confirmed, or reassured by it. Still less to be judge of its correctness, relevance, morality.

We may write *out of* moral or political conviction, but we cannot write about it. That discourse is for our lives, not our work. The dead again: Blake's Memorable Fancy, the voice of Isaiah: "My senses discover'd the infinite in everything, and as I was then perswaded, & remain confirmed, that the voice of honest indignation is the voice of God, I cared not for the consequences, but wrote."

The real task is to create worlds that *work*. More grave dust — the Baron rummaging in graves to assemble whole, beautiful creatures. It can be grotesque, it will never be pretty — but it's not impossible. Life can be created.

The only things which save Dante are his language and the fact that some of his victims *breathe*. Paolo and

Francesca subvert the *Commedia*'s moral structure by the pity they wrench from us.

Olivier and Guthrie stood on the Thames Embankment. "Oh well," Guthrie said. "If you don't learn to love Iago, you'll *never* get him right, will you?"

What else? Simply to love and dread the craft, never attempt the same thing twice, and exit laughing. For "Energy," said Saintly Billy (he was quoting the Devil)," is eternal delight."

November 1988
Holstein, Ont.

RON SMITH

From Beginning To Becoming

At this moment, the Second World War battleship *Missouri*, the great relic of the Pacific war with Japan, moves before my eyes into Nanoose Bay, is nudged and caressed into place by tugs, Canadian tugs, dwarfed by this piece of salvage from the rust heap of bad dreams.

The deck cannons are cosmetic, we are told by the media; this ship has been refitted with current hardware. Tomahawks, missiles, etc., that sort of thing. Weaponry is not my strong suit. Onlookers interviewed by CBC speak with breathless reverence of this opportunity to witness history in the raw. Golly. I just wish the guy on screen would take his hands out of his pockets, he's that excited. Erotic this sure ain't, I want to tell him, but he reminds me of the guys from my teens who drooled over customized cars, those with dual pipes, flames, balls, and raccoon tails. Just the thought of those sleek, low-slung, pussy wagons is enough to raise the hair on the back of my neck. (The top of my head should be so lucky.) But there were also artists, those who restored classic cars back to their original state. Who saw the automobile as something other than the proverbial phallic symbol. As large, motorized dildos, with stupefied pricks lodged behind the wheel.

But as I say, some saw beauty in machinery, it is possible, and loved their folly as others love gardens, words, fishing, story, etc. They saw beauty in machinery as some see beauty in ships. Artistry. But the *Missouri* isn't now, certainly, nor likely ever was, a work of art. It may have had utilitarian function in a passing nightmare or two, but now it anchors in our beloved bay with impunity and for many is clearly a source of recurring terror and bad dreams.

Our writers, those who challenge this "cordial transgression" (surely we can resort to the kind of euphemistic dodge that justifies "joint manoeuvres" under "bilateral treaties"), reject masters. Certainly many of our artists have discovered an individuality and liberty that dream, risk, and act our need to invent "songlines" that sing our vision into existence. Meanwhile, the majority of our politicians and militarists remain, sadly, confused and senseless in their irons. They, too, dream, but of ships that would be heroes. So they are enslaved by masters, by this scent of power, by what they fear. The self. The potential to invent themselves. To be huge in the world. Not to be a part of some diabolical machine.

So we must conclude that old soldiers never die. For many, the happiest days of their lives were spent in combat.

Perhaps this is why so many of the best artists in Canada are women. They are puzzled and sometimes outraged by the male passion to vanquish. To destroy, life! They understand that art is positive, constructive. Art doesn't avoid what is unpleasant, monstrous, or evil, but ultimately it manifests itself in affirmation. Women in our culture have understood this much more readily than men.

Too many of us still applaud the mass violation of the soul and attack those individuals who would encourage us in the collective celebration of the human spirit.

It is amazing that there are those who join paramilitary organizations or go to camps on weekends where they "play" war games. They tramp through forests, kill a few people, get killed themselves three or four times, and then return home to a dull life with the family. Better a few head butts on "Monday Night Football".

We protect those we consider misfits and invite others to assault what we cherish. Apparently we enjoy being mugged.

We claim to love nature. We tolerate poets because every developed culture needs at least a few hanging about the place. Inconspicuously, mind you. When will we realize that one addresses the other ? That our writers best articulate our "blood love" of the soil. Of the sea.

Tonight, as I write this, the first September storm is moving in, and the bay rumbles and groans as if protesting our violation.

Why do we tolerate the sons-of-bitches who would wage war? Or take their wages from war?

Why do we not embrace those who would have us love ourselves, now?

Our writers celebrate the love of men and women.

Our writers agonize over our feelings of bitterness and hatred.

Our writers are compassionate.

They understand the power of kinship and community. They have pushed beyond boundaries, geographically and aesthetically, in language and form.

The *Missouri* should be allowed to rust in peace, as the bumper-sticker reads.

Certainly Canadian literature struggles to accommodate all the current fads. Often it is dominated by world-view attitudes and consequently lacks spirituality and a sense of mythic purpose. It is stuffed with social purpose, which is *not* morality. Often it expresses our confidence in the social machinery of Europe and America, and, when this is the case, our literature is inaccurately mercantile. We fear the images that haunt our souls. We revel in those that reflect our daily business. We should distrust a language that merely reflects. The tricks done with mirrors can be far more deadly than those done with knives.

A sense of place. Canadian writing in many respects is about a sense of place. A literature of regions, which should not be interpreted synonymously with parochial. Inexplicably some critics view a lack of homogeneity as inexcusable. They would prefer that our literature emulate American daytime television. The soaps. Formulistic. They determine the aesthetic criteria; the writer conforms, or be damned. Even though mediocrity prevails, the critic is secure in his reputation, which was the point in the first place. More on this later.

Ezra Pound noted that "good writing, good presentation can be specifically local, but it must not depend on locality." Clearly, though, the role and emphasis given to place by writers varies, to the extent that it becomes a useful method of characterizing the difference between what can be termed "site known" (a term first used by David Jones) and world-view writing. The distinction is not qualitative, nor is it intended to be divisive.

Site-known writing is concerned primarily with the nature and experience of community within a well-defined landscape. A list might include Hardy and Faulkner; Marquez, Llosa, and Carpentier; and Canadian writers such as Ross, Watson, Munro, O'Hagan, Kroetsch. Perhaps it can be argued that site-known writing arises within those communities attempting to define themselves for the first time. Or is generated by a disaffection with old mythologies. Certainly this is true for many West Coast writers who convey the sense that they are discovering a literature of their own. They deliberately challenge the prescriptions of world-view writing, the kind of writing exemplified by Tolstoy, Dickens, Thackeray, and Drabble; and by Canadians such as Davies, MacLennan, Richler, and Atwood. Here the attempt to communicate a vision of a universal social and political morality does not satisfy the spiritual need that many writers feel to speak out of the unique images embodied in a specific site. It is from site that experience tends to be much more anarchistic than is implied in the ordered environment of the world-view writer. Solutions to problems cannot be legislated. In language and form it is an attempt to escape from a literature of heroes and villains, beginnings, middles, and endings, harmony through a received order. Site-known writing is a literature of process rather than system, of questions rather than answers. It is oral rather than alphabetical in its impulse. It is a way of coming to grips with historical tradition, conventions, and established mythologies.

It is healthy that we have diverse voices in Canadian literature. I despair when some critic would seek what he perceives as harmony by having us all think and write from within the same box.

In Canadian literature we have not yet learned the art of eating. Bouts of drinking, yes, but there are no great feasts in our stories. And we are still taking the weather personally. But everything else appears in order, in spite of the petty complaints of some of our critics. And there lies what must be our greatest regret. Criticism. We have too few good critics and too many who would establish reputations when given the opportunity to play the bully. It is okay to be disagreeable, less so to be the snake in the grass, but there is no excuse for being an insensitive and pompous ass. My daughter accuses me of swearing more these days than I used to, but how else deal with these cyclopses. Let them fashion thunderbolts but not hurl them until they have the wisdom, wit, and taste to be constructive. The critic's responsibility is to evaluate, with the awareness, as Pound suggests, that "no critic has the right to pretend that he fully understands any artist."

September 1988
Lantzville, B.C.

THE BAD TIMES

By *AL PURDY*

*I*t's strange to be talking about things that were momentous and important for you, occasionally even life and death for you. And when you get them down as words on paper, they sound commonplace. Or is it that after a bad time is over, you'll never duplicate such things on a typewriter? But I'm not trying to do that. I just want to remind myself of something. I don't know what it is. But when I come to it, I'll remember.

Al Purdy is working on a novel.

My wife and I had been living in Montreal for a year that ended in the summer of 1957. I was writing radio and television plays for the Canadian Broadcasting Corporation, with nearly a minimum of success. (I had to write eight or ten of them to get one accepted by hard-boiled CBC producers.) Eurithe worked as a secretary with the C.P. Railway for that period, sometimes showing symptoms of discontent with our situation.

We made a few friends in Montreal, mostly literary people: Frank Scott and Marian; Ron Everson and Lorna; Irving Layton and his wife; Louis Dudek; Milton Acorn; Ingrid Lewis; Henry Ballon and Annette; a few others.

There were parties. Doug Kaye (whom I had known while working at the same factory in Vancouver), Henry Ballon, and I made beer in an oak whiskey barrel. We produced fifteen gallons every five or six days, much more than we could drink. There was talk for a while of our home brewery becoming a commercial proposition.

Writers and a couple of painters. Marian Scott, Frank's wife, a very good artist. Louise Scott, no relation, whose work I thought impressive. A sort of bohemian art colony in Montreal, gradually becoming surer of its own abilities, or at least pretending to be sure.

We all made noises of genius of course: with the exception of Frank Scott, whose character made it unnecessary for him to brag. Louis Dudek had a direct pipeline to the one true God, Ezra Pound: and Louis was a carbon epiphany. William Carlos Williams also ranked high in this pantheon; but I was never able to appreciate him.

Irving Layton was the Montreal magnet for me: a large little man with a word for everything, never in the time of my knowing him was he ever at a loss. He seemed to hypnotize himself with his own voice, feeding on echoes of his own opinions. But warm, with a feeling for other people. And the warmth made the phoniness bearable. I felt about him as I had not about any other Canadian writer, a kind of awe and surprise that such magical things should pour from an egotistic clown, a charismatic poseur. And I forgive myself for saying those things, which are both true and not true.

Anyway: by the spring of 1957 it was obvious that I wouldn't make a fortune writing plays for the CBC. Alice Frick — she was some kind of executive producer in Toronto — had given all sorts of valuable advice and had accepted two or three plays. One of those was an adaptation of Thornton Wilder's *Woman of Andros*, a novel that shivered itself into my backbone.

My mother in Ontario was seventy-nine, and not in the best of health; she needed looking after. Therefore: Eurithe and I and our twelve-year-old son, Jim, moved into the old brick house in Trenton. It was a town of some 10,000 people. Eurithe's own parents were in Belleville, not far distant. She and I were both resolved to find a house, a plot of land, something of our own, after the feeling of having to rent the air itself in Montreal.

We were not entirely comfortable living with my mother. Eleanor Louisa Purdy: she had outlived the world of her youth and middle age. Coal-oil lamps for house lighting were replaced by electricity. Automobiles had nearly taken over from horse-drawn buggies and wagons. The roads around us were swiftly becoming paved. The people even *looked* different. Everyone seemed younger.

Her friends were mostly dead. Only God remained constant. He was the same. And she went to church three or four times a week, surprised to find the church locked tight on weekdays. Even her son — myself — was almost a stranger. And the town streets kept changing without warning; once in a while she'd get lost on her way to church, and have to be brought home by the town police.

The children next door, they were always shouting at her when she went downtown. She would smile and often give them pennies. But pennies would buy little in 1957; they wanted more. And the sun was so hot when she forgot to wear something on her head. Work around the house was hard, climbing the stairs so tiring . . . Alfred and his wife, they weren't much help. Off somewhere else in that red car, looking for something, always looking for something. . . . She was alone, except for God; she was alone.

The old red Chevy we had driven from Vancouver to Belleville and Montreal the year before made protesting noises but chugged on mufflerless. Eurithe and I explored the area within a thirty-mile radius of Trenton, looking for land, looking for anything, a place to end this displaced feeling. This belonging-nowhere-and-anywhere sickness.

Of course we didn't say that, even in the silence of our minds. The ostensible reason was more mundane: just a place to live within our financial means, which was around $1,200. (I had sold three plays in Montreal.) We wanted cheap land, a cheap house. . . . There was an element of desperation about the search. But I was a blustering sort of person, and would rarely admit such childish fears. Who am I? — saith the prophet, and What is the nature of reality? Sure, that's the sort of bullshit that droned in my head at the time. And it troubles me a little still: is it actually bullshit?

The south shore of Roblin Lake, a mile or so from the village of Ameliasburgh, in Prince Edward County. The place met most of our desired standards. Our lot bordered the lake shoreline, a teacup of water nearly two miles long. Dimensions of the lot were 100 feet wide by 265 long, with nobody else living within a few hundred yards. The lot cost $800. We paid $300 down to farmer Harry Gibson who owned the entire lakeshore. The other payments were to follow in two instalments.

Eurithe's father, Jim Parkhurst, in nearby Belleville, had suggested that we build our own house. He would supply know-how, and even some of the necessary carpenter tools. Obviously we needed a place. Co-habitation with my mother in Trenton was rather like a goldfish bowl, very little privacy.

James A. Parkhurst, known to his many friends and acquaintances as "Jim", was a study in character contrasts. Born on a farm in the Bancroft area eighty miles north of Belleville, he joined the army at age fifteen during the First World War. A lanky six feet three inches in height, with a mature manner and appearance: recruiting officers passed him with little more than a quizzical frown regarding his proofs of age.

World War I and the Canadian Army were the big adventures of Jim's life. He loved the army, romanticized European places, was promoted to sergeant, suffered serious shrapnel wounds, and was discharged with a pension in 1918. Disliking farm life, he became a door-to-door salesman for *Maclean's* magazine. He sold encyclopedias and whatever came to hand. Shortly after the war he married Ethel Ryan of Montreal. A production line of procreation was set up, and produced eleven children. They were still arriving when I met Eurithe in Belleville in 1941. She was the second-oldest.

Somewhere along the line, Jim Parkhurst had acquired small expertise in nearly everything imaginable. Hating to work for anyone but himself, he hauled cordwood from the north with an old truck when the sales jobs petered out. And he collected scrap iron for local junk dealers. The wartime shrapnel wounds had never properly healed, remained suppurating, and had to be treated and bandaged daily.

He was an impressive physical specimen, and possessed enormous strength. When I joined him for one of the scrap-iron-gathering expeditions, the lids of steel drums had to be cut out in circular fashion with an axe. He sliced out the sheet steel almost casually, with one arm, his expression never changing. I was little more than half his age, but I couldn't do that with both arms.

There's a kind of good-will ethos among some people. They'll do "anything for you", as the saying goes. In the country north of Belleville, especially in the fringe-quality farmland area, this so-called ethos is fairly common. People had very little money during the Twenties and "Hungry Thirties", but they helped each other at harvest time, made survival possible during bad periods, loaned and borrowed from each other as if everyone was their blood relative. I think it's one of the most admirable qualities of human beings.

Jim Parkhurst was part of this northern ethos, which of course is not confined to the north. (In selfish contrast, I've always had a strong feeling about ownership, the privacy of things, the inviolate object attached umbilically as a logical right.) Reactions to him by other people were not, however, always flattering. My own feelings about him were ambivalent. He was a puzzle to me at that time. My own somewhat sheltered life had not equipped me to deal with anyone like Jim Parkhurst.

These admirable qualities I've mentioned were only the visible tip of the Parkhurst iceberg. In many ways he was quite unscrupulous, and completely unaware of the dark side of his own nature. "I've never done anything in my life that I was ashamed of," he once told me. I interpret such a claim as the self-righteous quality some people have — of making either good or evil the same in one's own moral judgment. It means: if I did a thing or said it, then it's okay.

A large building complex was in process of being torn down in Belleville at the time. We paid $500 for a pile of used lumber, concrete blocks, studdings, beaverboard, and the like. Two of Jim's sons helped us dismantle the stuff and transport it to Roblin Lake.

At that time, if I had permitted myself to think of such things, it would have been to label myself as a failure. Despite the 1955 production of my first play, *A Gathering of Days*, by CBC in Toronto, I couldn't sell enough plays to make a living. But I refused to stop writing — not that anyone had asked me to stop. Eurithe didn't. I believe we both thought I might write a sexy best-seller one of these days; then we could retire from everything.

In the meantime, we stood on the shores of Roblin Lake, sombrely regarding this great pile of crap — I mean scrap; that is, reclaimed building materials. There was no shelter at the lake. We had to drive back and forth to Trenton every day. There was a shithouse, a small shed which I had adapted to this honourable usage. But the sunlit scene of lacustrine splendour was a bit grim in our eyes. Eurithe and I regarded each other that way, too.

Our personal relations were like that, somewhat wary and careful. Volcanic quarrels would be succeeded by armed truce, or a disguised tenderness. Sexual relations were always nocturnal, and occasionally resembled combat in their hostile preliminaries. But — let us say — there was love, although I avoided such words. If not, how could we possibly have tolerated each other?

Roblin Lake was turquoise and dazzling blue in mid-summer. Orioles, robins, sparrows, swallows, and gold-finches thronged our living-space, which was also *their* living-space. One morning on first arrival I saw a great blue heron stalking the shore, an ungainly native. And we saw muskrats. They pushed a wave ahead of them with their noses while swimming. It was idyllic. I looked at the delightful Eden landscape and longed for the grimy streets of Montreal. I was not a country boy, but a sallow-complexioned cigar-puffing expatriate banished from Montreal. It must have showed in my permanently dis-mayed expression at Ameliasburgh — I hate beautiful trees. Eurithe interrupted my contemplation of them: "Get to work!" The tone was imperative.

To build a house! My own carpentering skills were nearly minimal (I could saw a board more or less straight, and pound a nail without always bending it); Eurithe's were non-existent. We'd come across some architect's plans in a "house beautiful" magazine that appealed to both of us. It didn't look like every other house around Roblin Lake: a small A-frame structure with adjoining kitchen and bath. But in order to build on our lot, we had to prepare the land: it was a jungle of willows. So I became a temporary lumberjack, chopping, sawing, and burning.

After pondering, lucubration, and cogitation, we enlarged the house-plan foundation to 30 feet long and 17 wide. The A-frame section was 18 feet high, measuring from the floor to gable. It was erected on four-foot walls. And a 12-foot-square kitchen-bathroom was planned for one side. The finished house at that point was entirely in our heads, of course. And I've come more and more to realize: without Jim Parkhurst's help, it could never have been done.

His character was phlegmatic and almost unbearably calm; mine excitable and even mercurial. I'd come to him sometimes, despairing and despondent, with an insoluble problem. The difficulty would melt away and seem never to have existed: do this and do that in the ordinary course of building. It was almost possible for me to think I'd solved the puzzle myself: but not quite. He'd drive to the lake from Belleville once or twice a week, listen to our woeful account of difficulties. Our troubles simply disappeared in the face of his unchanging calm.

As will be obvious, I pondered the man. His mind worked on a different level from mine; he wasn't self-aware in quite the same way. To say that he was concrete and I abstract wouldn't explain it: he could at least imagine what our house should be, standing shadowy in his own pragmatic mind, ordinary as a bent nail. Whereas I thought the projected house was something marvellous, a factual dream of solidity. I think, therefore I am: I think a house and ergo the house am?

There was always a reserve about him, a foreignness even; some kind of dirt-poor grass-roots aristocracy, a northern nobility I couldn't quite understand. And of course I'm embroidering a bit here, searching for something about the man that may not exist at all. But I must forgive myself for doing it, since I'm saying as much about myself as about him.

Early summer, 1957. Eurithe and I stand near the shores of Roblin Lake. We measure the supposedly-equal sides of our house-footing with diagonal lines. That is, we stretch a cord kitty-corner from and to opposite ends of our wooden forms. Then we switch sides and do the opposite. This in order that all angles, lengths, and widths should match and measure true.

All this time, orioles and robins plunge the sun-bright air around us. They build their nest-houses in playful joy and love, without measuring a damn thing; ourselves in worry and suspense and labour. I grin at the thought, promptly messing up our diagonal measurements — forgetting to keep the lines taut.

Sometimes all the studding, fibreboard, planks, and nails danced in my head, like those ephemeral little flies that dance in bright sunlight. A dance of nothingness it seemed to me. And I felt dubious about the house ever being built. And I must do the things I do for their own sake, their own worthwhileness. Anything else was illusory. The poems I wrote must live in themselves, exist as entities and dance in their own sunlight. Without an audience, minus acclaim, even from a few. Thinking such things is treading gingerly close to a fifty-thousand-gallon tank of pure bullshit, teetering even. I wallow and rejoice in self-pity, my stiff upper lip is a dirty dishrag. In short, we built a house.

A mile away from our building site across Roblin Lake, the village of Ameliasburgh, once called Roblin Mills.

Owen Roblin, a United Empire Loyalist descendant, had settled as a young man with his family in the county's southern part. Riding his horse one day he happened on Roblin Lake (of course not named that at the time), and the settlement's few houses. There was already a mill, owned and built by one John Way. Roblin bought land overlooking the millpond below the hill. He built his own mill, married, and had sons and daughters.

I've seen Roblin's picture, taken when he was a very old man. I think I would have disliked him. Clean-shaven at the century's turn, with the look of a martinet, a domestic sergeant-major, pioneer become village artifact with an uneasy smile. He was the oldest postmaster in Canada when the photographer took that picture. Shake hands with Owen Roblin, our living fossil, the man who made this village go, the kindly boss of everything, a dead man whose name is alive on county maps.

The 1842 grist mill was the village's main attraction for me. I explored it from top to bottom, careful to avoid dangerous black holes in the floor. And marvelled at the twenty-four-inch-wide pine boards from the county's vanished forests. And carved wooden cog wheels, millstones, and rotting silk from the flour-sifting apparatus . . . Some dirty flour, unmilled grain . . .

I had the sense that those nineteenth-century people had just stepped out on some errand or other, and would be back soon. I could see the sunlit wagons, loaded with grain for milling, pulled up outside. At harvest time several wagons, the pioneer farmers joking with each other, their wives comparing recipes . . . Illusion based on an old reality. You realize you stand at the head of a long procession, the rear part of which is invisible, and those ahead of you do not yet exist, except as creatures of the flashing sunbeams.

When the stress of house-building lessened a little, I explored Ameliasburgh. As a writer, you made use of the materials composing your daily life and surroundings. My thinking went that way when I thought about it at all. Montreal and the Layton-Dudek-Scott-Everson friends were far away. I couldn't afford them at that distance.

Ameliasburgh had a post office and grocery. Fat, good-humoured Norman Sword was the postmaster, the person I saw most of in my yearning for city friends. The one main street stretched for nearly a mile.

Its architecture was commonplace: gables, board siding, and brick, with one stone house. And dogs. When I walked the mile or so to Ameliasburgh, they trailed me, and sometimes barred the road completely. Not little yapping curs. Cannibal dogs, seemingly hungry for human flesh. It was like facing nemesis or personal destiny, something you can't over-dramatize. And it was also a game of bluff. But you couldn't be quite sure of that. It was possible to lose two pounds of your own steak at a price you couldn't afford. I'd bend down, pick up stones from the road, make throwing motions, and hope. It worked sometimes: but when a dog faces you from six feet away, snarling at you with dripping teeth, it tends to ruin your sense of humour.

I talked to the old men about the village's beginnings. An ancient named Doug Redner supplied some details; the village blacksmith also filled in some gaps. It was like hearing a name, then having bits of knowledge about them piled on other bits of knowledge, until finally even their faces wavered through the dusk towards you. People existed there in the past, people with ambitions, anger and jealousies, achievements and failures. . . .

Below the highway and ruined mill, where the hill plunged down a hundred feet or so, there were still traces of that nineteenth-century village. Foundations of Sprague's carriage factory and several houses lay blurred in the long grass; a graveyard, some of whose markers reiterated village names; the millpond itself, black water sprinkled with dead tree-stumps, like an eye peering forward and backwards; garbage scattered down the hillside, a kitchen midden and repository of broken wornout things . . . Some village Babylon . . .

Once a week Eurithe and I drove to Trenton to visit my mother, a distance of eighteen miles. Her health and mental abilities were both fragile. She had made a last will and testament with the Victoria & Grey Trust Company. The will left me the interest on her money, while the principal remained with the trust company. At my behest, she made another will which gave me the principal. Some friends visiting us from British Columbia, Doug Kaye and his wife, witnessed this new will. But for the present, we had scarcely any money at all.

At our worst times, even food was scarce. When our new neighbours, the Eleys, ran over a rabbit, they gave us the corpse a couple of times. Eurithe's brother, Alvin, had the contract for removing garbage from an A & P supermarket in Belleville. Much edible food was buried in that rotting mess, and it was saved for us. Our sub-teenage son, Jim, fished the lake for bass and pike. Once he caught a huge eel which thrashed in the rowboat like a sea serpent. And once I shot a duck, and nearly threw up from the stink while cleaning it.

Among the most awful clichés that litter your mind: It was the best of times, it was the worst of times. . . . But yeah, it was. Both. The house became a ragged cobweb against the sky. We moved in long before it was finished; and really, it was never finished; still isn't. Eurithe and I poured concrete for the footings with a non-musical throb of cement-mixer pounding our nerves. And we quarrelled. About damn near everything. Name something we didn't quarrel over, and I still can't be sure we didn't.

But the house was important. We never thought of it that way, but it was. Our lives were involved and wrapped up in that silly house. Survival. When food gets scarce, that word survival lurks in the near periphery. Sure, Eurithe could have left me and taken safe refuge with her family in Belleville. But what kind of disgraceful defeat is that? You live, this is the way it is; make a fuss if you don't like it; scream at the world a little, exaggerate everything like I'm doing now. (Am I really?)

Alf Eley, our new neighbour, worked on the roads

for the township. Mrs. Eley (I omit her first name, because she was always Mrs. Eley to me) talked all the time. Mrs. Eley began talking the first time I met her. When I stumbled away, deaf and blind with the beauty of her wisdom, she visited Eurithe with scarcely a comma between past, present, and future. And brought us a dish of food, having surmised we might need it. And recurring echoes of Mrs. Eley have remained with me ever since.

Our half-built house was erected on low-lying land; after heavy rain the ground was flooded for a day or two. Jim Parkhurst and a helper were excavating a cellar in Belleville with jack-hammer and pick and shovel at that time. It was suggested that I raise our front lawn's altitude with the contents of that Belleville cellar. So I drove an old truck back and forth several times a day, loaded with limestone strata, dumping and returning for more. Our front yard became visibly higher.

And a box-car load of scrap lumber became available from C.P. Railway, courtesy of Gordon Parkhurst, a C.P. employee. I spent a week hauling the stuff to Roblin Lake, and additional days cutting it to stove length on an old belt-driven saw machine.

In Vancouver, and later in Montreal, I had always been a beer-drinker. Not a souse, someone who sits in a pub hour after hour and day after day soaking it up. But a few convivial beers with friends had always seemed a sociable way to spend eternity. But here I had no friends as such, only endless brothers-in-law and relatives by marriage.

Here I had very good health and strength, but no money. However, an abundant crop of wild grapes grew on countryside fences all around. For several weeks in the fall of 1957 our cottage industry was picking wild grapes and brewing home-made wine.

You could say that making wild-grape wine was labour-intensive. A bushel of grapes took six or eight hours to clean in addition to the original harvesting on farmers' fences. Ten-gallon plastic garbage cans replaced wooden barrels: pour them half full of cleaned grapes, plus fifteen pounds of sugar, add water to within six inches of the top. After a couple of days they sing a purple song, as if a whole hive of bees was contemplating marriage. Then scrunch the grapes to mush in your hands.

And presto, some invisible alchemist goes noisily to work on purple nectar that, if not divine, is certainly earthly.

During my top production period I had some twenty-five dozen twenty-five-ounce bottles ready to drink after a decent period of maturity. "Maturity" being when it was still working if I got thirsty. A night club near Belleville provided empty whiskey bottles, which it wasn't necessary to wash because of the previous alcohol content. From October to Christmas at Roblin Lake the house throbbed softly, an omnipresent alcoholic sound, a dreamy music that reached high C at about eleven per cent proof and sang to me in my sleep.

My mental condition was sometimes turbulent. I was sour and jubilant, depressed and ebullient by turns. Being broke continually was getting to me. As well, nobody noticed the poems I wrote. As much as I tried to tell myself that reward was in creation itself, my spirits sank at the complete silence that greeted my efforts.

However, I still believe it: if you don't enjoy feeling your own mind explore and create, if you must have continual outside stimulation, then you shouldn't be writing at all. And that is both true and not true; it's bullshit to some extent. One writes in a silent vacuum, and needs some small encouragement at least. But talking about writing makes me despair of saying anything relevant and authentic. So much is said, and nearly all of it worthless.

But those awful depressions I went through, sometimes lasting for several weeks! Poverty is like that. Reading Orwell's *Down and Out in Paris and London* and Norman Levine's *Canada Made Me* is depressing and exhilarating. To endure such experiences is to be transformed to a socialist or a nihilist. I was neither, but suicide sometimes did enter my mind. As something to think about, as a trapdoor if all else failed, as an ending for the unendurable present.

We ground it out, the time, the bad experiences, and poverty that seemed to have no ending. . . . At a later date I wrote a poem in the Arctic, on Baffin Island, one that seemed to say something about those bad days. It concerned the desolate sound of old squaw ducks, so mournful it's like a dirge for humanity. I was spending the night on an island in Cumberland Sound, inside a sleeping-bag. The Eskimo hunter I was with knew no English. I felt terrible. And those ducks were singing Mozart's *Requiem Mass* for Salieri in an eighteenth-century crazy-house. My line was: "I think to the other side of that sound. . . ." Which is really a lie, because on the other side of "that sound" is death, as it was for Mozart.

But what do you do, how do you stand it: poverty, failure, all the rest? There is no answer. You go on, or you don't.

My son Jim went to the country school at Ameliasburgh (and wasn't very happy about it either, which I didn't know at the time). Eurithe had her own kind of fortitude, which wasn't communicable to me. We talked, but not at the spiritual nails-on-the-blackboard level. I regarded her as a strong woman, myself as a not particularly strong man. I grumbled, made noises of protest and discontent in a kind of catharsis; she was mostly silent.

But we did reach each other on some unidentifiable level of feeling. It was not the ideal one hears about, the twin-feeling of male-female oneness. I'm not sure that exists anyway, that it isn't a much-wished-for myth. You settle for things, you make do: which unenthusiastic description is regarded as terrible cynicism by lovers lost in each other's bodies, and perhaps lost to reality. . . .

Three or four miles distant at Mountainview there was a military airport. The three of us, Eurithe, Jim, and I, scrounged its garbage dump for anything useful. It was amazing the good stuff we turned up. Boxes made of quarter-inch plywood; quarts and gallon cans of paint, sometimes only half used, black and red predominating; military emergency rations, instant coffee, different kinds of powdered milk and condensed soups, etc., all in little metallic envelopes for safe preservation. There were even small cans of vegetables.

This windfall of food joined our own meagre larder. The plywood was nailed to our living-room floor, in a kind of jigsaw pattern because of its different sizes. We painted it red and black from the garbage-dump paint, hoping for an artistic effect, I suppose. It looked like a checkerboard with odd-size squares, oblongs, even triangles made necessary when the plywood had been damaged. It was a job we enjoyed doing, making something useful from other people's discards.

On the surface of existence — if not underneath — we were enjoying life at Roblin Lake. Eurithe had spent her childhood on a farm near McArthur's mills, some eighty miles north of Belleville. As the second-oldest of eleven brothers and sisters, she had a more or less normal childhood — and I'm really not very sure what that "more or less" means. Perhaps family affection, relatives near by, berry-picking and swimming in summer, dogs and cows . . . Why don't I know more about her childhood? It seems inadequate.

Myself, I was a neurotic kid, and have a cousin's evidence on that point. Jean Woodsworth (née Ross) said, many years later, that I "was the most spoiled child she'd ever seen." It was probably my only distinction. I was an only child, and driven back into myself for recreation and amusement. I played with other children, and also joined the Trenton Library and did a lot of indiscriminate reading. I seem to myself to have created my own world, inhabiting several levels of existence. In none of these was I entirely comfortable, unless perhaps in the world of my own imagination.

Jimmy, our son, a blond twelve-year-old, was also very much self-contained. When he was at a very early age, his mother had made it plain that she intended to "raise" him in her own manner and method, without interference from me. Our relationship was sometimes explosive enough without me tempting fate unnecessarily. But the result was that Jimmy and I had very little communication. If he needed anything, whether advice or encouragement, he went to his mother. I was an intimate stranger, perhaps a person who stole time away from him with her that he thought should have been his time. Not an attractive picture, a recipe for disaster even.

But Roblin Lake in summer, planting seeds and watching things grow; doing a marathon swim across the lake while Eurithe accompanied me in a rowboat; working at the house, making it grow into something that nearly matched the structure already in my mind. . . . Owls came by at night, whoo-whooing in a row of cedars above the house; blue herons stalked our shallows; muskrats splashed the shoreline; and I wrote poems. Mrs. Eley showed up, unsurprisingly, bringing the gift of an inedible rhubarb pie, so sour it couldn't be eaten. . . .

And Mrs. Cannon, who lived down the long lane at the county highway. In her late seventies, with a no-nonsense voice other old ladies have achieved to hide fear. She lived with a male ancient in his late eighties, "for companionship", she said. The old man could scarcely walk, staggering down our laneway with a cane to watch the house-building, complaining about his infirmities and fear of dying. But Mrs. Cannon was sprightly, chirpy and bird-like; she was generous with her garden that first year at Roblin Lake. I remember her with affection.

Norman Sword, the village postmaster, was very fat; he must have weighed 250 pounds, and had a bad heart. Norman was genial. We got on well together. I'd stay talking with him until arriving customers made more talk impossible. Harry Gibson, the farmer from whom we had bought the lake property, would have been difficult to know. Irascible and reclusive, he once charged down on me when I left the party-line phone off the hook. His face very red, he charged me with crimes worse than murder in a shrill, high voice. I wasn't very polite to him with my own response.

The house was still a skeleton without flesh in the autumn of 1957: flesh being insulation, siding, paint, and other amenities. An old cookstove in the A-frame living-room supplied heat. We had scrounged coal-oil lamps for light (there was no electricity). Three of those lamps clustered together while you read a book meant your eyes wouldn't fall out of your head. But they were a smoky, dangerous fire hazard right out of the nineteenth century.

The surface of our lives was tolerable, bearable, even enjoyable, and producing occasional laughter. We were healthy, all three of us were, and a damn good thing too. Our original Montreal grubstake of some twelve hundred bucks had melted away, leaving a few measly dollars hoarded against emergencies. But ours was a permanent emergency.

A small chapbook of my poems was published that year by Fred Cogswell at the University of New Brunswick. He probably felt sorry for me; and I now think that little book was simply bad. (Alden Nowlan produced a much-superior first book the following year.) And I did a lot of writing in 1957. But poems about this traumatic period for me didn't appear until much later, during the early 1960s.

Winter, 1957. The county forests turned a brilliant scarlet and gold; the sky of autumn filled with hundreds and thousands of migrating Canada geese, squawking ceaselessly. And winter appeared without transition: Indian summer directly to frozen lake and miles of snow. We had to wake up at three-hour intervals to stoke the cook-stove when the temperature plunged far below zero. A few feet from the stove, wind whistled through openings I had neglected to caulk. My deficiences as a house-builder were very obvious.

Outside was white-magic: trees clothed in wedding gowns of snow, or a rattling armour of ice after freezing rain. When the lake had been in the process of freezing, partly covered with sheets of ice, wind lifted the ice at intervals, producing a sound like extraterrestrial animals wanting to return home. In deep winter and sinking temperatures, ice cracked with a terrifying noise as if a god were scourging the earth.

In the morning, when you emerged bleary-eyed from many-times-interrupted sleep to piss: the white damask was scrolled with a delicate tracery of artwork — animal footprints, bird hieroglyphs, your own deep-yellow calligraphy. Empty by day, the cold world was populated by rabbits, stray cats and dogs, squirrels and chipmunks by night.

When winter came like a lion, tiger, and tyrannosaurus combined, the lake we used for water became armoured with ice (it was three-foot-plus thick by March). I chopped through it with an axe all that first winter. When the ice was thickest, I had to chop a four- or five-foot circle in it, narrowing at the bottom to produce a huge funnel, from which water leaped upward in a reverse cataract at the final downward blow. I'd be sweating profusely as the work proceeded in fairly mild winter weather, discarding pieces of clothing one by one. At the end I'd often be stripped down to shorts. Mrs. Eley, observing me from her kitchen window, said I was "Mr. Tarzan". This flattered me inordinately.

But even in winter the weather sometimes turned suddenly warm. I remember one occasion like a spring evening, except that flakes of snow were drifting down softly as dandelion parachutes, and there was a luminous quality about the lighting. As if the white blanket was internally glowing, and a convention of white fireflies had decided that here was the place they wanted to sleep.

I was getting ready for bed, had removed all my clothes. Then on perhaps-a-whim put on my shoes and went outside into the falling world. . . . It was like being caressed by little white sparks, the touch no more than a ghostly awareness of touching. The feeling of having once had wings, or an additional sense beyond the ordinary five which enabled the possessor to be part of things instead of separate from them. But after five minutes or so the cold attacked my naked body, a thickening of perception and slowing down of movement. Retreating into the house, I felt as if I had glimpsed a human faculty we had lost when life was "dirty, brutish and short", but you could speak to snowflakes in their language. . . .

Money was an absent guest, also a necessity we didn't have. We were short of food, the car was empty of gasoline. Eurithe and I talked it over. "I'll have to hitch-hike to Montreal and get a job," I said. "Maybe," she said, "but not now, not when it's so cold."

So I delayed my departure until it got warmer. But it didn't get warmer. After a bleak Christmas, in which there were no gifts but good wishes that didn't cost money, January was a continuous Ice Age. I refused to think of how cold it was. Eurithe said don't go. I went, bundled up in scarf and overcoat; but no gloves; I had none.

It was Sunday. There were friends in Montreal with whom I expected to find temporary refuge. The sun shone like steel, a cold knife. I got a ride to Belleville. Another to Shannonville on #2 Highway. Then a long wait, and another twenty-mile hop eastward. One kindly motorist, noticing I had nothing on my hands in this bitter weather, gave me a pair of gloves. I was almost weepily sentimental thanking him. And I reached Kingston by noon of that January Sunday, while people went to church and prayed to the God of their fathers. . . . I stood by the roadside with thumb extended, wondering if it would help to pray a little. And decided it wouldn't.

Another ride to Gananoque, twenty miles east of Kingston. And there I stalled. Standing on the side of the road for an hour, for an hour and a half, for two hours, I lost track of time. Cold bored into my body; I jumped up and down to relieve numbness in feet and legs; I tried to think "good thoughts" and thought of food. I had eaten the sandwich lunch in my pocket, but food-thoughts made me hungry again.

After how long a time at Gananoque I don't know, and after no motorist even slowing down to examine me curiously, I switched sides of the road and attempted to hitch-hike back the way I had come. At that point I was feeling desperate and despairing, very very sorry for myself. The switch worked. I got a ride right away, and another after that. I walked the last six miles home. And entered the house ashamed. I suppose that amusing anecdote was my low point.

I'm bound to over-dramatize it, of course. But it's difficult to do that with the nadir, and what's lower than low. . . . Foolish grandiloquent writer reduced to penury, crying in his beer if he had beer. "Corpse discovered near Gananoque on #2 Highway"? Whaddaya think, Eurithe? "Would you like some hot soup, dear?"

Spring came, the birds returned, dandelions bloomed, frogs sang on the shores of Roblin Lake. The mating season, flashes of colour in the air, green and yellow on the ground, the sky blue and grey with sun and rain. Our financial situation was no better, but we survived.

During my year of exile from cities I renewed acquaintance with a cousin, Don Ross. A friend from childhood, Don ran an orchard farm between Wellington and Bloomfield in Prince Edward County. He'd spent most of the war in the Canadian army, the latter part of it plodding north on the Italian peninsula in pursuit of Germans. He emerged from the war an alcoholic, neurotic and often quarrelsome, his marriage broke up, and everything fell to pieces for him. . . .

Don's situation made me think how lucky I was by comparison. There had been a sympathy between us as children and teen-agers. Some of it still remained. We drank beer when I had the money for it. I listened to his stories about the horrors of the Italian campaign, which were indeed horrible. He visited us at Roblin Lake, sampling my wild-grape wine, amiable to a degree. But his manner seemed rigid; I felt his nerves were liable to fly apart at any time. He talked jerkily, not so much to me as to himself, his eyes focused elsewhere.

He ate dinner with Eurithe and me one Sunday, leaving a little drunken in early evening. On the way to his car I saw him stagger, climbing a little rise of land. I dashed out to help, make sure he didn't take a bad tumble. He turned, hearing me coming, fists rising and ready to strike. I stopped, bawled him out in as scathing terms as I could think of: and he went.

Later on I heard his girlfriend had been killed by a train, whose rail line bisected the middle of his farm. It was a curious story. The Prince Edward County railway spur was a "Toonerville Trolley" kind of train. It made only two trips a day between Picton and Trenton. Don's girlfriend — said to be his best friend's wife — had been sitting on the railway tracks when she was killed. Very odd! Something had been left out of the story that would make it more understandable.

Two years later Don was thrown from a horse, landed on his head, and was taken to hospital. He had been drinking at the time. I was about to visit him at Kingston General Hospital when I heard he was dead. His sister, Jean, said to me that she thought life had been wasted on him. I don't know. I remember our childhood friendship, and think of him now with strong affection.

Jim Parkhurst hated working for anyone but himself. He disliked bosses. I shared the feeling, although it provided no special bond between us. I am a verbal and rational sort of person — the latter to some degree anyway. Jim was instinctual, his speech slow and spoken after much apparent deliberation. When our house-building had been carried as far towards completion as it could be — given our low-ebb financial plight — Jim and I went on scrap-iron-hunting expeditions.

He drove an old stake truck, the same one I had used to transport gravel fill for our front yard and CPR waste lumber for winter fuel. We ranged all over the county in search of scrap metal, calling at any house whose backyard disclosed a derelict car rusting among the weeds. He knocked on doors or I did, asking householders if they'd like to get rid of that worthless hunk of iron which undoubtedly spoiled the view of their outhouse. If they did, we'd take it off their hands free of charge.

My own view of the world and time and human existence during that period was largely the angle visible from Jim Parkhurst's truck, limited and narrow. I've sometimes thought you can divide people into at least two camps because of their attitudes to life, whether buoyant and hopeful or depressed and down-looking. I was one of the world's losers at that time. I always expected the worst, despite a secret opinion that I was a pretty good writer. (No one at all shared that opinion.)

Among the more interesting questions that I now pose to myself: why and how did I change? Because I am no longer a defeatist, no longer a loser: I've expected to triumph at almost anything I do for years. Hooray for me, my psyche says to itself (if I needed to say it, which I don't). How did I change? Why did I change?

I hasten to amend and clarify any erroneous impression of my character resulting from the above passages. I think there is no way you (meaning me) can conduct your life over the long term that will not reveal exactly what you are. In other words, the way I screw myself up and lose track of my own thought in this sentence gives an unprofound insight into me (unless of course I revise the sentence later).

I think it is possible that if I were to act and speak in a particular way, it would endear me to women; people would shower money on me in large golden quantities; and I would be popular in all areas of society. All of us, we human beings, could act in such a way that we would be both rich and extremely popular. *If we just knew what way.*

But I would bore myself to death very quickly in such case. Having sometimes started a conversation resolved to keep my temper and patience in check, I nearly always forgot myself and lost both. Despite elementary politeness and manners, "I yam what I yam", in the quite unsuitable language of Popeye the Sailor. But somewhere in the past I changed from being a loser to someone who expected not to lose. At least not in the areas which I think important, having to do with human relations and attitudes toward my own writing. How and why did I change? One reason for this narrative is my own inquiry into that question.

Among the Parkhurst/Purdy expeditions were a couple to the Bancroft-Maynooth area with apples to sell. Despite its distance of only a hundred miles from Belleville, people there regard it as the true north. And certainly those northern people are different from those of more populous sections. They're much less prosperous for one thing, and perhaps a little more cordial. Jim regarded the north as something special, where nearly everyone knew him, and those that did loved him personally. He felt romantic about it. He had left to join the army when very young, and on return it seemed like a homecoming for him. People in the south were more or less anonymous, he felt; in the north they were human, with special, remembered quirks and idiosyncrasies.

On Highway 62 the paleolithic chin of the Canadian Shield pokes south to within forty miles of Belleville. (In the limestone county of Prince Edward there is, surprisingly, a small protrusion of the same Shield.) At century's turn the Ottawa government financed and built a colonization road through this area, called "The Opeongo Trail". The road was probably a mistake at the time, responsible for hardship and early death. The reason? Land there was only occasionally fertile enough to support farms; when thick forests were cut down, marginal grazing land was often the only result. But people rushed in to settle the cheap land, and once they arrived were never able to accumulate enough money to escape again. It was a rural trap, a grassy ghetto.

This section of the north has long been noted for weird religious cults, even witches. It's a northern Bible belt. Jim knew people's names; they greeted him with evidence of cordiality; many of them bought apples. I was impressed. Perhaps my own cultural education was given special instruction.

Eurithe and I both worked at Jay Sprague's Mountainview canning factory in 1958. She peeled tomatoes. I operated a machine which capped the twenty-eight-ounce cans. Earlier, I had picked tomatoes in county fields; but my back couldn't stand the continual bending.

My mother died that year. Since building our house the year before, we had driven the eighteen miles to Trenton every week to see how she was getting along. Her sense of time was mixed up; Sunday became any day of the week; her "Redeemer" was a non-paying boarder in the nineteenth-century brick house where I grew up. There was a little framed motto on the wall: "Christ is the head of this house, the unseen listener to every conversation". It made me very uncomfortable before my religious beliefs vanished.

This unseen guest seemed to have taken over the household. And my mother's health was worsening. Eurithe and I discussed things, wondering what to do.

But the possibility of doing anything was taken out of our hands near the end of 1957. My mother stumbled and fell in the upstairs bedroom. She remained on the floor unconscious for more than twenty-four hours. The neighbours noticed her non-appearance at windows and called police. She was taken to Trenton hospital. That long period on the bedroom floor had caused "pressure sores". Eurithe and I arrived shortly after she was admitted to hospital.

Three weeks later at age eighty, after removal to a nursing-home, she was dead. If we had been able to live with her in Trenton, I don't think it would have happened. As it was, my guilt feelings were pretty overwhelming. Understanding between us had always been incomplete. It seemed she had lived her life, at least the latter years, for my sake alone. It seemed also that she wanted many things from me, the chiefest of which was love. I sometimes felt beleaguered as a result, as if love could be doled out like a weekly money allowance. But that's a mean way to express it, since love is freely given or else takes the form of coercion.

Anyway, the United Church minister called on Eurithe and me at Trenton prior to the funeral. We talked briefly about very little, then I made a bad mistake: said I wasn't a very religious person. If I'd been watching closely, I'd probably have seen the man's face change expression. When he delivered his eulogy for my mother at the funeral chapel, his words were aimed directly at unbelievers, specifically me. And he knew I knew. I could tell from the look on his face, the eyes that sometimes looked directly into mine.

Relatives and friends of my mother had gathered in that chapel: the smell of flowers, the smell of people's Sunday best, the smell of the dead. I was very angry at that preacher. My face was hot with it. But I was trapped by circumstance, as if I'd been tied hand and foot. There was no escape. And I thought: if this is the sort of god and his representative on earth that my mother loved, that god is for her alone. In the unlikely event such a god actually existed, I'd mount an armed expedition to the Heavenly Gates to rescue my mother from his clutches.

In 1959 I published another small chapbook with the Ryerson Press. It had a title borrowed from Chaucer, *The Crafte So Longe To Lerne*. And by that year Eurithe and I were both certain that we'd finally starve to death if we stayed in this rural slum. Plans were made for a return to Montreal. Henry Ballon loaned us enough money to enrol Jimmy in a Quebec boarding-school. We lived with Henry and his wife for three weeks in Montreal. When Eurithe and I both got jobs, we found a place of our own.

Eurithe's job could have been called a "position" — secretary with Parke-Davis Pharmaceutical Company. Mine was at Johnston's Mattress Company in Montreal East. I had learned to operate all the various machines at previous mattress-factory jobs in Vancouver, but Johnston's kind double-crossed me: they gave me something totally unfamiliar — making box-springs by hand.

It was principally a matter of simple assembly. You stapled a spring to the wooden frame; you covered the spring with burlap; then cotten felt over the burlapped spring, with a tailored mattress cover fitted over the whole thing. Fairly simple; even a moron could do it; a moron did.

Beaudoin, a veteran upholsterer, worked next to me on the second floor. He was about forty, and used his mouth like a machine-gun, spitting out tacks for his magnetic hammer and talking at the same time. Beaudoin believed Jewish bankers controlled the world, and that they made wars happen.

On the floor below us Italian immigrants ran the

tape-edge and roll-edge machines, turning out mass-produced mattresses. Their English was sometimes a little thick and difficult to understand. French Canadians worked there as well. The cutting-room (for mattress and box-spring covers) was entirely manned by women, if one can so phrase it. A couple of those girls were very pretty.

Beaudoin was genial and likeable, but his anti-Semitism began to get to me. I started to drop seemingly accidental little hints about my own religion. I mentioned a friend's Bar Mitzvah, for instance; and eating kosher foods. He began to think about it, deciding that I was Jewish myself, and finally accused me of it. I didn't deny or affirm, but let him think whatever he wanted. And in Beaudoin's mind I became definitely a child of Israel.

But I couldn't keep it up; my brain was racing to anticipate what he would ask me next. Beaudoin knew more about Jews than I did, despite my having lived with a Jewish family and associating with others. I thought of asking Hymie Sloan, the Jewish foreman at Johnston's, for information. But I'd have to tell Hymie the reason I wanted the info, which was too much trouble. Beaudoin finally caught me in blatant factual errors. But for about a week I was a captive in Egypt with Joseph; and even climbed a mountain with Moses, and returned bearing the Tablets of the Law. It was exhilarating, since I was both amused and interested in the role I was playing.

Irving Layton, Louis Dudek, Frank Scott, Ron Everson — all the people I had known in Montreal on my first go-around — seemed not to have changed at all. Dudek was still worshipping Ezra Pound, the latter still incarcerated in St. Elizabeth's Hospital, New York, for treason. William Carlos Williams was Dudek's slightly lesser god. Irving was about to publish *A Red Carpet for the Sun*. His wife Betty and he had broken up; a young lady named Aviva of notable physical proportions was now installed in his apartment.

Milton Acorn had sold his carpenter tools against my advice, and was turning out science fiction. I ran into Jack McClelland at Irving's apartment one evening, attempting his temptation with my wild-grape wine. He pronounced it undrinkable.

When I wasn't bone-tired I wrote poems and plays. My first play, *A Gathering of Days*, was produced again on

CBC, and the six hundred resulting bucks made Eurithe and me briefly happy. But the work at Johnston's was beginning to grind me down physically. I applied for a Canada Council grant, with Layton and Frank Scott writing supporting letters. In late winter of 1960 I couldn't stand the job any longer, and quit. Milton Acorn came with me to the house on Roblin Lake; Eurithe stayed behind at Parke-Davis.

It was early March, snow and ice a cold blanket over everything. Milton and I set to work on the house interior, levelling and connecting joists, nailing wallboard between the studdings for insulation. And sawing stove wood with a hand saw — the only means available. The weather still like iron.

There was no subject whatever that Milton and I didn't argue about. Remembering those passionate "discussions", it's a wonder we didn't kill each other. And we read books by lamplight; chopped through lake ice armouring the planet for water; stayed up all night in three-hour shifts to stoke the wood-stove. And froze when we forgot.

I think Milton took himself more seriously than I took myself — which may have been a good thing, since no one else took either of us seriously. At the end of March there was a literary conference at Queen's University in Kingston, some fifty miles away. Milton wanted to go in order to escape me; I wanted him to go for the same personal reason. It was getting so we couldn't stand each other. He hitch-hiked to Kingston in near-zero weather.

I didn't hear from Milton for three days. I questioned him about it on his return. Too shy to attend the conference, he watched writers entering and leaving the university building; ate the sandwiches he'd taken with him; slept on a park bench near Lake Ontario; and spoke to no one. He wouldn't actually mention his shyness as the reason he hadn't gone inside the conference building, but his face reddened when we talked about it.

I've seen Milton years later — when some of his shyness was gone — walking across the floor of a crowded room, quite oblivious to where he was and to the other people around him. One could say he had spiritual qualities, which sounds ridiculous when you think of that red face and knotted body like an oak branch. But maybe not. Nobody ever thought I was very spiritual either.

I received a thousand dollars from a Canada Council grant in the spring of 1960. I bought a train ticket to Vancouver; Eurithe kept her job with Parke-Davis, but was transferred to Brockville, Ontario. During the tenure of my short-term grant I planned to revisit the place where I'd been stationed during the war, at Woodcock in the Hazelton area of northern B.C.

Driving an old 1948 Pontiac from a Vancouver used-car lot, I travelled north, sleeping in the car. In fact I lived in that car for nearly twenty-four hours a day. Parked on a side road in the Hazelton wilderness area, I set up literary shop. My idea was to write about Indians and whites, loggers and miners and trappers.

I drank beer with them in the local pubs, talked to everyone, from Mounties to railway workers. And wrote poems. Once I interviewed an Indian while drinking beer with him, asking questions about his life style, education (which seemed fairly extensive), and ambitions in life. His expression while I asked my questions was most peculiar. It turned out he was the son of the Chinese-Canadian hotel owner in Hazelton village.

It was a savage place. There were giant mountains towering in every direction. One of them was called "Rocher de Boule", and was shaped like a huge loaf of stone bread. The Skeena River roared, twisted, lisped, and foamed past, much the same as it had during my wartime exile there. When I drove back to my side-road haven one evening a horde of dogs appeared on the road, at least a dozen dogs of all sizes. They headed straight for the car, their leader a handsome white animal. I was certain they'd slow down and swerve aside before reaching the car. They did, all but one, a white Samoyed. He broke his neck slamming into fender and bumper. I turned into a service station farther down the highway, informing its operator about the accident. He owned the dog, and seemed unsurprised at its fate.

At my side-road camping spot, I had rigged some pots and wires as an alarm system while I slept in the old Pontiac. But there was no sound in the night. Wandering around next morning, I stumbled on the Samoyed's body in a nearby ditch. It gave me a jolt, this ghost dog I had killed seeking out its murderer. Of course the service-station operator had simply thrown the dog's body there, as a handy method of garbage disposal.

On my return trip east the American states slipped past slowly. Montana seemed to last forever at forty miles an hour. The Pontiac had a throttle, a gimmick you pull out, and the car keeps a steady speed as a result. I slid back in the seat, almost dreaming, thinking about poems. Those I had written in Hazelton seemed nothing special, but how can you ever tell about your own poems? And caught myself up: of course you can tell; if you can't, what's the use of writing at all? In this case, the poems were ordinary. I knew it, and didn't want to admit it. Or maybe they weren't so bad, repeating in my head the title of my 1959 chapbook, *The Crafte So Longe To Lerne*.

The big job that summer at Roblin Lake was getting electricity into the house. Jim Parkhurst had wired the place, using cheap second-hand electric stuff, with me helping as best I could. And the Picton Hydro was scheduled to run a line into the house from the lane two hundred feet away. But first I had to get a hydro pole in situ, ready for the electrical people.

A tall cedar near the house supplied a pole. I dug a hole some eighteen inches deep to receive the pole. At that depth I encountered — solid limestone. What to do? I talked to village people who'd used dynamite in their own work, and bought some myself. I rigged a fuse long enough to give me plenty of time to escape the blast. I lit it and ran, taking cover behind a breast-high pile of stones.

I waited and waited, but nothing happened. And felt extremely nervous. Maybe the stuff would explode the instant I got close to it; I stayed behind my protective stone barrier. After a few more minutes I began to feel quite foolish, but alive and intending to stay that way. I didn't dare climb down into the shallow hole I'd dug for my hydro pole; but sat on the edge and thought about the problem. The fuse had gotten extinguished somehow, and maybe it could be lit again. But not down in that hole, not by me. . . .

Newspapers? Maybe that would do it. I gathered an armload of them, scrunching them up and twisting as if I intended to light a fire. Which I did intend, to light a fire. When the dynamite hole was filled with crumpled newspapers, I threw in a match and ran like a rabbit before they got well ignited.

This time the results were more satisfactory. After a few moments the earth made a low baritone *crump* sound, as if in bad humour about something. Dirt and stones flew into the air. I started to breathe with less difficulty. And resolved to have nothing to do with dynamite in future. I've already forgotten how I crimped that fuse into place, in case anybody should ask me to do the same again. I won't. Cowardice is sometimes necessary for survival.

It took six years from my mother's death in early 1958 to get her will settled. Over that entire length of time Eurithe and I had been expecting our poverty to be lessened, even a season of mild prosperity. We had no idea how much money was involved. But apparently the Victoria and Grey Trust Company didn't intend to let us have it, whatever the amount.

During most of those six years, I had been driving the eighteen miles between Roblin Lake and Trenton once a week. My lawyer there kept making encouraging noises. Things were going well, he'd say: just a few months more, be patient a little longer. . . . That sort of thing. The Trenton lawyer's only advantage was that I didn't have to pay him any money until the will was actually probated. But I had very little anyway.

Over those six years after 1958, I published several small chapbooks. My style of writing had taken a ninety-degree turn in the direction of — what? — modernism? I don't like these labels anyway. Whatever the terminology, the change in me was radical. My reading had become omnivorous and carnivorous. As well as poems, I also wrote radio plays at the rate of at least one a month, sometimes more. On one memorable occasion I wrote an entire hour-long radio play overnight, finishing off a couple of bottles of my homemade wine in the process. It was a very bad play.

The image of myself I see reflected from then to now is not particularly attractive. Our small family was poverty-stricken. My own moods alternated between exaltation and depression. But I was writing excitedly and ferociously; it was a fever, an obsession, almost an illness. And I was probably neurotic as hell, a psychiatric mess.

That Trenton lawyer was hopeless: my impatience with him during interviews badly concealed. I can't look into his mind, but I wish this was possible. I boiled and simmered in his waiting-room; I chewed silent nails when I talked to/with him. . . .

Visiting Frank Scott in Montreal, I asked him for advice and the name of a good lawyer in Toronto. Scott mentioned Andrew Brewin. But shortly after that Brewin was elected to Parliament. He handed over this small probate job to a young lawyer in his office, Ian Scott. It was an excellent choice. After a trip to Belleville by Scott and a session with Judge Anderson, my mother's will was finally to be probated in 1964.

(In Toronto at an awards ceremony recently, I met Scott again after twenty-three years. Now Attorney General of Ontario, he asked me if I remembered him. Migawd! — In 1964 he saved my sanity. I'd almost vote Liberal in his honour — although not quite.)

A dozen radio plays of mine were produced during this approximate six-year period. Alice Frick and Doris Hedges at CBC Toronto were largely responsible for any small success I had with play-writing. They sent me scripts for adjudication as well; and to read bad plays and contrast them with good ones is a way of improving your own writing. I had so far to go that I couldn't help improving.

I published *Poems For All the Annettes* in 1962. And regard this book as a watershed in my own development. But I don't like the word "development", which sounds like a boxer or a pole-vaulter prepping for a big athletic meet. However, I admit to being almost fully aware of the changes taking place in my own mental equipment, changes that were partly the result of discontent with nearly everything about myself. The previous six-year period was one of turmoil and radical change, as I've intimated.

And some interesting questions might again be raised here: why and how does one change? Writing itself was part of the reason for my own small movements from what I was to what I am. Scribbling poems is supposed to be an occupation for the eternal amateur, even if the poet makes money at it and is regarded as highly accomplished. One might say the poem researches an adjacent universe for truth and beauty. And those last two words sound a bit ridiculous in this day and age. My own idea is that writing poems is a mental discipline that stretches the mind; although I don't regard myself as a very disciplined person. "Inspiration" is another word I dislike; but there is a mind-cloistered condition in which the physical world is extinguished like a match, thoughts float free like small clouds inside infinite space of the human skull. . . .

But enough maundering. *Poems For All the Annettes* caused some small comment in Toronto literary circles. Deciding that the timing was right, I submitted the manuscript of *The Cariboo Horses* to McClelland & Stewart in 1963. It was published two years later, winning an award. I borrowed a suit from my brother-in-law for a trip to Ottawa and the award ceremony.

In 1964 I went to Cuba, one of a dozen Canadians on that trip. They were guests of the Cuban government, which wanted people to look at the country unhampered by American prejudice. Fidel Castro had chased the previous dictator, Fulgencio Batista, into exile five years previously. Castro's long struggle from his mountain refuge in the Sierra Maestras against Batista had made him something of a hero, but a hero the United States disliked for his recently acquired communist politics.

In 1962 the U.S. had financed and armed a counter-revolutionary military force which landed at the Bay of Pigs. Castro took personal command of the Cuban army and militia, defeating the invaders and taking many prisoners. (A short synopsis of some complicated events.)

My own trip to Cuba was more or less accidental. Some months before, I had had a poem-reading at Ross Dowson's Trotsky bookstore in Toronto. And since my politics are NDP-leftist, Dowson asked me if I'd be interested in going to Cuba. I was. In fact I was ecstatic about the trip. Visions of new poems flashed in my head; maybe even a prose narrative about Cuba.

I visited Michel Lambeth, a Toronto photographer, one of the dozen Canadians invited. His photographs and my prose would go well together in a book; at least that was my thinking. But Lambeth, a few days before departure, decided not to go. He was afraid of being blacklisted as a Communist. He mentioned to me that the days of McCarthy witch-hunting were fairly recent, only ten years previous.

An organization called "Fair Play for Cuba" was the up-front sponsor of this Canadian trip to Cuba. Lambeth was nervous about that too, since "Fair Play" had been linked with the assassination of President John Kennedy a year earlier. (Ross Dowson was involved in that outfit as well.) Anyway, Lambeth was extremely jittery where the Red Menace was concerned. He was employed by Toronto newspapers, and thought blacklisting would destroy his livelihood. I had no such fears myself, not being gainfully employed anywhere. Besides, I think you take your chances when you feel adventurous and have enthusiasm for a project.

Travelling from Canada to Cuba couldn't be done in a straight line, across the U.S. to Miami, say, then south to Havana. American hostility to Fidel Castro and his nation precluded such a simple trip. One had to book for Mexico City, then wait for a scheduled Cubana Airlines flight instead. And there was a feeling of danger about the whole thing. Rumour had it that everyone Cuba-bound was being photographed at the Mexico City airport; the CIA was said to lurk behind every pair of tourist sunglasses.

Edith Firth, a York University professor who'd spent her teen-age years in Mexico, was visibly apprehensive. "I'm afraid they'll stop me," she said.

"Who?"

"You need a visa to leave Mexico for Cuba. Then you need another one for the return trip to Mexico City." And there was a film of perspiration — never sweat — on her forehead. She could not be reassured. Besides, she probably knew more about it than I did.

I stayed at a cheap hotel on Avenida Reforma, wandering across Mexico City on foot, excited about almost everything I saw. The market especially. Orozco paintings in government buildings. Cheap Mexican beer. And hovering over the entire city a cloud of dark pollution; the air so heavy and permeated with human smells, the stink of garbage and automobile exhaust, that you could almost weigh and package it. And the poor, the wretched, ragged, miserable poor! Beggars on every street corner and some in the middle of the block. Cripples begging, Indians begging for pesos, and me thinking: is this the reward for being human, for our supposed superiority to the animals, for having invented a kindly and benign God?

But I was too excited for continued depression. And the flight to Havana was exhilarating. Over the Gulf of Mexico there was thunder and lightning cannonading on one side of the aeroplane, a quiet rose-and-scarlet sunset on the other. The aircraft plunged and dipped; the sky splashed bright silver inside; longshoremen were piling beer kegs in my ears. I rushed from one side window to another for a better view. It was like my childhood times at Trenton during a storm: I'd spend hours on the veranda feeling that shaken silence when lightning struck somewhere else, a silence like the ringing of bells on the far-off moon. . . .

Cuba was a revelation for me, in several ways. We — several of the visitors had arrived on the same flight — were met at the airport, given drinks, had our hands shaken, and were grinned at — Friendly. And we met Alicia, blonde, generally smiling, and simply "nice". She was our translator and sometimes our guide.

Among the Canadian visitors, a union shop steward and his wife from Vancouver. Frank something. About thirty-five, but fresh-faced and looking years younger than that. Six feet two inches, he was very handsome, and had a talent for stating the obvious in portentous tones.

Barbara something was young and quite beautiful; she disliked me for some forgotten reason. Ralph was a union organizer and official, about fifty-five. When we visited a cigar factory, I was asked to speak to the workers, all being given a free moment from hand-rolling cigars. That embarrassed me. I didn't know what to say, and asked Ralph to speak instead. He spewed the usual Communist clichés that would have made Karl Marx blush. The cigar-rollers all banged metal spoons on their desks and made a big racket, although I'm sure few of them understood English.

Two Montreal lawyers were with our contingent, both French-Canadian. One spoke very little; the other was lean-faced, of middle height, and balding, his manner self-possessed and confident. During one long discussion I had with him, he described his formula for Quebec relations with the rest of the country. I was impressed but forgetful, and later asked him to repeat some key portions of his thesis. He refused, and nothing more could be said on the subject. His name was Pierre Trudeau.

Trudeau made me very careful of what I said around him. I had the feeling he'd notice anything foolish immediately. He might not mention it, but I'd know he'd know I'd been stupid. You encounter a few people like that from time to time; they keep you on your toes. Once during our Cuban stay, the eleven Canadians were sitting in a country schoolroom, cramped by those little hardwood desks they have, listening to a Communist official explain the *modus operandi* of things since the revolution. I raised my hand like a small boy, asking if they arrived at decisions by a majority vote. There was a little stir behind me, and Pierre Trudeau's voice said, "Don't be naive, Al!" I nearly blushed.

The Canadians attended a ballet performance before we left Havana for a motor tour of the island. The prima ballerina's name was Alicia Alonso. She was rather long in the tooth, but a big favourite with the audience. Before the show was over, Pierre and I walked out of the theatre, as stealthily as possible for politeness's sake.

We spent much of that cultural evening walking all the way across the city to the Habaña Libre Hotel. Along the route we admired ancient churches, bought cider from restaurants, and talked. I recited a poem of mine, written shortly before, "Necropsy of Love", feeling flattered when he seemed interested. I didn't dare remind him of his formula for Quebec as part of the Canadian federation; that would have been asking for a verbal rebuff. And yes, I was impressed with the guy.

In the past, whenever I've been similarly impressed with anyone, I've gone to some trouble in order to meet them again. And when you do that, the onus is on you to be interesting to them in your turn, and perhaps showing it in a way not flattering to yourself. You either remain silent, or else reveal enough of yourself to be thought a fool. And sometimes, too, you can read other people's thoughts about you while they're talking, quite different from those they are verbalizing. Of course, all this is conjecture, since a thought on someone's face is like a shadow on the sun: it vanishes before you can be sure it existed.

What it brings home again to you is something you already know, that you are a separate world. It's always been slightly incredible to me that other people also have a brightly coloured world in their heads similar to my own infinite personal universe. All the evidence says they do have such a world; but why don't their worlds and my own join at the edges in some sort of telepathic super-cosmos? The ancient Greeks used to believe that Delphi was the world's navel. So it's probably understandable that some people think the universe begins and ends with them. It would be an even more chaotic world if they acted on such a belief.

And when I look at what I am typing at this moment, then the infinite universe in my head focuses to pour onto the paper; even the things I can't remember any longer influence what I say here. Hemisphere-wide rain-bows and continent-spanning black clouds are just behind my fingertips. . . . And is this Narcissus speaking, or can I really project a thought of mine about a pork-chop lunch to the dark side of the moon?

May Day in Cuba was a chance for everyone to dress in their Sunday best; for the Cuban leaders to brag end-lessly about their accomplishments; for soldiers and their weapons to parade through downtown streets; while Marx and Lenin looked on approvingly from murals on the sides of tall buildings. Carnival. The equivalent any-way.

The foreign visitors from Canada sat in a concrete grandstand at one side of a monster city park. Visitors from other countries were placed near by, including ladies from North Vietnam in diaphanous summer dresses, and no doubt others from the Soviet Union. The sun, like a dull knife, pressed against your head. We sat there, and sat there, while people filed into the meeting-place, or marched, or rode in army vehicles, for hours.

In the row of seats below us, a man was moving like a small brown cloud among the foreign visitors. He stepped up to where the Canadians were seated. A short and stockily built man, wearing olive-drab army fatigues and black beret. He had a short beard and smoked a cigar. "Who is it?" I whispered to Pierre Trudeau. "Che Guevara."

There is something about meeting a legend! As if history resided in his handshake, as if, as if . . . Che Guevara. Fidel Castro's first lieutenant and comrade; the Argentine doctor who'd devoted his life to proletarian revolution, crouching with Castro in the Sierra Maestra Mountains, hunted daily by the Cuban dictator's soldiers. A small man, brown-eyed and unassuming, about thirty-five to forty, not bad-looking either. As he shook my hand at that moment, I could even smell the good cigar. And he was gone. Down the line of visitors, become a sudden giant among the tiny Vietnamese ladies.

Some people are perhaps not vulnerable to meeting legends. I was. Later on Guevara disappeared from Cuba. He was said to be leading uprisings against various South American governments. Which governments, which countries? The news media didn't know. But he finally turned up in Bolivia, one of the most backward countries in the southern continent. And leading a peasant army in the jungle, being shot at by the Bolivian army, with CIA advisers lurking in the shadow background. Being killed. His body destroyed. But first they cut off his fingers for fingerprint identification, to prove that the dead man was Che Guevara.

Of course I didn't know all this when we were shaking hands during the May Day celebrations. But there was something about the man: it was like turning a page of history and seeing a shadowy photograph, someone who looked like you, also present briefly.

Castro spoke. And spoke, and spoke. The sun burned down. Water poured downhill off my head. I manufactured a flimsy hat from newspaper, quite inadequate. Trudeau had a handkerchief around his head. At one point we looked at each other, then both made for the concrete bowels of the grandstand with a single mind, as if pleading "natural necessity". And it was natural necessity. Castro spoke on. The tanks and armoured gun-carriers baked in the heat. The bullets nestled in gun-belts; the bombs slept quiet.

The 1958 Cadillacs in which we joyrode around the island were wearing out. Spare parts were unobtainable because of the American trade embargo. But there was a decadent luxury about them, a feeling that we were being favoured and visibly appreciated. Of course, it was all laid on for propaganda. That was understandable, with Uncle Sam frowning down on us from Miami ninety miles away. Alicia's blonde smile was for sweet propaganda's sake. And so was everything else, so was our driver's easy grin, and so on.

But what would you? Besides, the Cubans were very likeable. Their enthusiasm impressed me. And when we stopped for lunch at country restaurants, so did their beer. Make an impression on me, I mean. Half the Canadians in our party didn't drink beer; therefore I was pleased to help them out of this difficulty, their non-appreciation of Cuban beer. Of course, it wasn't very good beer, being cloudy with sediment, it's taste indifferent. But it was alcoholic, undeniably. And the end of the lunch-hours sometimes left me slightly sozzled.

At Playa Giron — more familiar to Canadians as "The Bay of Pigs" — we toured the battle zones, as much as the swampy terrain would allow. Here the U.S.-backed and -advised invasion force landed, and was defeated in two days of furious fighting. An alligator farm was in operation there. A couple of jokes were made among us, to the effect that alligators resemble counter-revolution-aries or vice versa. Pretty feeble stuff.

Near the end of our three-week visit, we travelled by jeep across the Sierra Maestras, arriving at a coastal sugar mill that had been attacked by sea raiders two days before. The jeep ride was unnerving: clouds of red dust exploded behind us; pigs fled squealing from the careering vehicle; we caught a glimpse of shocked faces in our churning wake. When we disembarked, hands, faces, and clothes covered with red pigment from the dusty mountain road.

The sugar-mill town looked like a western movie set. Horses and riders clopped the main street; burros waited outside false-front buildings; but no six-shooters were buckled around waists. . . . Near the ruined mill, moun-tainous piles of raw sugar still smoked from gunfire; a black man clambered over the sugar, grinning at us with gold teeth. But the only human casualty from the sea attack was a woman, struck in the buttocks by a stray bullet. The entire scene was unreal to me, living in rural Ontario all my life; now suddenly transported to a war zone. Because that's what it looked like, a war zone.

Among the tangle of Cuban impressions, some

stand out. I was riding in our '58 Cadillac limousine over a mountain road late at night. We encountered an army convoy. Moonlight glittered on camouflaged troop-carriers and men; big guns trundling along behind trucks; tropical palms overhead. On reaching Havana I saw anti-aircraft guns lined up near the waterfront, their snouts like open mouths. An American warship, the *Oxford*, could be seen vaguely just outside the twelve-mile limit, its spy apparatus focused on the now-Communist island. It becomes a nightmare world, a place for dead lovers. . . .

I would never maintain that you can get to know a country in three weeks. But one can form a liking for some of the people. Over that time we saw palm-thatched huts, sheet-iron shanties, and modern apartment buildings. We travelled from one end of the country to the other, from Hemingway's chalet to Spanish-colonial-style hotels. If there was any racism among the blacks and whites on this island, it wasn't visible to me. Of course, we didn't see the prisons and camps for political detainees. The Cubans put their best foot forward, as one would expect. A country dominated by the United States for many years was slowly regaining its self-respect. And some would say, regaining it at a heavy cost.

My own outlook on the world changed as a result of visiting Cuba. Not to the extent that I became Communist, or ever expect to be more left than a socialist New Demo-crat in Canada. But I have an admiration and liking for the country and its people. They fume and froth around the edges when the U.S.A. is mentioned; the spy-ship *Oxford* was a constant thistle in their pants; and Castro in 1964 was a kind of legendary god. As is Che Guevara still. And of course, José Marti, hero of their war of independence from Spain. He is their patron saint.

No longer is Cuba a backwater of history, as it was before Castro. Not that there's anything wrong with being a backwater of history. In fact, I think it's admirable, like being the quiet eye of a hurricane world. And certainly preferable to being ravaged by wars and poisoned by atomics. I prefer the Canadian backwater to being a world power with its consequent inevitable abuse of power and emergence as a world empire like the United States.

However, Cuba has exchanged domination by one country, the United States, for domination by another, the

Soviet Union. Their pride has blossomed nevertheless; their name is known in the world; they haven't lain down in the centre of the road waiting to be run over. One doesn't have to be a Communist to admire the people, standing on their defiant little Caribbean island waiting for the barbarians to arrive. Armed to the teeth and waiting.

There's a demarcation or bench-mark in my life at the years 1965-66. Before that my wife and I managed to survive poverty; and we built a house together (thanks largely to Jim Parkhurst) in a kind of desperation; my book *The Cariboo Horses* was published in 1965, and won the Governor General's Award. From that time on life became very different.

During those bad years my own character changed as well. As if everything that happened before 1965 was an apprenticeship, an uncertain testing of my footing, a mysterious waiting-period. And I do not mean to imply that after 1965 my writing program would produce nothing but masterpieces. It's just that the changes inside myself were so obvious, at least to me. . . .

During the 1950-55 years in Vancouver I was writing silly doggerel. And my own ineptitude was beginning to dawn on me during that period. But I was reading Dylan Thomas, T. S. Eliot, and others; I was growing even more interested in and curious about other people. I was also a navel-watcher, narcissistic as hell. Sure, I was fascinated by myself. It's been a metamorphosis — not to produce a butterfly but, I hope, a writer.

Curiosity seems to me my most salient characteristic. I'd like to use it for a few years more. I want to go on exploring my own limitations and boundaries. And in all my writing, there's a shadow self I'm trying to get in touch with, the other self who lives in all of us, friend, foe, or neutral judge. A doppelganger of the soul, that absurd word designating something that doesn't exist. Therefore I invent him.

1988
Ameliasburgh, Ont.

AL PURDY

HERODOTUS OF HALICARNASSUS

This fever in the veins
         this running fire
flickering on the sea
this rumor on the wind
in Ephesus Babylon Persepolis
this whisper in the night
about murdered kings
                — is news?

Belshazzar's overthrow
riding the backs of dolphins
across the sea from Asia
                — is news?

No presses roll
no harried editor snarls
Where?   When?   Who?   How?
                   only
a mild-mannered middleaged observer
listener rather than talker
quietly deciding what he really thinks
about things other people have
already decided
staring bemused among sleepy herdsmen
near a mountain village at Thurii
wandering the agora at Athens

He fantasizes headlines:
PERICLES IN CROOKED LAND DEAL (No!)
AGAMEMNON A YELLOW COWARD (Very unlikely)
CROESUS CONSULTS DELPHIC ORACLE (True)
XERXES FLOGS HELLESPONT WITH WHIPS
WHEN WATER REFUSES OBEDIENCE
(Informant swears truth of this
on his honor — which may be insufficient)

News of Wars:
Thousands dead on battlefields
Wolves feast on torn bodies
Children die of starvation
The world a desert . . .
Why?

He considers the recent past:
Nicaea   Salamis   Marathon   Thermopylae
Xerxes and the Persians
invading Greece
Headline —: WE WIN
(sub-heading)
WE KNOCK HELL OUTA THE PERSIANS
but why — *why* did we win?
Consider some reasons:
— the phalanx?
sterling character of Greek hoplites?
leadership of Leonides and Themistocles?
But I say the ships
that old man on the docks
muttering to himself
(interview him later)
"Three banks of oars much
superior to double row of oars"
(seems logical)
that doddering old shipwright
who invented triremes
— a new design
paid for with Greek silver
— paid for with death
one always pays for victories

But why Greeks and Persians?
Well now
It's like we got into bad habits
and kept kidnapping each other's women
until someone's husband
got really annoyed
— that might be one Why

A reasonable man
listening to what people say
in the marketplace
at peddlers' stalls
at the docks talking to fishermen
off-shift miners
plowmen in springtime
taking notes and considering . . .

(For gawd's sake
they're talking about a statue
on the main street
for the ol bastard
I mean why?
— that sloppy old man
staring at women's legs
wine-bibber
"old father of lies"
buttonholing everyone
asking the world questions . . .)

Quietly in a vineyard at Thurii
Herodotus
dreams life never ends
— in the Islands of the Blest
of the Western Sea
all his loves waiting
the fair and not so fair
the dark ones with lips like flames
their faces shining on him
their eyes like springs of light
Let it be so!

VERTICAL VERSUS HORIZONTAL

Never mind why
pay no attention to when
only that it did happen
— that little mammal sucking
dinosaur eggs at early dawn
trying to figure out a new method
for safecracking those eggs
and leaving the burglary undetectable
— that minuscule creature
with beady treacherous eyes
stood suddenly upright
and proclaimed his own importance
in a series of one-decibel shrieks
no self-respecting carnivore
even noticed

Think more on the matter
be advised in anthropogenesis jargon
that when the lil bugger stood upright
his position relative to the world
changed to right angles with the horizon
(in geometry preferred term is "perpendicular")
and in the first employment of admass
became "the far-seeing one"
before such language was
in general usage

The advantages of verticality were several:
lower vegetation — ferns and such
small shrubbery — could be looked above
danger glimpsed while still far-distant
and it was really marvellous for the ego
While gentle ungulates grazed
and remained belly-plumb with earth
and the carnivores made rude noises
but stayed horizontal
The far-seeing one remained upright
and praised his own perspicacity
and forgot that other world

Remember the morning? —
our shadows long in the long grass
our bodies swift in the leaping distance
how we overtook our own beginnings
in sweetness of dew and morning
and so still we heard god's heartbeat
in the wet near earth
Remember the noonday?
— the trees were green sentinels
and birds warned us of danger
and we raced the west wind over the grasslands
and discovered the east wind in earth's turning
in springtime everything was shining
as if it had just been born
and it had been
Remember the evening?
— how it was in that great blaze of sun
horizon embroidery
blue green purple orange mixed with blackness
being born as a colour
asking ourselves who we were
and knowing anyway
— and quietness in the forest
when leaves talked together
and the words they said
were sleep sleep sleep
and we slept
our bodies joined to each other
and were parallel with the earth
— we slept
and dreamed a strange dream
and woke and were not ourselves

LOK

It was after our fathers had been listening
a long time to the rain
to birds chirping and the silence between
and they listened to the wolves
crying at night to the wolf-mother
and the glacier-spirit whispered to them
and our fathers made words
Then we looked at each other
and knew from the sounds
that came from our mouths
how the beasts were made nervous
with ears lower than their tails
when we approached them
we knew we were men

A long time after
one among us was called Lok
— when Lok fell from a tree
many sleeps ago he landed
near a bear and ran for his life
we pointed at him after that
we pointed and said Lok
When the bear returned again
we scrambled up a tree
and all of us said "Lok-Lok-Lok"
The bear was very angry
and tried to climb after us
his mouth frothed foam
his claws wounded the tree
then we pointed at the bear
and the sound came again
we jumped up and down in the tree
we were very happy

For a long time after
we pointed at each other often
we said "Lok-Lok-Lok"
— and the sound changed in our heads
we could not plead with it to stay
we could not command it to go
it belonged to itself
but sometimes when things are most serious
most solemn and most important
the sound returns among us
and will not be silent
Lok himself said nothing
his face became haunted
from the sound that was his name
and was not his name any longer
he went away into the forest
and did not return
until his memory grew faint among us

For a long time after
we wondered about it
this gift that was given us
but denied the beasts
we wondered what it might mean:
and the gods speak within us
when we least expect their voices
when we know there is no other help
Listen Listen Listen
under the moon we say his name
solemnly seriously we say his name
the man who left us and never came back
"Lok-Lok-Lok"
and the gods are listening
until the name returns from the mountains
and lives again among us

IN A DRY SEASON

The juices inside women's bodies
are the condiments of heaven and earth
whose formulae remain secret in the skulls of dead alchemists
Those woman-juices
must well from springs deep inside earth
they are the unimaginable and certainly unwritten
proof that a god or gods do exist as corollary
to unseen orchids waiting to be stepped on
by men with cork helmets in imaginary jungles
— a young god who has discovered in unmapped regions
of Venus this shimmering source
of all his questions about death and life hereafter
the answer that contains always its own opposite
and circles back on itself to become a question
— and the young god being celibate
must wander mad across parched deserts of earth
until the great rains come
— and Jesus wept

HORSES

— stand beside yourself
your other self
the waiting child
in an imaginary town
and nobody there no one
except the dead
everyone dead
except —

And they'd come
you knew they'd come
out of empty streets
into the sun
my quick steppers my thunder-footed
ones wearing all shades of copper
gold umber satin covered grey
and black tar babies shining
and me in my plural child's disguise
watching them
in calm sun watching
the wild eye in its rolling heavens

These were the steady cloppers
these were the prancers
going whusp-whusp-whusp all four
feet together like one along
and I was a witness
in the whispery winter morning
with the shadow beside me
being born over and over
every day outside the warm house
every blink of the eye

Moving to market and slaughter
of ducks and upsidedown chickens
in summer the dainty ones
with clover breath
every step a dance step

their feet loved each other
their feet were lovers
before the road was paved
and the great beasts came

(They are of course dog food
and cat feed long since
while the planet cycle
repeats and repeats and vultures over
my head are cancer-stroke-heart disease
but I pay no attention
now is parenthesis
now is going backward)

— and sometimes when I was older
I ran beside them a little
way and they knew they knew
eye blinkers notwithstanding
they knew the small boy
they remembered they remembered
my quick steppers my thunder-footed
ones wearing gold and silver
jewellery brother and sister
to the wind and jingle jingle
in cold weather went the bells
went the years went the child
all the way to the world's edge
all the way home

— and the body-clock ticks on

ON THE FLOOD PLAIN

Midnight:
it's freezing on the lake
and wind whips ice eastward
but most of the water remains open
— and stars visit earth
tumbled about like floating candles
on the black tumulus
then wind extinguishes the silver fire
but more flash down
and even those reflections reflect
on the sides of waves
even the stars' reflections reflect stars

Ice:
far older than earth
primordial as the Big Bang
— cold unmeasured by Celsius and Fahrenheit
quarreling about it on a Jurassic shingle
— before Pangaea and Gondwanaland
arrived here in the 20th century
born like a baby
under the flashlight beam
Bend down and examine the monster
and freeze for your pains
— tiny oblong crystals
seem to come from nowhere
little transparent piano keys
that go tinkle tinkle tinkle
while the wind screams
— and you feel like some shivering hey
presto god grumbling at his fucked-up weather
hurry indoors hurry indoors to heaven

People have told us we built too near the lake
"The flood plain is dangerous" they said
and no doubt they know more about it than we do
— but here wind pressed down on new-formed ice
trembles it like some just invented musical instrument
and that shrieking obbligato to winter
sounds like the tension in a stretched worm
when the robin has it hauled halfway out of the lawn
I stand outside

between house and outhouse
feeling my body stiffen in fossilized rigor mortis
and listening
thinking
this is the reason we built on the flood plain
damn right
the seriousness of things beyond your understanding

Whatever I have not discovered and enjoyed
is still waiting for me
and there will be time
but now are these floating stars on the freezing lake
and music fills the darkness
holds me there listening
— it's a matter of separating these instants from others
that have no significance
so that they keep reflecting each other
a way to live and contain eternity
in which the moment is altered and expanded
my consciousness hung like a great silver metronome
suspended between stars
on the dark lake
and time pours itself into my cupped hands shimmering

THE FREEZING MUSIC

There is a music no Heifetz or Paganini knew
it never occurred to them to think of it
— at night when man-sounds fade
the lake is trying to decide about itself
whether it is better to be ice or water
and can't make up its mind
it yearns toward both of them
And little two-inch tubular crystals form
phantoms in the water
when the merest hint of wind comes
they *sing*
they sing like nothing here on earth
nothing here on earth resembles this
this mingled weeping and laughter
sighing between the planets

On earth
I have maneuvered myself near them
my face close to the little tubular crystals
kneeling uncomfortably
on this rocky shoreline near Ameliasburgh
temperature 32 degrees Fahrenheit
shining my flashlight on them
trying to observe the exact instant
water becomes ice
intently observing metamorphosis
but unable to escape myself
Running into the house to escape cold
clapping both hands on my breast grandiloquently
"I have heard the music of the spheres"
But yes I have
yes I have

Paulette Jiles was born in Missouri in 1943. She came to Canada in 1969. Between 1973 and 1983 she worked in the Arctic and sub-Arctic, mostly with Cree and Inuit communications organizations. She also taught creative writing at David Thompson University Centre in Nelson, B.C. She won the Governor General's Award for poetry in 1984 with a collection entitled *Celestial Navigations*.

A TOURIST EXCURSION TO THE BADLANDS *BY PAULETTE JILES*

I. On the Way

Along the way advertisements will insist you do something; eat, or
surrender, back off from the bluffs, sleep, go forward, undress,
invest in something, catch a flight to Minneapolis or Butte, have
an adventure in an abandoned mining town. Take heart; ahead is the
REPTILE GARDENS, and the apple, and the expulsion, and the whole
   damn
show.

Along the way are cattle sales; the panicked ranchy calves with similar
big eyes all looking in double units, the apostolic auctioneer searching
the crowd of hats for converts, the riders back in the pens wearing
antennae on their galloping heads. You ask yourself, will I never get
to the Badlands, or the REPTILE GARDENS, with all the distractions and
fooling around? Fooling around the bed full of bedsheets in the cowboy
motels, travellers in hats like flying minds on their way to *les liaisons
dangereux*.

And on your way to the Badlands every night you can stop at western
bars, change sliding down the old walnut counters like lost silver
children, and the army-colored pennies, and listen to the heavy and
soft musician's weapons of melody and chord, playing out their hidden
agenda.

And I know these musicians work harder at their sorry art than I ever in
my life have worked at poetry, and take more personal risks, and are paid
about the same, all told. All told,

you get handtooled by life and its graving instruments, marked by odd,
random designs which can't possibly mean anything unless seen from an
altitude of 1,000 feet,

and so sometimes our lives look like a REPTILE GARDEN, a roadside
   attraction
on the way to Hell's Half Acre.

The musicians in the fake-adobe bar open their instrument cases
and from time to time remain completely silent.

II.   Park Service Brochures

Grey clouds go running by, herded by thunder,
ruined and torn,
and sunlight flashes out between them
over the Badlands
as if somebody were throwing it out of a drawer

and the chest of drawers were in an empty room
and the room were in an abandoned house
the color of brushed steel
and the high Dakota wind were banging the doors shut
and open and shut again
bouncing Styrofoam cups hellbent for apocalypse
I dreamed last night
you lay beside me
and said honey I'm going back
home to Corpus Christi.

The Parks Service has left brochures
with the names they give the canted earth
and its layering business
describing the way
whole gullies have sat down to rest
on the bones below
— and this is the extract of vermillion
— this is the aperture of the world's eyebone
    spying out at the ridges of baking powder

with ash icing and red happy birthday dear Badlands stripes
on them

the gold-sequin parts shaped like ovens
and people hoarding unspent light
unliving their lives in the pressure
of dark talk
who try and try to unshutter
who are looking for the Goodlands

after all the divorces and the wars, who have been silly and mad and
spendthrift, forgetting their birthdays, losing their way home from
foreign countries, who get into cul-de-sacs and desert highways, who pray
without thought to whatever divinity comes along, the One that looks
    like
a Soft Touch, the One that appears the most Tender-Hearted, or Who
    has
the most Coins in Its Pockets, the One who would pull you through the
REPTILE GARDENS and the stretches of the bony country; but you are
    already
in it and what pressure forced you here, what gambles? Let us suppose
we are people walking across the Badlands. We are for sure those people
walking across the Badlands, watching the big pearly ridges of buff and
opal for hawks, pulling all our lives behind us, baggage trains,
and these are my brains
which have seized at everything with dry plans
and maps and calculations
how to get out of here
and I have come so far in my life
and have loved nothing but my life
until now
and I think I will begin to rain on this place
until I am empty
or it gives over.

III.   The Goodlands

YOU ARE HERE   → ○   aren't you?

And from here you have to invent the Goodlands, because there is no
    other
place to go, unless you are going to just pull up and sit here, like a
calf in the pens ready to go to pieces, jammed up in the crowding alleys,
you have to keep on and walk out of the bad standing water rimmed white
as an eye with alkali

toward a river in its own alluvial body, between two sets of mountains;
the Wind Rivers, The Bighorns, a valley with swales and the weird batty
machinery of ducks going through the air like roaching shears, and all
the paths along the river plated with October leaves, the salt cedar
yellow as Crayolas,

cottonwoods throwing their leaves of large denomination out over the
crowded world, as if the Pope Of Jupiter would arrive in a Starmobile
and bless the bowing peasant grass;

all the grass of the valley and the benches, the buffalo grass and the
little short grasses with curly starter knobs and the level-headed
grasses holding up gemwork stems, and the tall ones in the swales,
also bowing, wet-footed;

your mind is a nation, populated, with standing armies, post offices,
reptile gardens; and some parts are a wilderness and other parts are
dark as railroad clinkers, and parts are a valley like this where
we are going, dreaming about going someplace, not home, but one parsec
to the side of it;

many people have died to hold this place, they are still finding pieces
of coin and horse in Medicine Tail Coulee. But this is why we eat and
keep up our strength; to cross into Montana, like people without papers,
or reasons, without a fixed address, people at large, expendable nomads,
jingling with coins and horses, into the valley of the Little Big Horn
thinking, we could have dinner there. We could win this time.

THE YEAR IN REVIEW

BY SMARO KAMBOURELI

Reviewing is something like gossip: it involves the telling of truths and half-truths, the making or damaging of reputations, the sharing of one's own private pleasures or dislikes in the reading of a text — all in the absence of authors. There is no innocence involved in this telling; there is pleasure and, often, a certain kind of incivility, even malice. "The 'public' form of a private mode", "gossiping" about reading books is an activity that empowers reviewers. They bless or damn, their appraisals often depending not on the books they review but on their own reading expectations or their personal laws of familiarity.

Such is the case with Michael Darling's review essay in the first volume of The Macmillan Anthology. His review, complete with an epigraph that claims "prose in Canada is sadly undistinguished," proceeds to judge — it would be more accurate to say, throw mud at — all Canadian literature.

Professor Darling lacks a sense of occasion, to say the least. His "critical" assessments are based on his premise that "a memorable work of art requires a sense of wholeness and undiluted harmony." Professor Darling must be either innocent or blind. He must scrap not only Canadian literature but some of the best writing of our century if he still insists on seeking wholeness and undiluted harmony in a world that has already undone the largely fictional strings that held it together. What is supposed to read as high and solid literary standards in Michael Darling's review is in fact élitism of a suspect sort.

Smaro Kamboureli teaches Canadian literature at the University of Victoria. Her critical writings are widely published. She edited (with Shirley Neuman) *A Mazing Space: Writing Canadian Women Writing,* and is the author of *in the second person,* a book of poetry.

"I would point out," he concludes his review of fifteen books, "that my general impression of Canadian writing in 1987 is not so much that it is bad but that the worst of it has been grossly overpraised." I don't view my task as reviewer for this anthology to be as judgemental as Michael Darling's. Literature is largely a matter of taste, and I choose not to talk here of books about which I have nothing to say.

Dany Laferrière's *How to Make Love to a Negro* is a horny book. Sex and writing, not always in this order, are the protagonist's *raison d'être*. A first-person narrative that unravels sometimes in quick spurts of meditation on political and literary ideologies and sometimes by way of leisurely and elaborate descriptions of the black protagonist's state of being (inspired, horny, hungry, desperate, pleased with himself, cynical, aloof), *How to Make Love to a Negro* badly wants to be provocative and irreverent. And it succeeds. Part of its success, however, is due not only to its vivid portrayals of racial, cultural, and sexual politics in contemporary Montreal, but also to the humorous and satirical approach it takes toward these very serious issues.

No doubt, man is an unnatural animal. The Koran asks, "How many generations have We destroyed before them! Can you find one of them still alive, or hear so much as a whisper from them?" I try to think unpleasant thoughts; I think of *The Critique of Pure Reason*. Kant becomes porno. *The Critique* gives me a hard-on. It grows. Miz Literature stares straight ahead. We hear the double gasp of Beelzebub and his accomplice. Like a slow dance. They're doing it in slow motion. In some movies they show the violent parts in slow motion to increase the effect. Like violence shot into our blood. A hypodermic. In our veins. We sense their movements in a mad modern ballet. Two naked bodies violently intertwined in a pas de deux of death. My sex keeps rising, obeying a secret command beyond my will. Miz Literature turns slightly on her axis, watching it rise with a disconcerting stare. She lowers herself towards me, reducing the angle to fifteen degrees. In the sitting position. Her eyes still staring. I close mine and Miz Literature, in a trance, takes me in her mouth. Between her beautiful pink lips. I'd dreamed of it. I'd licked my chops over it. I didn't dare ask her. An act so . . . I knew that as long as she hadn't done it, she wouldn't be completely mine.

That's the key in sexual relations between black and white: as long as the woman hasn't done something judged degrading, you can never be sure.

Because in the scale of Western values, white woman is inferior to white man, but superior to black man. That's why she can't get off except with a Negro. It's obvious why: she can go as far as she wants with him. The only true sexual relation is between unequals. [Laferrière's ellipses]

There are no winners in this book, for despite all its cursing and sexual bravado, it is a claustrophobic text simulating, while parodying, the voyeuristic settings of pornography: a pig-sty of a room shared by two blacks, one the narrator/writer writing "not a real novel" but "a kind of autobiographical grab-bag", the other, Bouba, "lying on a couch meditating, reading the Koran, listening to jazz" — both of them "screwing when it comes along". It is a book that fears naming, that sets out to explore not real characters but types, yet a book that unabashedly names its own origins and making. From *Kama Sutra* to Marguerite Duras, from Mishima to Henry Miller, this novel is at once self-referential and intertextual. Whether obscene or lyrical, the narrative cannot keep itself from thrusting toward sociopolitical translation. Yet the reader wonders why the "white man", who is the colonizer of both "negroes" and women, gets off scot-free in this narrative. In fact the narrator emulates the white man's mythologies. But what disarms the reader is that this "negro" lover/writer is fully conscious of how he is co-opted and co-opting. Despite the title's tantalizing promise, the book never tells you "how to make love to a negro". Instead, it tells you how you can no longer make love only for pleasure's sake. Writing and sex subvert themselves, showing their "true colors".

Gail Scott's *Heroine*, like Laferrière's novel, is also a Montreal book whose greatness derives partly from the naturalness and ease with which Scott recreates the toughness and sophistication of her characters' urban lives. The title is at once apt and deliberately misleading, for Gail, the novel's "heroine", is non-heroic. A young woman who has lived through the turbulence of the seventies in Quebec, Gail, while soaking in a bathtub on an October day in 1980, tries to come to terms with her past political actions and relationships. But this is not just a novel of reminiscences, of jealousy and betrayal, of being politically correct or living "on the fringe of a new era". The emphasis lies on "how to be a modern woman living in the present", how to distinguish between personal and public politics. The "clarity" Gail seeks is achieved through her telling of her story — "The trick is to tell a story. Keeping things in the same time register" — which becomes the novel she has always wanted to write, the novel we read. Such a narrative can only be labyrinthian, and Gail Scott controls the different narrative threads remarkably well.

"The point is we have to create new images of ourselves," Scott's heroine says, "even if at first they're superficial, in order to move forward." Notes from the "black book" Gail kept over the years find their way into *Heroine*, but the "heroine" emerging from them keeps changing faces and moods. Often she's a "heterosexual victim", at other times "strong and passionate, her own person", or confused by the sexual and political codes of a lesbian community. Scott does not attempt to resolve her heroine's attempt to image the modernity of her own character. Gail's most important question — "is it possible to create Paradise in this Strangeness?" — echoes throughout this extraordinary novel, which, although poignantly realistic, constantly questions the precarious balancing of reality and realism, of the direction feminism has taken.

Ann Rosenberg's second novel, *Movement in Slow Time*, is as experimental as her first one, *The Bee Book*, if not even more so. But while it is a book that "makes strange" all our expectations from novelistic writing, it is also deeply embedded within our western visual and literary traditions. Although it defies summation, one could easily say that *Movement in Slow Time* is structured after Dante's *The Divine Comedy*, thus leading the reader through the "Hell", "Purgatory", and "Paradise" of an array of characters who are observed through the events (I use this word with hesitation) of a single day. At once episodic and philosophical, erotic and cerebral, social and literary, fictional and autobiographical, this book not only challenges what a novel is but also invites us to question our reading practices. *Movement in Slow Time* is a textual amalgamation of prose, poetry, stage directions, charts (found and made-up), diagrams, and drawings and pictures by Rosenberg herself and painters like Bosch. From a transcription of the wind that blows in Dante's Hell — "OOOOOOOOOOOOooooooO OOOOOOOooooooOOOOOOOWWWWWWWWWWW OOOOOOAAAAAAAWWWWWW" — we move to a lyrical passage that approximates Renaissance iconography:

As she ceased her speaking, the winds began to move and sigh.

With a gentle hand Francesca rubbed the back of her wailing lover as softly, as surely as a mother comforts a child. She knelt before him, rocked him in her arms. Her hand stole up his slender body to claim the one that lay across his heart. She kissed each finger reverently. Then with one sure movement she drew him up and with another pulled him swiftly, certainly, into the sky.

What follows it, in bold print, is "You've got the libido of a pig!" Quotations out of context like these can only distort the complex ways in which Rosenberg orchestrates the visual, phonetic, and verbal dimensions of her book. Rosenberg's versatility with form and structure may seem puzzling and gratuitous to most readers, but there is no doubt that she succeeds in what she sets out to do.

Marion Quednau's *The Butterfly Chair* and Constance Beresford-Howe's *Prospero's Daughter* are both novels dealing with daughters and fathers. Quednau's novel begins with what marks the end of the protagonist's childhood: Else Rainer is the witness of her mother's murder by her father and of his own suicide. But through the journey into her past that the adult Else undergoes, the reader discovers that Else's complicity is not only that of a witness. Else tries to relive her troubled childhood in an attempt to appease her sense of guilt for turning in her abusive and introverted father to the police, an act she fears precipitated her parents' deaths. The strength of this novel lies precisely in its sustaining Else's narrative despite its giving away, so early in the story, the two most important facts of the plot. But whereas Else's imaginative recreation of the past is engaging, the narrative shifts from first-person to third-person accounts are often awkward, if not gratuitous. Else emerges from the silence she practised for years as a traveller in space and memories, and most of the time the reader follows her real and psychological meanderings with interest. There are times, however, when her experiences remain puzzling, as when she imagines an encounter with Carl Jung:

Else is fingering the dead flowers in the vase on the table, the buds of the cornflowers break off in her hands, the dry bits of stem litter the table. "I used to play a little game with myself that I would meet you [Jung] someday, in a garden. My mother was an avid gardener, you see. But she always left it looking partly overgrown, partly wild. Whether that was because she ran out of time to tend it, I don't know — I like to think the wild look of her daisies and Black-eyed Susans and morning glories was intentional. So I imagined us meeting in my mother's garden. You and I sitting in the golden butterfly chairs, facing the house. It was a very safe game, because you were so out of reach, already in the past, and I was never ready."

Nothing prepares the reader for this admittedly ingenious encounter, nor is it clear how, if at all, her dream of Jung resolves her personal anxieties. Putting aside the "games" Quednau plays with the reader, the novel is indeed an evocative exploration of the whole gamut of human emotions.

The psychological authenticity that is the strength of *The Butterfly Chair* is totally lacking in Beresford-Howe's novel. *Prospero's Daughter* also deals with the problematic relationship of an emancipated but strangely timid daughter and an autocratic father, but it does so in an entirely literary fashion. Here the drama of the characters' lives derives from the egocentric and manipulative actions of Montague Weston, a Canadian author of world fame who resides in England in great luxury and formality. He is the Prospero in the novel, but a Prospero who creates magic to hide his indiscretions and failures. Full of literary allusions, the sexual ploys of literary agents and writers, gourmet meals, and a film crew from Canada that tests the ego, patience, and national affinities of Montague Weston, the novel celebrates nothing but literary conventions. This is a novel of manners, not a novel of substance.

Similar problems arise from Robertson Davies's *The Lyre of Orpheus*, which completes his trilogy that began with *The Rebel Angels* and *What's Bred in the Bone*. Here Robertson Davies imitates Robertson Davies. And he does so exceptionally well. The reader is assigned a seat from where she or he can passively observe the antics of the classic Davies characters: yes, there is the erudite bachelor lovingly playing the role of a catalyst in the troubled lives of his friends; the uncivilized young female artist whom self-satisfied benefactors help to get ahead; and, of course, the other recognizable type of the Davies cast of characters, the bisexual woman who succeeds because she is more male than female. Like Beresford-Howe's novel, this is also about art, specifically opera; but it denies one the pleasure of finding out for oneself what the novel is about. It is a novel about sanitizing a woman artist's habits that her rich patrons find offensive, about completing unfinished works of art. If you don't mind that the characters and plot situations in this book don't seem to move beyond the archetypes of characters and themes that Davies has explored in his earlier works, then *The Lyre of Orpheus* is a good read.

Margaret Atwood's *Cat's Eye*, a fairly subdued novel in terms of action, is also about an artist. Elaine Risley, back in Toronto (where she was brought up) for a retrospective show of her paintings in a feminist gallery, relives her childhood and her formative years as an artist. With the distance that middle age and artistic success afford her, Elaine fluctuates between her troubled past and her stable present:

There are several diseases of the memory. Forgetfulness of nouns, for instance, or of numbers. Or there are more complex amnesias. With one, you can lose your entire past; you start afresh, learning how to tie your shoe-laces, how to eat with a fork, how to read and sing. You are introduced to your relatives, your oldest friends, as if you've never met them before; you get a second chance with them, better than forgiveness because you can begin innocent. With another form, you keep the distant past but lose the present. You can't remember what happened five minutes ago. . . .

I sometimes wonder which of these will afflict me, later; because I know one of them will.

For years I wanted to be older, and now I am.

The consistent use of the present tense renders the narrative vivid and captures the flux of life, but also functions as a reminder of the protagonist's attempt to understand how the past still lives within her, has survived, in fact haunts, her art:

Cordelia. . . . The same folded arms, the same immobile face, the blank-eyed stare. Cordelia! Put on your gloves, it's cold out. *So?* I can't come over, I have to finish my homework. *So?*

Cordelia, I think. You made me believe I was nothing.

So?

To which there is no answer.

Cordelia's taunting question offered as an answer is the very puzzle that Elaine seeks to understand. But whereas Atwood writes very astutely about the secrecies and cruelties of a child's world, there is a certain aloofness about her character that manifests itself when Elaine tries to account for the origins of her art. Elaine's artistic vision, effectively configured through the descriptions of some of her paintings, is rich, but she is anxious to denounce any influences that could be traced to either the feminist movement or specific artistic schools. In this respect she displays an independent spirit, but also a kind of solipsism that belies her claims. Elaine does not believe in polarizing female and male artists — "I hate party lines, I hate ghettoes. Anyway, I'm too old to have invented it." In this respect, Elaine seems to emulate her own author; but Elaine's readiness to deny the extent to which the same gender roles that shaped her childhood now surface in her art and that she is indeed part of the times that gave rise to feminism remains problematic.

Janice Kulyk Keefer's *Constellations*, the first novel by this accomplished short-story writer, is a compelling story about one of the oldest literary themes, the upheaval a stranger's appearance can cause in a small community. Bertrand, the "Français de France" who shocks and gradually alienates even the few people in Spruce Harbour, Nova Scotia, who offer him their friendship, is "the Compleat Aesthete and Intelligentsius", a photographer who remains blind to what lies on the other side of his camera lens. His brief sojourn in Spruce Harbour and its disastrous effects are related primarily through the biased point of view of Claire Saulnier, herself a misfit in her own community.

A small woman, living alone, beginning to grow old. A woman immured, not in herself, but in her fear of herself — you could see it in the hurried way she walked, as if there were someone shadowing her. He'd never known a person so walled off, with so many intricate defenses. In her more bitter moments his mother had said things to him about Claire being a crazy old maid, grabbing at a boy because she'd never be capable of getting a man. But even his mother couldn't really believe that — there was no person less sexual than Claire Saulnier. He imagined her body smooth, white as that of an old-fashioned porcelain doll, without any hairs or openings at all. As sexless, in her way, as Bertrand France was in his — a perfect couple.

Hector, the speaker above, is himself an intricate character with equally strange explanations as to why, like Claire, he abandons an urban and intellectually gratifying life for the pettiness and small-mindedness of his hometown. But *Constellations* is not the average Canadian novel about small-town lives. Besides being well written, it confronts the reader with complex problems of manipulation, misdirected or frustrated love, and, above all, how one's self-understanding entails an understanding of and respect for others.

Neil Bissoondath's *A Casual Brutality* is an equally satisfying first novel. In the words of the narrator, Raj Ramsingh, in this book "Time kaleidoscopes. The past is refracted back and forth, becomes the present, is highlighted by it, is illuminated by it, is replaced by it. In this rush of sparkle and eclipse, only the future is obscured, predictability shattered. Yesterday becomes today, today steps back from itself, and tomorrow might never be. I think: Sharpen the edge." The eloquent writing in this novel is a delight, but in order to fully enjoy it the reader must bracket the fact that its speaker is also presented as a reticent man, a medical student who feels at home neither in Toronto nor in Casaquemada, his fictionalized Caribbean island. Raj's double citizenship typifies his personal predicament: orphaned but brought up by adoring, if not doting, grandparents; married without love but an affectionate father to his son; responsible but a victim of his own actions of integrity. Raj's narrative, which begins as he boards a plane to return to Toronto, unfolds smoothly, every single detail further enhancing this gripping tale about his native island where corrupt political and economic forces accelerate their ruthless devastation of its people. At once lyrical and harshly realistic, *A Casual Brutality* is a novel of great virtuosity.

Linda Spalding's *Daughters of Captain Cook* has the same lyricism. The story it tells can only be told in poetic language. What shocks the reader about this novel emerges from the dark recesses of a love that blossoms between bodies sharing the same blood. Set in the sensuous and fragrant landscape of Hawaii, this novel is about the complexity of filial and parental allegiances, about the terrifying power and seductiveness of taboos and how they can destroy while creating something beautiful. Whether Jessie, the narrator and protagonist, reminisces about her American past or tries to make sense of her marriage to Paul, born in Hawaii, *Daughters of Captain Cook* hardly ever fails to draw the reader into the increasing mysteries of its plot. Perhaps the most fascinating character in the novel is Mihana:

Her long hair dark and thick, worn down or braided

under an old lauhala hat, her long muumuu fastened with a crescent-shaped bone pin. It was a lucky pin, she said. Her face was like no face I had known. There was in it, at the same time, benevolence and fury; there was an odd expression in it as if, within her, she combined beatitude and crime. All those wrinkled cotton coverings concealed a woman I couldn't understand — a mind that was old and tough and a body that was still soft, still in its prime. She radiated strength, as if at any moment she might change the weather or cause the ocean to rise.

Mihana remains for the reader as unfathomable as she is for Jessie, and this is my only regret about this novel. But then, how can we expect Jessie, an outsider to this world of lushness, to break the code of one of the daughters of Captain Cook? Only intuitively, and with considerable daring on her part, does Jessie realize that she bears within her the injuries of all those she loves — "I am Julia, my mother, and Mihana. Kit. I am Maya. I too looked for a god. I looked for a platter and a house. I looked for the resurrection of the body in a child." Powerful and disturbing, Spalding's novel shows how our contemporary sensibility cannot rid us of the puzzling realities of myth as history.

Daphne Marlatt's *Ana Historic* is a real treat, a novel many of us have waited for for years. But it is not a novel, if Annie, its narrator, is right when she says that "a book of interruptions is not a novel." The novelistic form of this book is deliberately meant to tease the reader's expectations. Marlatt, never losing sight of the thematic and ideological possibilities of form itself, interlaces autobiography and fiction with the historical material her narrator Annie retrieves about a Mrs. Richards, a single woman who presented herself as a widow in order to get a job as a teacher in 1873 in British Columbia. Mrs. Richards's life story blends with, and illuminates, Annie's own story as well as the story Annie tells of her mother Ina — "whose story is this? (the difference of a single letter)/ (the sharing of a not)." This story is about the telling of stories:

she keeps insisting herself on the telling because she was telling me right from the beginning stories out of a life are stories, true, true stories and real at once — this is not a roman/ce, it doesn't deal with heroes.

Marlatt, as she does in her earlier writing, fictionalizes history and historicizes fiction. She writes with the (woman's) body about the body while, at the same time, letting (her) language tell its own tales of distortion, of appropriation, of a "home from the beginning". Marlatt's exactitude with words, the sharpness of her perceptions, the uniqueness with which she challenges her reader both intellectually and sensuously, make this novel one of the best to appear this year.

Two of the poetry books I received for this review were late 1987 publications and both were nominated for the Governor General's Award. Roy Kiyooka's *Pear Tree Pomes* and Sharon Thesen's *The Beginning of the Long Dash* are indeed both wonderful books — if "wonderful" sounds too trite or too vague for you, you'll just have to read them and find out for yourselves. In fact, all the poetry books I'll briefly discuss here are wonderful, and this is the main reason I'm limiting myself to them. (I received a number of other poetry books, some of them recommended by their publishers as being "readable" and "down to earth", and they truly were. Poetry shouldn't be deliberately opaque or obscure, but a down-to-earth poem somehow defies its *raison d'être*. Or, at least, so it seems to this reader.)

Sharon Thesen's *The Beginning of the Long Dash* is grounded in her day-to-day experiences and immediate environment, but there is always surprise lurking at the end of her lines — the moment a line breaks to become another, its otherness never fully given away, teasing the reader:

Being adults
we share our toys.
Nothing is better
than this. This
delicate sliding out
of the pick-up stick
from the small chaos
on the floor. . . .

Thesen writes of the "small" things that are also great, of those "exclamation marks" that can signal both beauty and the quiet agony of life's repetition. There is a relentlessness in the way she images even an "imageless" self against a landscape of lilac bushes and the poetic terrain of gentlemen's handkerchiefs:

He uses his
handkerchief —
gentlemen do —
large ones almost
the size of diapers.
This has always
moved me — that and
shined shoes.

One of Thesen's great accomplishments is her ability to combine, with great ease and sophistication, humour and irony with intellect and imagination. Nothing is forceful in the way she evokes tradition; she subtly and gracefully inscribes herself within its gaps, signing her name with the delicate strokes of her language:

I kept falling from swings
my breath took away so often
I got bored
with seeing eternity
in a blanched instant,
looking up
into Okanagan hedges.

A fine romance
this is. As a mode
of understanding one confusion
speaks for another.
I never did get the drift,
the allegory of the cave.

Roy Kiyooka's *Pear Tree Pomes*, a long-awaited collection by this artist and poet, is stunning in the way it moves and stirs the reader. A long elegiac poem about a beloved who has moved "to another neighborhood", it resonates with the inner music of the poet's solitude. But although the poem circles around the seasonal changes of the pear tree outside the poet's study, there is an absence of time from where eternity seeps into the poem. Just as a statue glorifies marble, so does Kiyooka's pear tree illuminate his solitude: "an appall'd lover bends his/ear to the pear tree's trunk to hear a lost rhetorick." The poet lives neither within nor without himself, but within the sidereal space the pear tree and its "rhetorick" of "skeletal branches", of "dangling" fruit, create. There is no longer an immanence of disaster; just the quietude of the poet's vigil for a love that was once measured by the ripeness of the pears; only his meditation about his enchantment with the pear tree, itself a lone figure in the urban landscape.

love the aurora of these late september nights

as i write this lovely suffusion of twilight colors down
it changes before my very surmise from rose into translu-
*   cent amber .*
by the time i get to the end of this petite colonnade of words
all the amber will be stained a deep violet and in a few
*   moments . . .*
the pear tree's branches will have knit the night-sky
*   around*
themselves to catch a falling star . such as they are these
*   words bear*
a testimonial to all the weather we lived through together .
not even your leaving me for a woman will erase their
*   intrepid*
measure . love, the night-wind is winding up the spindle of
*   another*
dream . . . . where o where do you think it will spin us?
[the poet's ellipses]

In this book, beautifully illustrated by David Bolduc, the ruse that love is for the poet becomes a welcomed and treasured gift for the reader. Silence gives rise to utterance, what is undecipherable about loss creates the fissure that gives birth to these poems.

what i have been given to do will bear

its own felicities and ancient midden i've dreamt about
utterly enfolds . otherwise silences abound —
& the bounty is this hissing rain this whining midnight
*   siren*
& these my twice emptied-out clay hands . i would
write a cantata for a harp & a small bronze bell if i could
sound the unpeel'd silence when the last pear falls. . . .

There is nothing superfluous about this book. No reader could turn away from it.

Erin Mouré's *Furious* is equally competent. The sureness of her imagery, the versatility of her language, do not come as a surprise, for her earlier collections left no doubt that we're dealing with an accomplished poet. Mouré's poetry is euphoric and angry, and it combines, in her own words, "the colloquial expression with the words of the intellect".

It's the wood & paint of the chairs
speak loudest,
when we are not wearing them.
Where the grass stops at the edge of desert.
Trying as if for the first time, on the lawn, the
fault-lines of the heart
where two continents fit & push overboard
touching

In Mouré's poetry when objects speak they speak of the arbitrariness of linguistic signs — they "ain't true. Truly. True blew" — of the tentative line separating the physical body from the tangibility her imagination discovers in the intellect:

It's the way people use language makes me furious. The
ones who reject the colloquial & common culture. The ones
who laud on the other hand the common & denigrate the
intellect, as if we are not thinking. The ones who play
between the two, as if culture is a strong wind blowing in
the path of **honour**. *It takes us nowhere & makes me*
furious, that's all.

These lines come from the last part of *Furious*, called "The Acts", a gloss on the earlier poems, which presents Mouré's "feminist aesthetic". Yet her political relationship to language and culture can persuade the reader that feminism has the power to potentially exceed what is specifically feminine to embrace a body whose very life will depend on its resistance to appropriation. As is the case with the body of her poems. "I want to write these things like *Unfurled & Dressy* that can't be torn apart by anybody, anywhere, or in the university. I want the overall sound to be one of making sense, but I don't want the inside of the poem to make sense of anything." The dynamism of her poetry lies precisely in that centre of resistance, at once seductive and elusive.

David McFadden's *Gypsy Guitar*, subtitled "One Hundred Poems of Romance and Betrayal", is a *tour de force* of the idiosyncratic humour and wry wit that have long been McFadden's poetic trademark. Technically balanced on the edge separating long poetic lines from poetic and often deliberately non-poetic prose, these poems speak of unrequited love. McFadden deconstructs the courtly love tradition, infusing it with his failures to romance his lover at a time when romancing takes place as easily in front of a TV set as in a garden:

She writes she had a dream in which I inherited a million dollars and was driving around in a chocolate-coloured Maserati. I tell her it's true but the money is all in a trust fund for my many children, and the problem with the Maserati is its colour: the kids think it's real chocolate and tend to slobber over it. I tell her I'll never forget a moment of the year of "absolute insanity" and "incredible joy" we shared, but in truth by golly I've forgotten nine-tenths of it, like dumping soggy excess baggage. I reminded her, speaking of chocolate, how we used to get up at noon and head down to the village for boxes of chocolate bars for breakfast and that if we'd seen a chocolate Maserati in those days we'd have tried to eat it. After I mailed the letter I remembered that she (and I) never ate chocolate.

Yet he also whimsically insists on feeling bereft and forlorn:

Oh, the danger you are in. Listen to the angels, they will keep you safe. You say your grief has made you puerile, but if you hadn't been so puerile you would never have felt such grief. Listen to the angels, listen to their innocent chatter, for they have been attracted by the ridiculous power of your love. For years they have been calling you to awaken to their light. And now, finally, life has you checkmated, blocked off in all directions, enchained, imprisoned. And this is what you have wanted all along, this is what you have lived for, strived for. And now you have it. Be silent.

Although these poems "strive" for the ultimate break and revolt that would effect separation from what haunts the poet, nothing in these poems verifies that desire. Instead, their wealth of imagery incessantly repeats, with orchestrated variations, how interminable desire is, how desire more than love is one's greatest affliction. An affliction that often becomes a blessing, that transforms dissonance into song.

Words are tropical fish that disport and distort themselves beneath the surface. And so I swim in a pool of thick warm words and at night dream of wondrous pigmented sentences lying in tubes waiting to be uncapped and squeezed. Every word I write will have to be cancelled and I hope it can be by me. Yet there is a Great Word from which all words come and that word is the unspeakable word that means you-at-rest-in-my-soul-and-I-in-yours.

McFadden constantly crosses the precarious line marking both the difference and the sameness between reality and illusion, dream and imagination. Although one could call these poems "readable", it is their unreadability, the degree to which they invite and at the same time resist an immediate response, that insinuates the uniqueness of McFadden's poetic voice.

I took immense pleasure from most of these books, and I've been "gossiping" about them in cafés, in the classroom, in the privacy of living-rooms, in bed. Yet this does relatively nothing to appease my sense of guilt for not speaking about the other books I read, those I cannot possibly review here because of time. . . . But, then, Barthes says, "the pleasure of the text: *never apologize, never explain*."

Books Considered

Allen, Robert. *Magellan's Clouds: Poems 1971-1986.*
Montreal: Signal Editions, 1987. 97 pp. (paper)

Anderson, Hope. *Slips from Grace.* Toronto: Coach
House, 1987. 82 pp. (paper)

Atwood, Margaret. *Cat's Eye.* Toronto: McClelland and
Stewart, 1988. 421 pp. (cloth)

Beresford-Howe, Constance. *Prospero's Daughter.* Toronto:
Macmillan, 1988. 256 pp. (cloth)

bissett, bill. *Animal Uproar.* Vancouver: Talonbooks, 1987.
128 pp. (paper)

Bissoondath, Neil. *A Casual Brutality.* Toronto:
Macmillan, 1988. 384 pp.

Bowering, Marilyn. *Grandfather Was a Soldier.* Victoria:
Porcépic, 1987. 79 pp. (paper)

Brewster, Elizabeth. *Entertaining Angels.* Ottawa:
Oberon, 1988. 118 pp. (paper)

Burnard, Bonnie. *Women of Influence.* Regina: Coteau
Books, 1988. 109 pp. (paper)

Coles, Don. *K. in Love.* Montreal: Signal Editions, 1987.
69 pp. (paper)

Cooley, Dennis. *Perishable Light.* Regina: Coteau Books,
1988. 73 pp. (cloth and paper)

Conolly, L. W., ed. *Canadian Drama and the Critics.*
Vancouver: Talonbooks, 1987. 320 pp. (paper)

Davies, Robertson. *The Lyre of Orpheus.* Toronto:
Macmillan, 1988. 472 pp. (cloth)

Dennis, Ian. *The Prince of Stars.* Toronto: Macmillan,
1988. 232 pp. (cloth)

Downie, Glen. *An X-Ray of Longing.* Winlaw, B.C.:
Polestar, 1987. 96 pp. (paper)

Dyck, E. F. *Apostrophes to Myself.* Lantzville, B.C.:
Oolichan, 1987. 46 pp. (paper)

Flood, Cynthia. *The Animals in Their Elements.*
Vancouver: Talonbooks, 1987. 165 pp. (paper)

Gotlieb, Phyllis, and Douglas Barbour. *Tesseracts*[2]. Press
Porcépic. 304 pp. (paper)

Hillis, Rick. *The Blue Machines of Night.* Regina: Coteau
Books, 1988. 70 pp. (paper)

Jiles, Paulette. *The Jesse James Poems.* Winlaw, B.C.: Polestar, 1987. (paper)

Keefer, Janice Kulyk. *Constellations.* Toronto: Random House, 1988. 266 pp. (cloth)

Kiyooka, Roy. *Pear Tree Pomes.* Illustrations by David Bolduc. Toronto: Coach House, 1987. 68 pp. (paper)

Laferrière, Dany. *How to Make Love to a Negro.* Translated by David Homel. Toronto: Coach House, 1987. 116 pp. (paper)

Marlatt, Daphne. *Ana Historic.* Toronto: Coach House, 1988. 153 pp. (paper)

McFadden, David. *Gypsy Guitar.* Vancouver: Talonbooks, 1987. 100 pp. (paper)

McKay, Ally. *Human Bones.* Ottawa: Oberon, 1988. 108 pp. (paper)

Meigs, Mary. *The Box Closet.* Vancouver: Talonbooks, 1987. 223 pp. (paper)

Moon, Bryan. *The Grapefruit Tree.* Part One: *Seeds.* Ottawa: Oberon, 1987. 160 pp. (paper)

———. *The Grapefruit Tree.* Part Two: *The Western Kingdom.* Ottawa: Oberon, 1988. 126 pp. (paper)

Mouré, Erin. *Furious.* Toronto: Anansi, 1988. 101 pp. (paper)

Powe, Bruce Allen. *The Ice Eaters.* Toronto: Lester & Orpen Dennys, 1987. 278 pp. (cloth)

Priest, Robert. *The Mad Hand.* Toronto: Coach House, 1988. 128 pp. (paper)

Quednau, Marion. *The Butterfly Chair.* Toronto: Random House, 1987. 202 pp. (cloth)

Rosenberg, Ann. *Movement in Slow Time.* Toronto: Coach House, Underwhich, 1988. 218 pp. (paper)

Saul, John Ralston. *The Paradise Eater.* Toronto: Random House, 1988. 270 pp. (cloth)

Scott, Chris. *Jack.* Toronto: Macmillan, 1988. 288 pp.

Scott, Gail. *Heroine.* Toronto: Coach House, 1987. 183 pp. (paper)

Skelton, Robin. *Fires of the Kindred.* Victoria: Porcépic, 1987. 160 pp. (paper)

Smart, Elizabeth. *Juvenilia.* Edited by Alice van Wart. Toronto: Coach House, 1987. 80 pp. (paper)

Smith, Douglas Burnet. *Living in the Cave of the Mouth.* Riverview, N.B.: Owl's Head Press, 1988. 51 pp. (paper)

———. *Ladder to the Moon.* Brick Books/Coldstream. n.d. 51 pp. (paper)

Solway, David. *Modern Marriage.* Montreal: Signal Editions, 1987. 63 pp. (paper)

Spalding, Linda. *Daughters of Captain Cook.* Toronto: Lester & Orpen Dennys, 1988. 218 pp. (paper)

Stratton, Allan. *Words in Play, Three Comedies.* Toronto: Coach House, 1988. 211 pp. (paper)

Thesen, Sharon. *The Beginning of the Long Dash.* Toronto: Coach House, 1987. 83 pp. (paper)

Towell, Larry. *Gifts of War.* With Photographs by the Author. Toronto: Coach House, 1988. 112 pp. (paper)

Walker, George F. *Nothing Sacred.* Toronto: Coach House, 1988. 112 pp. (paper)

Wynand, Derk. *Heat Waves.* Lantzville, B.C.: Oolichan, 1988. 67 pp. (paper)

Young, Patricia. *All I Ever Needed Was a Beautiful Room.* Lantzville, B.C.: Oolichan, 1987. 71 pp. (paper)

Submissions

Submissions for consideration for inclusion in next year's *Macmillan Anthology* may be sent to:

John Metcalf,
P.O. Box 2700,
Station "D",
Ottawa, Ont.
K1P 5W7

or

Kent Thompson,
Department of English,
University of New Brunswick,
P.O. Box 4400,
Fredericton, N.B.
E3B 5A3

All material to be returned or answered must be accompanied by a stamped, self-addressed envelope. Cut-off date for submissions is October 1989.